THE
EVERYTHING
ICE CREAM, GELATO, AND FROZEN DESSERTS COOKBOOK

Dear Reader,

I'll never forget my first taste of real Italian gelato. Soon after I was married, I was fortunate enough to travel for several weeks across Europe with my husband and our close friends. Our first night in Italy comprised of a gondola ride, pizza margherita, and two scoops of the most decadent coconut gelato I have ever eaten. Since then I've had more than my fair share of the frozen delight, and I make it a point to sample new and exciting flavors whenever I find myself in any Italian city. As research, of course!

Since beginning my food blog three years ago, I have experimented at great lengths with ice creams, sorbets, and gelatos in my own kitchen, and have loved the results. Everything from the simplest granitas to fresh sorbets to decadent ice creams and, of course, gelato have been included in this book, as well as special chapters for vegans and those requiring sugar-free recipes. You'll also find wonderful ice cream cakes, pies, and other spectacular frozen desserts here, too!

It is my hope that you will experiment with my recipes, stir up your own childhood (or adulthood!) memories, and perhaps create a few special memories for your own children or grandchildren. *Buon appetito!*

Susan Whetzel

Welcome to the EVERYTHING® Series!

These handy, accessible books give you all you need to tackle a difficult project, gain a new hobby, comprehend a fascinating topic, prepare for an exam, or even brush up on something you learned back in school but have since forgotten.

You can choose to read an Everything® book from cover to cover or just pick out the information you want from our four useful boxes: e-questions, e-facts, e-alerts, and e-ssentials.

We give you everything you need to know on the subject, but throw in a lot of fun stuff along the way, too.

We now have more than 400 Everything® books in print, spanning such wide-ranging categories as weddings, pregnancy, cooking, music instruction, foreign language, crafts, pets, New Age, and so much more. When you're done reading them all, you can finally say you know Everything®!

QUESTION

Answers to common questions

FACT

Important snippets of information

ALERT

Urgent warnings

ESSENTIAL

Quick handy tips

PUBLISHER Karen Cooper

DIRECTOR OF ACQUISITIONS AND INNOVATION Paula Munier

MANAGING EDITOR, EVERYTHING® SERIES Lisa Laing

COPY CHIEF Casey Ebert

ASSISTANT PRODUCTION EDITOR Melanie Cordova

ACQUISITIONS EDITOR Lisa Laing

ASSOCIATE DEVELOPMENT EDITOR Hillary Thompson

EDITORIAL ASSISTANT Matthew Kane

EVERYTHING® SERIES COVER DESIGNER Erin Alexander

LAYOUT DESIGNERS Erin Dawson, Michelle Roy Kelly, Elisabeth Lariviere, Denise Wallace

Visit the entire Everything® series at *www.everything.com*

THE EVERYTHING®

ICE CREAM, GELATO, AND FROZEN DESSERTS COOKBOOK

Susan Whetzel

Avon, Massachusetts

An Everything® Series Book.
Everything® and everything.com® are registered trademarks of F+W Media, Inc.

Published by Adams Media, a division of F+W Media, Inc.
57 Littlefield Street, Avon, MA 02322 U.S.A.
www.adamsmedia.com

ISBN 10: 1-4405-2497-1
ISBN 13: 978-1-4405-2497-4
eISBN 10: 1-4405-2568-4
eISBN 13: 978-1-4405-2568-1

Printed in the United States of America.

10 9 8 7 6 5 4 3 2 1

Library of Congress Cataloging-in-Publication Data
is available from the publisher.

Readers are urged to take all appropriate precautions before undertaking any how-to task. Always read and follow instructions and safety warnings for all tools and materials, and call in a professional if the task stretches your abilities too far. Although every effort has been made to provide the best possible information in this book, neither the publisher nor the author are responsible for accidents, injuries, or damage incurred as a result of tasks undertaken by readers. This book is not a substitute for professional services.

Many of the designations used by manufacturers and sellers to distinguish their products are claimed as trademarks. Where those designations appear in this book and Adams Media was aware of a trademark claim, the designations have been printed with initial capital letters.

This book is available at quantity discounts for bulk purchases.
For information, please call 1-800-289-0963.

Contents

Introduction 9

1 Ice Cream Basics 11

History of Ice Cream 12

Ice Cream Varieties and Other Frozen Desserts 12

Tools and Techniques 14

Ingredients for Success 18

Tips for Special Diets 21

Successful Storage 21

2 Essential Ice Cream Recipes 23

3 Gelato 41

4 Frozen Yogurt 61

5 Fanciful Flavors 73

6 Sorbet 99

7 Sherbet 111

8 Granita 127

9 Vegan Ice Cream 149

10 Sugar-Free Ice Cream. 163

11 For the Kids 177

12 Cakes, Ice Cream Cakes, Cupcakes, and Trifles . . 191

13 Ice Cream Pies .211

14 Decadent Frozen Confections 229

15 Milkshakes 243

16 Smoothies. 253

17 Toppings and Mix-Ins. 265

Appendix A: Glossary 285
Appendix B: Resources. 291
Standard U.S./Metric Measurement Conversions 295

Index. 296

Acknowledgments

A huge thanks to my husband, Jon, and my son, Seven. They have overlooked my messy kitchen, my undone chores, and my lack of sleep since the beginning of this cookbook undertaking! I also appreciate my parents for stepping in and helping as much as they have: I am a very lucky woman to have such a wonderful family.

I am also grateful to my amazing friends, both online and in real life. I could *not* have made it without the generous help from Carrie Fields and Paula Jones, whom I met through my blog over two years ago. They are amazing friends and talents whom I admire in so many ways. And, to my Doughmesstic readers—thanks for the inspiration! I hope to keep the recipes coming!

Introduction

THE HISTORY OF FROZEN desserts is widely believed to date back nearly 2,000 years, when the feared Emperor Nero sent his slaves high in to the surrounding mountains. There they would collect snow and ice to transport it back to their master, where it would be mixed with nectar, fruits, and other sweets, such as honey, and served as a form of sorbet. Hundreds of years later, Marco Polo is said to have brought several recipes for frozen concoctions with him from his travels to Asia, where natives had been using the recipes for thousands of years.

Despite the early and often disputed beginnings, ice cream and other frozen desserts have come a very long way. Modern technologies, especially the invention of electricity and refrigeration, have created an abundance of icy sweets that are now available to just about anyone, no slaves or mountain climbing required.

While it gained notoriety in Europe for several hundred years in the finest of courts and palaces, the Quakers are credited with finally bringing ice cream to America. In Colonial times, sweet shops in New York, Philadelphia, and other larger cities would sell the frozen concoction. Benjamin Franklin, Thomas Jefferson, and even George Washington were documented fans of this early ice cream, often seen eating or serving this treat. Dolly Madison, wife of President James Madison, is said to have served ice cream at her husband's inauguration in 1813.

Much advancement took place over the next hundred years, including the invention of the hand-cranked ice cream churn and improved recipes. The waffle cone made its debut in the very early 1900s, creating a new and delicious vessel in which to enjoy the chilly dessert. It is believed that the first cone was created by accident at the 1904 World's Fair in St. Louis, when an ice cream vendor ran out of bowls and partnered on a whim with the waffle vendor, who created a "cornucopia" style waffle vessel. While a charming story, there is belief that the Europeans had been using cones for many years prior to 1904.

It was not until refrigeration became widely available that the boom in ice cream happened. Companies and chains such as Howard Johnson and Baskin Robbins began competing for the most flavors, and customers fell in love with the varieties. Later, the development of "soft-serve" ice cream became a favorite treat, as it is softer, airier, and decidedly different from the scoop. Dairy Queen and Tasty-Freez were pioneers in introducing soft serve to the masses, and it is still incredibly popular today.

With all this ice cream available, frozen desserts were soon to follow. Ice cream cakes filled with cookies; frozen pies full of sweet sherbets and cream; delectable bombes and Baked Alaska can all be found in the smallest of eateries to the finest luxury cruise liners. In the mid 1900s, soda shops serving milkshakes were rampant in both big cities and small towns. Today, though the soda shops are far less the norm, milkshakes, smoothies, ice cream sodas, and floats are still as popular as ever.

With the resurgence of gourmet tastes, a move back to the days of home-made and fanciful flavors has resurfaced. High-end restaurants dole out their frozen delicacies at high prices to their eager patrons on a daily basis. With a few recipes, an ice cream machine, and a little effort, you too can be in ice cream and frozen dessert heaven.

CHAPTER 1

Ice Cream Basics

Anyone can successfully make ice cream, gelato, sorbets, and other frozen delights, thanks to the affordability of commercially available ice cream machines. Unlike baking, preparing frozen treats is less exact and offers room for lots of experimentation. Trade out spices, add your favorite ingredients, and use fresh and ripe produce as it becomes available. As long as it tastes great going *into* the machine, it's guaranteed to come *out* tasting great as well. Experiment!

History of Ice Cream

The history of ice cream is one consisting of legend, myth, and handed-down stories based on some fact, some fiction, and a lot of debate. Many historians believe that ice cream dates back to thousands of centuries B.C. in ancient China, when snow was the major factor in freezing creams. Over the years, ice cream made its way to Europe; Marco Polo (1254–1324) is usually credited with bringing the concept to Italy after his travels to the Orient. From there, ice cream spread north into France (Catherine de Medici is often cited as the person behind the spread from Italy to France), to Britain, and finally, to the United States.

Before modern refrigeration, ice cream and frozen desserts were a treat only for the wealthy, as ice was a true luxury item. Not until the late-nineteenth century did ice cream become a widely consumed confection in the United States, when more modern technologies made it possible to keep foods frozen at cheaper prices. Before this, ice creams were often served as elegant and exciting desserts at presidential dinners and high-society soirees in specialty glasses or carved and/or piped into fanciful shapes.

Since then, ice cream has transformed into the treat we know and love today, served in scoops alongside birthday cakes, atop giant cones, or in parfait glasses with chocolate and bananas. Culinary visionaries have transformed basic vanilla scoops into ganache-covered bombes and meringue-topped Baked Alaska, while clever moms have filled drinking cups with juice and created frozen pops. No matter the history, no matter the level of sophistication, one thing is for sure: Frozen desserts are here to stay.

Ice Cream Varieties and Other Frozen Desserts

There's no denying that frozen desserts are a popular and well-loved treat: Supermarket freezer sections have dedicated more and more valuable space to these concoctions over the years due to consumer demand. Everything from the standard vanilla ice cream to rainbow sherbets to Italian ice and freezer pops are purchased every day in mass quantities. While these store-bought options are certainly convenient, they simply pale in comparison to the quality of home-produced alternatives that can be made from the freshest ingredients with no added chemicals. Not only will these homemade versions be healthier, they will also *taste* vastly better than store-bought ice cream.

ALERT

Many ice cream recipes are easily tweaked, so feel free to use your creativity to make your own recipes. Try using whatever you have available, or experiment with new flavor combinations. For example, a basic vanilla recipe is wonderful on its own but welcomes mix-ins such as chocolate syrup, butterscotch, fresh fruits and jams, and chopped candy bars. For best results, add these ingredients toward the end of churning.

Ice Cream

There is no one definition of or recipe for ice cream. However, ice cream typically contains cream (hence, ice *cream*). From there, there are basically two directions to take: French style, which is egg- or custard-based, and Philadelphia (or American) style ice cream. French style is often considered smoother, thanks to the yolks used to create the creamy custard base, though it is more complicated to make. Philadelphia style tends to be firmer in texture and lighter in taste, but is a lot easier and faster to produce. Both are wonderful in their own way.

Gelato

You will be hard pressed to find two authorities who agree on a single, true definition of gelato. Some experts believe gelato should contain eggs, while others strongly disagree. What *can* be confirmed about gelato is the airiness. Gelato incorporates less air than ice cream, creating denser, more flavorful results. Standard ice cream machines can create gelato by simply turning off the machine when the ingredients are just frozen, incorporating less air than if it were left to continue the churning process.

Sorbet

Sorbets contain very few ingredients and are primarily composed of fruit and sugar or syrup. Typically, sorbets do not include any dairy, though this isn't a hard and fast rule. After granita, sorbets typically include the fewest ingredients, and are incredibly simple to produce. You will find that removing sorbet from the freezer 8–10 minutes before serving aids in scooping, as sorbets freeze harder than ice creams or gelato do, due to the fact that they contain no fatty ingredients.

Sherbets

Sherbets are similar to sorbets in that they contain few ingredients. The difference? Sherbets tend to contain milk or cream. Fresh, ripe fruits are the stars here, and it's as simple as puréeing all ingredients together in a blender or food processor and freezing in an ice cream machine. Like sorbet, it is a good idea to remove sherbet from the freezer a few minutes before serving for best results.

Frozen Yogurt

Frozen delights composed of—you guessed it—yogurt. Cream and/ or milk are also common ingredients in this variety of dessert. Both Greek yogurt and standard yogurts are excellent bases and can be used inter-changeably if desired. In a pinch, or as an added twist, sour cream can be substituted for part (or all, if desired) of the yogurt for either variety. This will of course result in a more sour end product, but is quite refreshing when paired with a variety of fruits, such as blueberries.

Granita

Granitas are frozen juices scraped into crystals. Granita is also commonly labeled as Italian Ice. Found in almost every country, these ices most closely resemble the original frozen desserts, when snow was mixed in with fruit juices as refreshing desserts and drinks. The wonderful thing about granita is that it is a snap to make, and requires nothing more than a fork and a freezer to obtain quality results.

Tools and Techniques

With the exception of granita, every ice cream, sorbet, sherbet, gelato, and frozen yogurt found throughout this book requires the use of special equipment. An ice cream machine, whether hand-cranked, self-cooling, or requiring prefreezing of canisters, is a staple in the production of these frozen concoctions. You will also find it handy to have a few other products, from mixers to whisks to baking pans, to make the process a little bit easier.

Ice Cream Machines

There are many ice cream makers on the market today. With a little research, you'll be able to find one that suits your needs and budget. Chain stores, such as Wal-Mart (*www.walmart.com*), Target (*www.target.com*), and Macy's (*www.macys.com*) are great places to find a variety of machines at several price points. A multitude of options are available on Amazon.com and other online retailers. It never hurts to shop around!

Most home kitchens will opt for the popular ice cream makers that require prefreezing of the canisters. These machines typically produce 1–2 quarts of ice cream at a time, and can be stored away when not in use, relinquishing valuable countertop space. The downside? Canisters must be frozen for several hours before using, thereby requiring some advance planning. It's a con that many will gladly accept, however, due to the value and convenience. All recipes in this book were prepared using this type of ice cream machine, and all with great results.

FACT

Cuisinart makes several quality machines, including one that will churn two flavors at the same time by using two canisters. If you own a KitchenAid stand mixer, KitchenAid offers a sturdy and well-loved ice cream bowl attachment for its versatile machines. Both Cuisinart and KitchenAid ice cream makers can be purchased for $150 or less and are of very good quality. See Appendix B for details on where to purchase.

If you are serious about your ice cream making and intend to make more than a few batches per week, you may prefer a self-refrigerating model. The cost is substantially higher than the above models, and there's no getting around the extra space it will consume. But no advance planning is needed, and batch after batch of sorbet and gelato can be produced with no wait.

Nonelectric ice cream makers, like those used in the past, are still on the market. These models typically allow a larger batch to be made than the countertop models, but be prepared: Rock salt and ice machines are a labor of love. Ice creams must be cranked for quite some time to produce the end result, and require a large amount of ice and rock salt. Motorized varieties are available, but they tend to be very loud and do not allow for adding ingredients, as they cannot be opened until the end.

Stand Mixer

A stand mixer is a luxury, but it makes whipping cream, meringue, and batters a breeze. KitchenAid is world-renown for their iconic mixer, which has changed very little since its early days. Beaters, whisks, and dough hooks come standard with these machines. Cuisinart, Sunbeam, Hamilton Beach, and Viking are also popular brands. As a bonus, Cuisinart and KitchenAid mixers both offer freezable canister attachments for ice cream making.

Hand Mixer

Without at least a hand mixer, whipping meringues to stiff peaks is quite a chore. Hand mixers are readily available, and many are quite inexpensive. The more expensive models tend to be a bit quieter and have more speeds.

Blenders and Food Processors

A blender or food processor is absolutely essential for making many of the recipes in this book. The two can be used interchangeably, since they are being used to combine and purée ingredients into a uniform state. Blenders tend to be less expensive, as well as offer a larger standard capacity. If using a food processor, choose a model with a 6-cup or larger container.

ALERT

Using a blender can turn into a messy situation if you're not careful. Cover the top of the blender with a dishtowel while using, and never fill a blender more than halfway up the bowl. Always have approximately half liquid in the blender to offset the solids, and remember to leave a crack open at the top. To begin blending, "pulse" a few times to make sure the blades can turn freely.

Saucepans

Many recipes, especially those requiring the creation of custards, must be made in a saucepan. Heavy-bottomed or enameled cast-iron pots and pans are well worth their added expense.

Zesters

While box graters are okay to use for zesting the peel off citrus fruit, a hand-held microplane zester does the job in less time and with better results.

Baking Sheets, Baking Pans, and Muffin Pans

Baking sheets are used for cookie creations in this book. A good non-stick, shiny pan is a quality investment and leads to better results for both cakes and cookies. Muffin pans are used for ice cream cupcakes and Nutty Buddies.

Silicone Mats

Silicone mats are becoming more and more popular, and for good reason. These reusable mats prevent burning and sticking of baked goods. They are also a breeze to clean up.

Parchment Paper

Parchment paper is a great nonstick product used in a variety of applications. Place it on baking sheets to prevent sticking.

Waffle Cone or Pizzelle Maker

There's virtually no way to make a waffle cone without a waffle cone maker. Pizzelles—thin, fanciful cookies that are similar to the waffle cone—are made with a pizzelle maker. Both waffle cones makers and pizzelle makers involve pouring a thin batter into the iron, cooking, and immediately wrapping the warm product around a cone tool, shaping by hand, or placing into a bowl to create an alternate vessel.

Ingredients for Success

When it comes to frozen desserts, what you put into it is what you get out of it. The better ingredients you use, the better your result will be, so use the best quality ingredients you can. Your efforts will be rewarded in fantastic flavor!

Fresh Fruit and Berries

If the recipe calls for fresh fruit, please think twice before substituting canned or frozen; the results will not be the same. For berries, purchase locally (or pick your own, if you can) for the most flavorful results; in season is best, and backyard is better. Shopping at a farmer's market is a wonderful way to support your local community, as well as to ensure that you get the tastiest and ripest fruit available.

ESSENTIAL

Dutch-processed cocoa powder simply means that the cocoa powder has been treated with an alkali to reduce the acidity. The process makes the color a bit darker, and the flavor is more mellow than natural cocoa powder. Many brands are available, from Hershey's, found in most groceries, to Valrhona, an exceptional quality recommended by numerous chefs.

Citrus Fruits

The heavier the fruit feels, the juicier it probably is. Allow citrus to come to room temperature before attempting to squeeze for fresh juice: You'll get more return on your investment. Rolling an orange or lemon on the counter with a little palm pressure will also help release juices before squeezing.

Chocolate

High-quality chocolate can be expensive, but once you've had it, you'll appreciate the difference. Companies such as Scharffen Berger and Ghirardelli offer excellent chocolates for the price, and they are readily available in most supermarkets.

Milk

When milk is called for in a recipe, whole milk should be used. If you must, substitute 2%, but expect possible faults. In no instance should 1% or skim milk be used. Condensed milk and half and half are also used in some recipes. These should not be substituted for other ingredients.

Cream

Heavy or double cream should be used when cream is called for. The high milk fats create a more delectable, rich, and creamy result.

Sugars

Standard white granulated sugar, light brown sugar, dark brown sugar, and powdered sugar, also known as confectioner's sugar, are used throughout this book. A few recipes will call for specialty sugars, such as unrefined or super fine sugar, available at many large grocers or specialty food shops. Other than swapping out dark for light brown sugars, you should not substitute one variety for another. Measure white sugar simply by scooping, but brown sugars should be packed tightly for measuring.

FACT

Some ice cream recipes may call for the zest of citrus fruits and the sugar to be pulsed in a food processor, but a similar and effective method is to use your fingers. Simply add the zest to the sugar, and continue to knead and squeeze the mixture until the zest has released its scent and become a part of the sugar. Then continue with the recipe as directed. This method is also very useful when making baked goods, such as pie crusts, where you may like a little extra kick of flavor.

Sugar Substitutes

Agave, Splenda, honey, and stevia are all sweeteners used in some recipes for special diets. If you are comfortable using another artificial or natural sweetener, experiment as you see fit. While a few of the recipes included in the sugar-free chapter do not contain refined sugars, please note, agave nectar, fruits, and honey still have sugar. They make for a healthier substitute for sugar, as they are natural, but those on a restricted diet should consult with a doctor before adding such ingredients to their own diet.

Yogurt

Both plain yogurt and Greek yogurt are used in this book. For recipes calling for Greek yogurt, Oikos brand was used, though there are many other acceptable brands on the market. You can certainly experiment, opting to change plain for Greek and vice versa. Sour cream can also be used in a pinch, cup for cup. Greek yogurt, even nonfat or reduced fat, is thicker, making it ideal for frozen desserts. Use caution if substituting nonfat or reduced-fat regular yogurts in recipes calling for Greek yogurt, as the liquid content can result in a less-than-desirable consistency.

Flour

Flour is required for the cakes, cookies, and brownies found in this book. Most recipes will call for all-purpose flour, though whole-wheat flour can be substituted for up to half of the all-purpose if desired. To measure, sift the flour first, then scoop and level, without packing it down.

Eggs

Recipes were tested using large eggs, available in all groceries. You can find cage-free, organic, white, brown—use any variety you wish.

Herbs

Mint, basil, lavender, and other herbs are used throughout this collection of recipes. Unless otherwise noted, assume fresh herbs are being used, and not dried. Most, if not all, are available in most chain grocery stores in the produce section. They are also quite easy to grow in your own garden or in windowsill pots for year-round enjoyment.

Vanilla

Vanilla is the most common flavoring in this book. When a recipe calls for vanilla extract, use extract, not imitation flavoring. Vanilla beans are also readily available in most supermarkets, though they can be found at very good prices in many online shops. See Appendix B for details.

Tips for Special Diets

In recent years, thanks to advances in medical science and the population's desire for better health, many new diets have become wildly popular. Whether an allergen has been isolated (such as nuts) or an intolerance detected (such as dairy), many consumers are finding themselves in a quandary about how to prepare and enjoy the foods they used to love. The same holds true for those who have opted for a vegetarian or vegan lifestyle. Included in this book are two chapters dedicated specifically to vegan and sugar-free readers.

QUESTION

If I have to remove an ingredient, what can I add to enhance my ice cream?
Chefs often add a splash of acid, such as orange or lemon juice, to desserts to highlight the sweet elements of the recipe and add a layer of complexity. The next time you find your frozen dessert "missing something," try drizzling fresh-squeezed citrus juice over the top.

If you're allergic to nuts, you will find that almost all ice creams and sorbets included in the book are nut-free, with only a few exceptions. Most of these are flexible, and the nuts can be omitted if necessary. You will also find that the sorbet and granita chapters are very friendly for vegan and vegetarian diets, as well as for those persons needing nut-free recipes. These recipes can also easily be adapted to sugar-free, using equal parts Splenda for sugar, or by using other sweeteners, such as stevia, agave, or honey.

Successful Storage

Should any of your concoctions remain uneaten, be sure to store them properly. The best containers will have tight-fitting seals and create suction when closed. Lock & Lock, Tupperware, and Rubbermaid are three companies that make quality containers for better freezer storage, and all are available in most groceries and big-box stores.

To ensure the best results, press a piece of plastic wrap tightly against the ice cream or sorbet in its container before freezing to prevent ice crystals from forming. Most frozen treats featured in this book can be frozen for 1–2 weeks with no discernible reduction in quality.

All homemade ice creams, sorbets, and other frozen desserts will benefit from being removed from the freezer 5–10 minutes before serving, as no artificial additives have been incorporated to keep them soft. A warm scoop (or knife for cakes and pies) that has been run under hot water and dried makes serving a breeze.

CHAPTER 2

Essential Ice Cream Recipes

Simple Vanilla Ice Cream
24

Dreamy Orange Cream
Ice Cream
24

Simple Strawberry Ice Cream
25

Simple Chocolate Ice Cream
26

Rich Vanilla Bean Ice Cream
27

Decadent Chocolate Ice Cream
28

Butter Pecan Ice Cream
29

Peaches and Cream Ice Cream
30

Milk Chocolate Ice Cream
31

Coffee Ice Cream
32

Peanut Butter Ice Cream
32

Fresh Peach Ice Cream
33

Lemon Ice Cream
34

Black Cherry Ice Cream
35

Mint Chocolate Chip Ice Cream
36

Cookie Dough Ice Cream
37

Mudslide Ice Cream
38

Rocky Road Ice Cream
39

Nutella Ice Cream
39

Rum Raisin Ice Cream
40

White Chocolate Ice Cream
40

Simple Vanilla Ice Cream

The quintessential ice cream flavor, this quick and easy recipe is perfect for times when you are yearning for ice cream but don't want to spend a lot of time making it. Often, you'll see this type of eggless ice cream labeled as Philadelphia style.

INGREDIENTS | YIELD: 1 QUART

2 cups heavy cream
2 cups whole milk
¾ cup granulated sugar
2 tablespoons light brown sugar
1 tablespoon vanilla extract
Pinch salt

1. Combine all ingredients in a medium saucepan over low heat. Do not allow to boil.

2. Whisk continuously to combine.

3. Remove from heat once sugars are dissolved.

4. Allow to cool in refrigerator.

5. Add to ice cream maker and follow manufacturer's instructions for freezing.

Dreamy Orange Cream Ice Cream

If you are looking for a trip down memory lane, look no further. This creamy orange ice cream will take you back to summer vacations and ballgames in the park when nothing but that tangy popsicle could remedy the afternoon heat.

INGREDIENTS | YIELD: 1 QUART

⅔ cup sugar
Zest of 4 medium oranges
1½ cups freshly squeezed orange juice
½ cup cream cheese
½ cup sour cream
½ cup heavy cream
1 tablespoon vanilla extract
1 teaspoon Grand Marnier, optional

1. Combine the sugar and orange zest in a food processor, and pulse until very well combined.

2. Add in remaining ingredients and pulse thoroughly for several minutes, until all of the sugar has dissolved. Allow to chill for 1–3 hours.

3. Once chilled, add to ice cream maker and follow manufacturer's instructions for freezing.

Simple Strawberry Ice Cream

Sweet and summery, this easy ice cream is a wonderful treat when made with berries fresh from the garden, although grocer's berries are still delicious! Frozen berries are not an option—fresh is the only way to go.

INGREDIENTS | YIELD: 1 QUART

2 cups heavy cream

2 cups whole milk

Pinch salt

¼ cup strawberry jam/preserves

¾ cup sugar

1 cup puréed fresh strawberries

1 cup chopped/crushed fresh strawberries

1. Combine all ingredients in a large mixing bowl or the bowl of a stand mixer.

2. Once combined, allow to chill in refrigerator for 3–4 hours or overnight.

3. Once chilled, add to ice cream maker and follow manufacturer's instructions for freezing.

But It's Not Pink!

Fresh, homemade strawberry ice cream, unlike store-bought ice cream, is not pink. The chunks of berries add a nice bit of color on their own, but if you are itching for that familiar pink hue, simply add a couple drops of red food coloring to the mix.

Simple Chocolate Ice Cream

Lots of heavy cream makes this recipe smooth and luxurious. For extra decadence, toss in a half cup of dark-chocolate chips to the final few spins of the ice cream machine.

INGREDIENTS | YIELD: 1 QUART

3 cups heavy cream

1 cup whole milk

¾ cup sweetened cocoa powder

2 tablespoons cocoa powder

¼ cup brown sugar

⅔ cup sugar

Pinch salt

1 tablespoon vanilla extract

1. In a saucepan over medium heat, combine all ingredients except vanilla until sugar is dissolved. Remove from heat and add vanilla. Stir to combine.

2. Allow to chill in refrigerator for 3–4 hours, or overnight.

3. Once chilled, add to ice cream maker and follow manufacturer's instructions for freezing.

Sweetened Cocoa Powder

Not to be confused with regular or Dutch-processed cocoa powders, sweetened cocoa powder is not interchangeable in baking recipes that call for unsweetened or natural cocoa. Sweetened cocoa powder is not as intense, it is sweet, and is intended for use in drinks and goods that are typically unbaked.

Rich Vanilla Bean Ice Cream

Unlike the Simple Vanilla Ice Cream recipe, this version incorporates a generous amount of egg yolks to add a true richness and very developed flavor. The addition of a steeped vanilla bean not only increases the flavor but adds the speckled appearance that many people love to see in homemade ice cream.

INGREDIENTS | YIELD: 1 QUART

1 cup whole milk

¾ cup sugar

Pinch salt

1 vanilla bean, split and scraped

4 large egg yolks

2 cups heavy cream

2 teaspoons vanilla extract

Vanilla Beans

Vanilla beans are a versatile ingredient in cooking and baking. In this recipe, once you remove the steeped pod from the milk, pat it dry and save it for future use, such as adding to a container of sugar. Just shake the container once or twice a week, and you'll have a delicious vanilla sugar to add to your baked goods or morning coffee. Don't throw those pricy beans away!

1. In a small saucepan, combine the milk, sugar, salt, vanilla bean seeds, and empty bean pod. Stir over medium heat. Once simmering, remove from heat, cover, and allow to steep for 1 hour.

2. After 1 hour, remove bean pod (save for later use). Reheat milk mixture over medium-low heat.

3. In a separate bowl, whisk egg yolks. Once milk mixture is hot, temper the yolks by adding half of the mixture into the eggs, whisking constantly. Return mixture to saucepan, and heat until thickened.

4. Pour heavy cream into a large mixing bowl over an ice bath. Strain custard into the cream, stirring until cooled. Add vanilla extract, stir, and place in refrigerator until thoroughly chilled, about 5 hours or overnight.

5. Once chilled, add to ice cream maker and follow manufacturer's instructions for freezing.

Decadent Chocolate Ice Cream

Smooth and delicious, this custard-style chocolate ice cream is made with tempered egg yolks for a wonderful richness. You'll never want to go back to store-bought after one bite of this!

INGREDIENTS | YIELD: 1 QUART

1 cup whole milk

¾ cup sugar

2 tablespoons Dutch-processed cocoa powder

Pinch salt

3 egg yolks, beaten

3 ounces chopped dark or semisweet chocolate

½ cups heavy cream

4 ounces cream cheese, softened

1 tablespoon vanilla extract

1. Combine the milk, sugar, cocoa powder, and salt in a saucepan over medium heat. Stir to combine. Do not allow to boil; simmer until sugar and cocoa are dissolved.

2. Beat the egg yolks in a medium mixing bowl.

3. Drizzle half of the cocoa mixture into the eggs to temper, whisking constantly. Return mixture to saucepan, and heat until thickened.

4. Remove from heat. Add in chopped chocolate and cream. Stir until chocolate is melted. Chill in refrigerator, stirring occasionally, until completely cooled.

5. Stir in the softened cream cheese and vanilla until well combined. Add to ice cream maker and follow manufacturer's instructions for freezing.

Butter Pecan Ice Cream

Rarely will you find an ice cream parlor that doesn't have butter pecan on the menu, as it is the most popular flavor after chocolate, vanilla, and strawberry, and certainly the most popular ice cream with nuts. This recipe is easy to pull together and is packed with nutty, buttery flavor.

INGREDIENTS | YIELD: 1 QUART

1 cup chopped pecans

2 tablespoons butter

1 cup whole milk

1¾ cups brown sugar

Pinch salt

3 egg yolks, beaten

2½ cups heavy cream

1 tablespoon vanilla extract

1. Sauté pecans in the butter in a medium skillet until aromatic and lightly browned. Set aside; do not drain any remaining butter.

2. Combine the milk, brown sugar, and salt in a medium saucepan, and warm over medium heat until sugar is dissolved. Do not allow to boil.

3. In a separate bowl, whisk egg yolks. Once milk mixture is hot, temper the eggs by adding half of the milk mixture into the eggs, whisking constantly. Return mixture to saucepan, and heat until thickened.

4. Pour heavy cream into a large mixing bowl over an ice bath. Strain custard into the cream, stirring until cooled. Add vanilla extract and butter-pecan mixture. Stir, and place in refrigerator until thoroughly chilled, about 5 hours or overnight.

5. Once chilled, add to ice cream maker and follow manufacturer's instructions for freezing.

Peaches and Cream Ice Cream

Cream cheese added just before the freezing adds a nice tanginess to the sweetness of the fresh peaches. A bit of caramel sauce drizzled over would be the perfect topping on a warm summer evening!

INGREDIENTS | YIELD: 1 QUART

1 cup whole milk

½ cup sugar

¼ cup brown sugar

Pinch salt

1 vanilla bean, split and scraped

3 large egg yolks

2 cups heavy cream

2 teaspoons vanilla extract

4 ounces softened cream cheese

5 fresh peaches, pitted and chopped

Peaches

For this recipe, yellow peaches provide a "peachier" hue and a tangier result than white peaches, although either are fine choices. Yellow peaches are more common than white in North America, but white is becoming more readily available. Look for clingstone peaches versus freestone for softer, sweeter, juicier fruit.

1. In a small saucepan, combine the milk, sugars, salt, vanilla bean seeds, and empty bean pod. Stir over medium heat. Once simmering, remove from heat, cover, and allow to steep for 1 hour.

2. After 1 hour, remove bean pod (save for later use). Reheat milk mixture over medium-low heat.

3. In a separate bowl, whisk egg yolks. Once milk mixture is hot, temper the yolks by adding half of the mixture into the eggs, whisking constantly. Return mixture to saucepan, and heat until thickened.

4. Pour heavy cream into a large mixing bowl over an ice bath. Strain custard into the cream, stirring until cooled. Add vanilla extract, cream cheese, and peaches; stir well, and place in refrigerator until thoroughly chilled, about 5 hours or overnight.

5. Once chilled, add to ice cream maker and follow manufacturer's instructions for freezing.

Milk Chocolate Ice Cream

Most gourmet chefs snub their nose at milk chocolate, but it is the taste from our childhood. There are few people who can't recall with glee their first taste of a milk chocolate candy bar, and this ice cream serves up a frozen version of that memorable bite.

INGREDIENTS | YIELD: 1 QUART

2 cups heavy cream

1 cup milk chocolate, chopped

1 cup whole milk

¾ cup sugar

¼ teaspoon sea salt

3 large egg yolks

1 tablespoon vanilla extract

Milk Chocolate

Many brands of milk chocolate are available, with Hershey's, Nestlé Toll House, and Ghirardelli being staples in most supermarkets. Any of these will work, but for best results, try to find chocolate containing at least 30% cocoa solids. The cocoa content will be labeled on the packaging.

1. Heat the cream over medium-low heat. Once simmering, remove from heat and add in chocolate. Allow to rest for 1 minute, then stir to combine until smooth. Set aside.

2. Combine milk, sugar, and sea salt in a medium saucepan and heat over medium-low heat until sugar and salt are dissolved.

3. In a separate bowl, whisk egg yolks. Once milk mixture is hot, temper the yolks by adding half of the mixture into the eggs, whisking constantly. Return mixture to saucepan, and heat until thickened.

4. Strain custard into the chocolate over an ice bath, stirring until cooled. Add vanilla extract, stir, and place in refrigerator until thoroughly chilled, about 5 hours or overnight.

5. Once chilled, add to ice cream maker and follow manufacturer's instructions for freezing.

Coffee Ice Cream

Served after a decadent evening meal, this ice cream combines both dessert and an after-dinner cup of coffee. For an extra shot of flavor, consider adding a tablespoon of Baileys Irish Cream or Kahlua just before freezing.

INGREDIENTS | YIELD: 1 QUART

1½ cups sweetened condensed milk
¼ cup milk
⅓ cup heavy cream
1¼ cups very strong brewed coffee
Pinch coffee grounds
2 teaspoons vanilla extract

1. Combine all ingredients in a mixing bowl, then chill 5–8 hours, or overnight.

2. Once chilled, add to ice cream maker and follow manufacturer's instructions for freezing.

Flavors Await

Thanks to the abundance of flavored coffees that are readily available, this ice cream recipe is easily changed simply by using different coffee flavors. One particularly nice choice is hazelnut coffee, which can be found in most groceries.

Peanut Butter Ice Cream

Nothing beats the smooth flavor of peanut butter combined with icy cold cream. This popular favorite is the perfect filling for chocolate ice cream sandwiches or a layered ice cream pie.

INGREDIENTS | YIELD: 1 QUART

1 cup peanut butter
1 cup sugar
2 cups half and half
¾ cups heavy cream
Pinch salt
1 teaspoon vanilla extract

1. Combine all ingredients in the food processor, and purée until very smooth. Chill in refrigerator for 2–4 hours, or overnight.

2. Once chilled, add to ice cream maker and follow manufacturer's instructions for freezing.

Peanut Butter

Natural peanut butter is not advised for ice cream recipes. When combined with other ingredients, natural peanut butter will release much of its oil, so it is best to stick with commercial brands for your ice cream making.

Fresh Peach Ice Cream

A Saturday morning trip to the farmers' market often yields a bounty of fresh local peaches, the perfect ingredients for this intensely flavorful ice cream. If you can't buy local, just allow your store-bought peaches to ripen in a brown paper bag for a couple of extra days.

INGREDIENTS | YIELD: 1 QUART

1 cup peaches, peeled
⅔ cup sugar
½ cup water
1 cup heavy cream
1 teaspoon vanilla extract

1. Peel and chop the peaches. Set aside in medium mixing bowl.

2. Combine sugar and water in a saucepan, and cook over medium heat until all sugar has dissolved.

3. Add reserved peaches to the sugar syrup, and continue to cook for 5 minutes. Remove from heat and chill in refrigerator for 30 minutes. Once chilled, purée the mixture in a food processor until very smooth. Strain through a mesh strainer, if desired.

4. Combine all ingredients in the food processor, and purée until very smooth. Chill in refrigerator for 2–4 hours, or overnight.

5. Once chilled, add to ice cream maker and follow manufacturer's instructions for freezing.

Lemon Ice Cream

Summer days in the South conjure up sweltering afternoons on shady porches, rocking chairs, and sweet memories. The subtle tang of this lemon ice cream is just the thing to cool off after a long, hot summer's nap. For a little variety, pair this with a gingerbread cone and a dollop of homemade meringue.

INGREDIENTS | YIELD: 1 QUART

Zest of 4 lemons
¾ cup sugar
¾ cup milk
2¼ cups heavy cream
Pinch salt
4 large egg yolks
½ teaspoon lemon extract

Aging Egg Whites for Meringue

Most great chefs will tell you to age your egg whites before attempting to whip them into mounds of meringue: three days seems to be the general consensus, with the whites left covered in the refrigerator. The aged whites become more stable and easier to whip, and tend to hold their shape. However, if you are in a rush, you can gently microwave the whites for 5 seconds, stir, and repeat twice more to achieve similar results.

1. Combine the lemon zest and sugar with your fingers until aromatic and well combined. In a small saucepan, combine the lemon/sugar mixture, milk, ⅔ cup of the cream, and salt. Stir over medium heat. Once simmering, remove from heat, cover, and allow to steep for 1 hour.

2. After 1 hour, reheat milk mixture over medium-low heat.

3. In a separate bowl, whisk egg yolks. Once milk mixture is hot, temper the yolks by adding half of the mixture into the eggs, whisking constantly. Return mixture to saucepan, and heat until thickened.

4. Pour rest of the heavy cream and lemon extract into a large mixing bowl over an ice bath. Strain lemon custard into the cream, discarding the zest, and stir until cooled. Place in refrigerator until thoroughly chilled, about 5 hours or overnight.

5. Once chilled, add to ice cream maker and follow manufacturer's instructions for freezing.

Black Cherry Ice Cream

Sadly, the season for fresh, ripe cherries is brief, so be sure to seek them out early. Once you've made a batch of this delectable ice cream, you'll certainly want more, and possibly still have time to buy fresh cherries before the season is over!

INGREDIENTS | YIELD: 1 QUART

1 pound black cherries, pitted and chopped

2 teaspoons lemon juice

1¾ cups whole milk

2 cups heavy cream

4 large egg yolks

1 cup sugar

2 teaspoons vanilla extract

2 drops almond extract

Pitting Cherries

Ever wondered where the term "It's the pits" came from? You've obviously never pitted cherries by hand! Several great cherry-pitting devices are on the market, but if you prefer to go gadgetless, you still have options. You can halve each cherry with a sharp knife and remove the pit. Another option is to use a large sturdy drinking straw. Simply insert the straw through the cherry, capturing the pit. A small bit of cherry may be lost with this method, but it's quick and easy and worth the loss.

1. Toss the chopped cherries with lemon juice and set aside.

2. In a medium to large saucepan, combine the milk and cream, and stir over medium heat.

3. In a separate bowl, whisk egg yolks with the sugar until thick and foamy. Once milk mixture is hot, temper the yolks by adding half of the mixture into the eggs, whisking constantly. Return mixture to saucepan, and heat until thickened.

4. Add three-quarters of the reserved cherries to the saucepan, cook for 10 minutes, and then remove from heat. Allow to cool for 15 minutes, then add vanilla and almond extracts.

5. Place mixture into a blender. Purée until smooth. Place in refrigerator until thoroughly chilled, about 5 hours or overnight.

6. Once chilled, add to ice cream maker and follow manufacturer's instructions for freezing. Near the end of the freezing cycle, add remaining cherries and allow to mix.

Mint Chocolate Chip Ice Cream

Combining the cool, fresh zing of mint to cold cream is a match made in heaven. The addition of dark chocolate chips makes it rich and delicious, a summertime favorite around the world.

INGREDIENTS | YIELD: 1 QUART

1 cup whole milk
¾ cup sugar
Pinch salt
20 mint leaves, washed
4 large egg yolks
2 cups heavy cream
2 teaspoons vanilla extract
½ teaspoon mint extract
1½ cups dark chocolate chips

Mint Varieties

Mint is a very hearty plant, and is available all over the world. There are many varieties, and most would be great in this recipe. One particularly tasty choice is chocolate mint, which smells and tastes subtly of cocoa. Wintergreen and peppermint are also wonderful choices. Or try spearmint for a twist!

1. In a small saucepan, combine the milk, sugar, salt, and mint leaves; stir over medium heat. Once simmering, remove from heat, cover, and allow to steep for 1 hour.

2. After 1 hour, remove the leaves. Reheat milk mixture over medium-low heat.

3. In a separate bowl, whisk egg yolks. Once milk mixture is hot, temper the yolks by adding half of the mixture into the eggs, whisking constantly. Return mixture to saucepan, and heat until thickened.

4. Pour heavy cream into a large mixing bowl over an ice bath. Strain custard into the cream, stirring until cooled. Add vanilla and mint extracts, stir, and place in refrigerator until thoroughly chilled, about 5 hours or overnight.

5. Once chilled, add to ice cream maker and follow manufacturer's instructions for freezing. Toward the end of the freeze cycle, add in the chocolate chips.

Cookie Dough Ice Cream

What is it about raw cookie dough that turns us all into kids? The sugary rush, the texture? Or is it just the feeling of being naughty? Whatever the reason, Cookie Dough Ice Cream is a true delight, and the quickest way to recapture that sneaky feeling of childhood.

INGREDIENTS | YIELD: 1 QUART

2½ cups heavy cream

1½ cups whole milk

⅔ cup sugar

⅓ cup light brown sugar

1 tablespoon vanilla extract

Pinch salt

1 package refrigerated cookie dough, frozen

Cookie Dough Caution

This recipe calls for prepackaged cookie dough, which contains raw eggs. It is the simplest way to gain that cookie-dough chewiness that we all crave, but, if concerned about the raw eggs, you can prepare an eggless cookie dough to use instead. In many cities, you may be able to find egg-free or vegan cookie dough in groceries or specialty stores.

1. Combine all ingredients except the cookie dough in a medium saucepan over low heat. Do not allow to boil.

2. Whisk continuously to combine.

3. Remove from heat once sugars are dissolved. Allow to cool in refrigerator for 4 hours or overnight.

4. Add to ice cream maker and follow manufacturer's instructions for freezing.

5. Chop frozen cookie dough into small pieces and add toward the end of the freeze cycle.

Mudslide Ice Cream

Based on a popular adult drink, this ice cream has satisfying "night out" flavor when you opt to stay in.

INGREDIENTS | YIELD: 1 QUART

1 cup Irish cream liqueur
1 cup coffee-flavored liqueur
3 cups heavy cream
1 cup half and half
¾ cup sugar
6 large egg yolks
7 ounces dark chocolate, finely chopped
1 tablespoon vanilla extract
⅓ cup mini chocolate chips

Mudslide Drinks

The Mudslide's delicious origin can be traced back to the Caribbean in the 1950s where it was allegedly invented at the Wreck Bar & Grill in the Cayman Islands.

1. Bring Irish cream and coffee-flavored liqueurs to a boil in a medium saucepan, and allow to reduce by half.

2. Add cream, half and half, and sugar to a steaming simmer. Remove from heat.

3. Whisk eggs in a large bowl. Slowly stream hot milk mixture into eggs until fully incorporated. Return mixture to heat, and cook over medium heat until thick, being careful not to boil.

4. Strain into a clean bowl. Add the chopped chocolate and vanilla; stir until smooth. Refrigerate 4 hours to overnight.

5. Add to ice cream maker and follow manufacturer's instructions for freezing. Fold in the mini chocolate chips.

Rocky Road Ice Cream

This is a classic ice cream for all ages. Chocolate ice cream; fluffy marshmallows; crunchy, toasty almonds; and chocolate chips are a perfect combination.

INGREDIENTS | YIELD: 1 QUART

1 cup half and half

⅓ cup Dutch-processed cocoa powder

4 egg yolks

12 ounces high-quality dark chocolate, finely chopped

1½ cups heavy cream

1 tablespoon vanilla extract

½ cup mini marshmallows

½ cup chopped toasted almonds

¼ cup mini chocolate chips

1. Heat the half and half and cocoa powder in a medium saucepan to a simmer.

2. Whisk the egg yolks in a medium bowl, then slowly pour the half and half into the egg yolks to temper them. Return mixture to the pot and stir constantly over medium heat until thickened, being sure not to boil. Remove from heat and add chocolate. Stir until smooth.

3. Add cream and vanilla. Cover and refrigerate 4 hours to overnight.

4. Add to ice cream maker and follow manufacturer's instructions for freezing. Just before storing, fold in the marshmallows, almonds, and chocolate chips.

Nutella Ice Cream

Popular for years in Europe, Nutella recently has started making a name for itself in the United States. Made of hazelnuts and chocolate, this delicious spread is a delightful alternative to peanut butter in a peanut butter and jelly sandwich, as well as in ice cream.

INGREDIENTS | YIELD: 1 QUART

1 cup Nutella

¾ cup sugar

1¾ cups half and half

1 cup heavy cream

Pinch salt

2 teaspoons vanilla extract

1. Combine all ingredients in the food processor, and purée until very smooth. Chill in refrigerator for 2–4 hours, or overnight.

2. Once chilled, add to ice cream maker and follow manufacturer's instructions for freezing.

Rum Raisin Ice Cream

Sweet and plump raisins are soaked in tummy-warming rum in this decadent adult treat.

INGREDIENTS | YIELD: 1 QUART

¾ cup raisins, chopped
¼ cup dark rum
2 cups cream
2 cups half and half
¾ cup sugar
¼ teaspoon fresh-grated nutmeg
1 teaspoon vanilla extract

1. Soak raisins in dark rum overnight.

2. Stir everything together. Refrigerate 2 hours. Add to ice cream maker and follow manufacturer's instructions for freezing.

Rums, Light to Dark

For a more robust flavor in your recipe, choose dark rum. For a more subtle taste, go with something a little lighter.

White Chocolate Ice Cream

This recipe is an elegant addition to your ice cream collection. It's sweet but decidedly unchildlike, and excellent when served alongside Peach Compote or Cherry Compote (see Chapter 17).

INGREDIENTS | YIELD: 1 QUART

1 cup half and half
4 egg yolks
12 ounces high-quality white chocolate, finely chopped
1½ cups heavy cream
1 tablespoon vanilla extract

1. Heat half and half to a simmer in a medium saucepan.

2. Whisk the egg yolks in a small bowl, then begin to slowly pour the half and half into the egg yolks to temper them. Return mixture to the pot and constantly stir over medium heat until thickened, being sure not to boil.

3. Remove from heat and add the white chocolate. Stir until smooth.

4. Add cream and vanilla extract. Cover and refrigerate 4 hours to overnight.

5. Add to ice cream maker and follow manufacturer's instructions for freezing.

White Chocolate

A few years after World War I, white chocolate was first introduced in Switzerland. This white chocolate was produced in 1930 by the Nestlé company. The bar's name was *Galak*. Perhaps it sounds unappealing, but we all know better!

CHAPTER 3

Gelato

Caramel Apple Gelato
(*Gelato di caramello mela*)
42

Orange Infused Olive Oil Gelato
(*Gelato di arancia olio
d'oliva infuso*)
43

Fresh Fig Gelato (*Gelato di fichi*)
44

Herbed Tomato Gelato
(*Gelato di herbes e tomati*)
44

Basil Gelato (*Gelato di basi*)
45

Rice Gelato (*Gelato di riso*)
46

Hazelnut Nutella Swirl Gelato
(*Gelato alla Nutella*)
47

Pumpkin Gelato
(*Gelato di zucca*)
48

Pistachio Gelato
(*Gelato di pistacchio*)
49

Honey Swirled Pear Gelato
(*Gelato di miele roteato pera*)
50

Gianduja Gelato
(*Gelato di gianduja*)
51

Limoncello Gelato
(*Gelato di limoncello*)
52

Espresso Gelato
(*Gelato di espresso*)
53

Sage Blackberry Swirl Gelato
(*Gelato di leggenda e mora*)
54

Chianti Gelato
(*Gelato di chianti*)
55

Toasted Coconut Gelato
(*Gelato di noce di cocco tostata*)
56

Cherry Limeade Gelato
(*Gelato di bere ciliegia e calce*)
57

Dark Chocolate Bourbon Gelato
(*Gelato di cioccolato
scuro borbone*)
58

Blood Orange Gelato
(*Gelato di arancia rosso*)
59

Caramel Apple Gelato *(Gelato di caramello mela)*

Few things say autumn and harvest festivals like caramel apples. Here, those joys of the season are frozen in a delectable, dreamy dessert.

INGREDIENTS | YIELD: 1 QUART

3 cups peeled, cored, and cubed green apples (about 10)

¼ cup brown sugar

½ teaspoon cinnamon

¼ teaspoon cardamom

Pinch salt

2 tablespoons fresh-squeezed orange juice

1 cup milk

2 cups heavy cream

½ cup sugar

4 large egg yolks

2 tablespoons butterscotch-flavored liqueur

½ cup Caramel Sauce (see Chapter 17)

Caramel Apples

The caramel apple was created in the 1950s by Dan Walker, a sales representative for Kraft Foods. This treat has evolved today with many people dipping and decorating them in chocolate, nuts, and other candies. Feel free to garnish your sweet treat similarly. Have fun!

1. Combine apples, brown sugar, cinnamon, cardamom, salt, and orange juice in large pan. Sauté over medium heat until apples are tender. Set aside to cool, then purée in a blender until smooth. Strain through a fine-mesh sieve and refrigerate purée.

2. In a medium saucepan, combine milk, cream, and ¼ cup of the sugar. Bring to a simmer and remove from heat.

3. In a separate bowl, whisk egg yolks and remaining ¼ cup sugar. Once milk mixture is hot, temper the yolks by adding half of the mixture into the eggs, whisking constantly. Return mixture to saucepan, and heat until thickened. Remove from heat and stir in the butterscotch liqueur.

4. Add apple purée and chill 4 hours or overnight.

5. Add to ice cream maker and follow manufacturer's instructions for freezing. Just before gelato is frozen, swirl in the Caramel Sauce. Stop the churning as soon as the gelato is just frozen.

Orange Infused Olive Oil Gelato *(Gelato di arancia olio d'oliva infuso)*

Olive oil is delicious and versatile, but when infused with complementary flavors it is out of this world. This is a beautiful, subtle, yet complex ice cream that is even more stunning when drizzled with just a bit more infused olive oil.

INGREDIENTS | YIELD: 1 QUART

3 cups milk
1 cup heavy cream
6 large egg yolks
1 cup sugar
⅔ cup orange-infused olive oil
Pinch salt

Olive Oil

There are several grades of olive oil: extra virgin, virgin, pure, and olive oil. Extra virgin is the strongest of flavors and is recommended for this particular recipe to allow the flavors to shine through. It is easy to infuse olive oil yourself, but Nudo offers several flavor-infused oils that can be purchased online. See Appendix B for details.

1. In a medium saucepan, bring milk and cream just to a boil and immediately remove from heat.

2. With an electric or stand mixer, beat egg yolks and sugar on high until tripled in volume. Scrape down sides of bowl occasionally. Reduce speed to low and slowly drizzle in olive oil and salt.

3. Slowly add the hot milk mixture to the egg mixture until combined, then add it back into the saucepan. Whisk constantly over medium-low heat until it coats the back of a wooden spoon. Be careful not to overheat or the eggs will curdle.

4. Place fine-mesh sieve over a large bowl. Strain gelato mixture. Chill 4 hours or overnight.

5. Add to ice cream maker and follow manufacturer's instructions for freezing. Stop the churning as soon as the gelato is just frozen.

Fresh Fig Gelato *(Gelato di fichi)*

Fresh figs are extremely perishable, and easily damaged when shipped long distances. Therefore, if your local supermarket doesn't carry any, try a farmers' market. The closer to home your figs grew, the better they will be.

INGREDIENTS | YIELD: 1 QUART

1 pound fresh figs, peeled
Juice and zest of ½ lemon
¼ cup honey

1. In small bowl, combine the peeled figs, lemon juice, and honey. Stir and allow to macerate at room temperature for 1–2 hours.

2. After figs are ready, place all ingredients in a blender or food processor, and blend until smooth.

3. Add to ice cream maker and follow manufacturer's instructions for freezing. Stop the churning as soon as the gelato is just frozen.

Herbed Tomato Gelato *(Gelato di herbes e tomati)*

Don't forget, tomatoes are fruit! In all seriousness, tomatoes make for a delicious and unusual frozen dessert ingredient. Give it a try!

INGREDIENTS | YIELD: 1 QUART

3 cups strongly flavored tomatoes, peeled, seeded, and diced
1 tablespoon balsamic vinegar
½ cup simple syrup
¼ teaspoon onion powder
¼ cup fresh basil leaves
¼ teaspoon dried oregano
Pinch salt and pepper
½ cup heavy cream

1. In a medium pot over low heat, reduce the tomatoes for about 45 minutes to 1 hour. Remove from heat and cool to room temperature.

2. Once cooled, combine all ingredients in a blender or food processor until very smooth. Taste, and adjust seasonings as necessary. Refrigerate mixture 4 hours or overnight.

3. Add to ice cream maker and follow manufacturer's instructions for freezing. Stop the churning as soon as the gelato is just frozen.

Basil Gelato *(Gelato di basi)*

Though it may seem like a surprising ingredient for gelato, basil is actually a member of the mint family. Its powerful flavor creates a wonderfully complex treat that will leave you wanting more.

INGREDIENTS | YIELD: 1 QUART

3 cups whole milk

1 cup sugar

Pinch salt

1 vanilla bean, split and scraped

5 large egg yolks

1 cup heavy cream

3 cups fresh basil

2 teaspoons vanilla extract

Say What?

The ancient Greeks and Romans had some odd philosophies when it came to basil. They believed that basil would only grow if loud cursing and shouting accompanied the sowing of the seeds!

1. In a small saucepan, combine the milk, sugar, salt, vanilla bean seeds, and empty bean pod. Stir over medium heat. Once simmering, remove from heat, cover, and allow to steep for 1 hour.

2. After 1 hour, remove bean pod (save for later use). Reheat milk mixture over medium-low heat.

3. In a separate bowl, whisk egg yolks. Once milk mixture is hot, temper the yolks by adding half of the mixture into the eggs, whisking constantly. Return mixture to saucepan, and heat until thickened. Pour ½ cup of the heavy cream into a large mixing bowl over an ice bath. Strain custard into the cream.

4. Blanch the basil in boiling water for 10 seconds, then shock in an ice bath. Towel the leaves dry. Add leaves and remaining ½ cup of heavy cream to blender and process. Add basil mixture and vanilla extract to the prepared custard, allowing the basil to infuse into the mixture. Strain after 2 hours, and place in refrigerator until thoroughly chilled, about 5 hours or overnight.

5. Add to ice cream maker and follow manufacturer's instructions for freezing. Stop the churning as soon as the gelato is just frozen.

Rice Gelato *(Gelato di riso)*

The feature of this recipe is rice, and therefore it offers an unusual texture. You'll find it unlike any other gelato, as it is subtle and yet distinctive in a very delicious way.

INGREDIENTS | YIELD: 1 QUART

3 cups milk

½ cup sugar

½ cup rice, rinsed

½ cup heavy cream

Pinch salt

4 large egg yolks

2 teaspoons vanilla extract

Pinch nutmeg

Rice

Italians have a bit of a love affair with rice when it comes to desserts, unlike many Americans. Sweet but not too sweet seems to be the trend in Italian sweet desserts, known as *dolci*. Many pies, tarts, and cannoli in Italy feature a substantial amount of the grain.

1. In a medium saucepan, bring 2 cups of the milk to a boil with ¼ cup of the sugar until sugar is dissolved. Stir in rice and simmer for 1 hour. Set aside to cool, stirring occasionally. Stir in cream, and cover. Refrigerate for 2 hours or more.

2. Bring remaining milk, sugar, and salt to a simmer over medium heat.

3. In a separate bowl, whisk egg yolks. Once milk mixture is hot, temper the yolks by adding half of the mixture into the eggs, whisking constantly. Return mixture to saucepan, and heat until thickened. Remove from heat and stir in the vanilla.

4. Chill 4 hours or overnight. Stir in the rice mixture and nutmeg.

5. Add to ice cream maker and follow manufacturer's instructions for freezing. Stop the churning as soon as the gelato is just frozen.

Hazelnut Nutella Swirl Gelato *(Gelato alla Nutella)*

Nutella is to Italy what peanut butter is to the United States. It is used in sandwiches, pastries . . . you name it. Made of hazelnuts and cocoa powder, it makes the perfect complement to hazelnut gelato.

INGREDIENTS | YIELD: 1 QUART

1½ cups toasted hazelnuts, skins removed

¾ cup sugar

1 cup milk

2 cups heavy cream

Pinch salt

4 large egg yolks

2 tablespoons Frangelico or other hazelnut liqueur

½ cup Nutella

Nutella

Nutella was created by Pietro Ferrero in the 1940s to extend the chocolate supply due to rationing of cocoa. Nutella was originally made in loaves and wrapped in foil (much like butter is today) so that it could be cut and spread on bread. It has since evolved into the much-loved creamy, silky spread that it is today.

1. Combine hazelnuts and sugar in blender or food processor, and pulse until well chopped. Add milk, cream, and salt to a medium saucepan. Add hazelnut mixture and bring to a boil over medium heat. Remove from heat and steep for 1–2 hours.

2. Place a strainer over a medium saucepan, and pour the hazelnut milk mixture into it. Wring the juices out of the strained hazelnuts into the saucepan. Discard nuts and bring mixture to a simmer.

3. In a separate bowl, whisk egg yolks. Once milk mixture is hot, temper the yolks by adding half of the mixture into the eggs, whisking constantly. Return mixture to saucepan, and heat until thickened. Remove from heat and stir in the Frangelico.

4. Chill 4 hours or overnight.

5. Add to ice cream maker and follow manufacturer's instructions for freezing. Just before gelato is frozen, swirl in the Nutella. Stop the churning as soon as the gelato is just frozen.

Pumpkin Gelato *(Gelato di zucca)*

Ah, the fall season: falling leaves, crisp air, cider, and pumpkins. This recipe is perfect for when you want the fall feeling but in deliciously cold, creamy form.

INGREDIENTS | YIELD: 1 QUART

3½ cups whole milk

1 can pumpkin purée

⅔ cup dark brown sugar

Pinch salt

1 teaspoon grated fresh ginger

2 teaspoons cinnamon

½ teaspoon cardamom

¼ teaspoon ground cloves

4 tablespoons cornstarch

1. Combine 2 cups of the milk, pumpkin purée, brown sugar, salt, ginger, cinnamon, cardamom, and cloves in a medium saucepan. Bring to a boil.

2. While pumpkin mixture heats up, make a slurry with the remaining milk and cornstarch.

3. When pumpkin mixture comes to a boil, add slurry and stir. Bring back to a boil while stirring constantly, then remove from heat. Bring to room temperature, seal tightly, and refrigerate 8 hours to overnight.

4. Add to your ice cream maker and follow manufacturer's instructions for freezing. Stop the churning just as the gelato is just frozen.

Pistachio Gelato *(Gelato di pistacchio)*

Believe it or not, despite their nutty appearance, pistachios are not nuts. They are actually the seeds of a plum-like fruit, the flesh of which is removed during processing.

INGREDIENTS | YIELD: 1 QUART

1 cup unsalted shelled pistachios

1 cup sugar

2 cups milk

Pinch salt

4 large egg yolks

2 teaspoons vanilla extract

1¼ cups heavy whipping cream

1 cup toasted unsalted shelled pistachios, chopped

1. Combine untoasted pistachios and sugar in a blender or food processor, and pulse until well chopped. Place into a medium saucepan. Add milk and salt, and bring to a boil over medium heat.

2. In a separate bowl, whisk egg yolks. Once milk mixture is hot, temper the yolks by adding half of the mixture into the eggs, whisking constantly. Add egg mixture to saucepan, and heat until thickened. Remove from heat, and stir in the vanilla.

3. Chill 4 hours or overnight. Stir in the cream and chopped toasted pistachios.

4. Add to ice cream maker and follow manufacturer's instructions for freezing. Stop the churning as soon as the gelato is just frozen.

Honey Swirled Pear Gelato *(Gelato di miele roteato pera)*

The floral notes of the honey and pear dance together like Fred Astaire and Ginger Rogers. Give it a twirl!

INGREDIENTS | YIELD: 1 QUART

2 cups whole milk

½ cup heavy cream

⅓ cup sugar

⅔ cup honey, divided

Pinch salt

4 large egg yolks

1½ cups pear nectar or purée

¼ teaspoon cardamom

1 (15-ounce) can pears, drained and roughly smashed

Honey

Honey dates back in history as far as 10–20 million years ago. Egyptians sacrificed honey to their gods, Roman soldiers used it as a healing aid for wounds, and kings and lords would reserve it for their private use. Honey has always been precious. We are fortunate these days to have easy access to delicious, golden honey.

1. Combine milk, cream, sugar, ⅓ cup honey, and salt in a medium saucepan. Bring to boil. Remove from heat.

2. In a separate bowl, whisk egg yolks. Temper the yolks by adding half of the hot milk mixture into the eggs, whisking constantly. Add egg mixture to saucepan, and heat until thickened.

3. Add pear nectar, cardamom, and smashed pears. Refrigerate 4 hours to overnight.

4. Add to ice cream maker and follow manufacturer's instructions for freezing. Stop the churning as soon as the gelato is just frozen. Swirl in the remaining ⅓ cup honey and freeze.

Gianduja Gelato *(Gelato di gianduja)*

Not familiar with the term gianduja? Gianduja is a chocolate mixture containing about one-third hazelnut paste. There is no real "law" about the proportion, however, and most gianduja recipes will simply call for both chocolate and hazelnut as featured ingredients.

INGREDIENTS | YIELD: 1 QUART

1½ cups toasted hazelnuts, skins removed

¾ cup sugar

1 cup milk

2 cups heavy cream

pinch salt

4 ounces milk chocolate, chopped

4 large egg yolks

2 teaspoons vanilla extract

1. Combine hazelnuts and sugar in blender or food processor, and pulse until well chopped. Add milk, 1 cup of the heavy cream, and salt to a medium saucepan. Add hazelnut mixture, and bring to a boil over medium heat. Remove from heat and steep for 1–2 hours.

2. Bring the remaining 1 cup of cream to a simmer in a separate saucepan, then pour over the chopped milk chocolate. Stir to combine until very smooth.

3. Place a strainer over a medium saucepan, and pour the hazelnut milk mixture into it. Wring the juices out of the strained hazelnuts into the saucepan. Discard nuts and bring mixture to a simmer.

4. In a separate bowl, whisk egg yolks. Once milk mixture is hot, temper the yolks by adding half of the mixture into the eggs, whisking constantly. Return mixture to saucepan, and heat until thickened. Remove from heat, and stir in the vanilla and melted milk chocolate mixture. Stir until smooth.

5. Chill 4 hours or overnight.

6. Add to ice cream maker and follow manufacturer's instructions for freezing. Stop the churning as soon as the gelato is just frozen.

Limoncello Gelato *(Gelato di limoncello)*

The perfect ending to the perfect Italian meal is limoncello, an Italian lemon liqueur.
This gelato variation steps it up and gives you a creamy dessert to boot!

INGREDIENTS | YIELD: 1 QUART

3 cups whole milk

1 cup sugar

Pinch salt

Zest of 2 lemons, finely chopped

5 large egg yolks

⅔ cup heavy cream

¼ cup limoncello

Fresh-squeezed juice of ½ lemon

Limoncello

There are several differing stories as to the origin of limoncello. What does remain consistent is that limoncello was first created in the 1900s. It originated on Italy's southwest coast, in either Capri, Sorrento, or Amalfi. In Italy, it is commonly used as an apéritif and a digestive before and after meals.

1. In a small saucepan, combine the milk, sugar, salt, and lemon zest. Stir over medium heat. Once simmering, remove from heat, cover, and allow to steep for 1 hour.

2. Reheat milk mixture over medium-low heat.

3. In a separate bowl, whisk egg yolks. Once milk mixture is hot, temper the yolks by adding half of the mixture into the eggs, whisking constantly. Return mixture to saucepan, and heat until thickened. Pour ½ cup of heavy cream into a large mixing bowl over an ice bath. Strain custard into the cream.

4. Stir together limoncello, lemon juice, and remaining cream. Stir into gelato mixture. Refrigerate 8 hours to overnight.

5. Add to ice cream maker and follow manufacturer's instructions for freezing. Stop the churning as soon as the gelato is just frozen.

Espresso Gelato *(Gelato di espresso)*

*When you think of Italy, gelato and espresso may instantly come to mind.
Here, they go hand in hand to give a cool and delicious pick-me-up.*

INGREDIENTS | YIELD: 1 QUART

3 cups whole milk

1 cup sugar

Pinch salt

⅓ cup coarse-ground espresso beans

1 tablespoon espresso powder (do not use instant coffee)

5 large egg yolks

1 cup heavy cream

2 teaspoons vanilla extract

1. In a small saucepan, combine the milk, sugar, salt, ground espresso beans, and espresso powder. Stir over medium heat. Once simmering, remove from heat, cover, and allow to steep for 1 hour.

2. After 1 hour, strain the milk mixture to remove all of the coffee grounds. You may want to do this a few times to ensure you get out the maximum amount of grounds. Reheat milk mixture over medium-low heat.

3. In a separate bowl, whisk egg yolks. Once milk mixture is hot, temper the yolks by adding half of the mixture into the eggs, whisking constantly. Add egg mixture to the saucepan, and heat until thickened. Pour ½ cup of the heavy cream into a large mixing bowl over an ice bath. Strain custard into the cream. Add remaining ½ cup cream and vanilla, and stir to combine.

4. Add to ice cream maker and follow manufacturer's instructions for freezing. Stop the churning as soon as the gelato is just frozen.

Sage Blackberry Swirl Gelato *(Gelato di leggenda e mora)*

With the deep flavors of the blackberries and the refreshing earthy flavors of the sage, this gelato will have you swooning.

INGREDIENTS | YIELD: 1 QUART

3 cups whole milk

1 cup sugar

Pinch salt

1 vanilla bean, split and scraped

5 large egg yolks

1 cup heavy cream

3 cups fresh sage

2 teaspoons vanilla extract

⅔ cup seedless blackberry jam

3 tablespoons blackberry brandy or dark berry liqueur

Sage

Sage is an astringent, an antiseptic, and a tonic herb, with a camphor-like aroma. Sage is said to prevent spasms, improve liver function and digestion, and have anti-inflammatory, antidepressant, and estrogenic effects. So not only is this sage gelato delicious, some might say it has health benefits as well!

1. In a small saucepan, combine the milk, sugar, salt, vanilla bean seeds, and empty bean pod. Stir over medium heat. Once simmering, remove from heat, cover, and allow to steep for 1 hour.

2. After 1 hour, remove bean pod (save for later use). Reheat milk mixture over medium-low heat.

3. In a separate bowl, whisk egg yolks. Once milk mixture is hot, temper the yolks by adding half of the mixture into the eggs, whisking constantly. Return egg mixture to saucepan, and heat until thickened. Pour ½ cup of the heavy cream into a large mixing bowl over an ice bath. Strain custard into the cream.

4. Blanch the sage in boiling water for 10 seconds, then shock in an ice bath. Towel the leaves dry. Add leaves and remaining ½ cup of heavy cream to blender and process. Add sage mixture and vanilla extract to the prepared custard, allowing the sage to infuse into the mixture. Strain after 2 hours, and place in refrigerator until thoroughly chilled, about 5 hours or overnight. Just before churning gelato, stir together jam and liqueur thoroughly in a small bowl.

5. Add to ice cream maker and follow manufacturer's instructions for freezing. Stop the churning as soon as the gelato is just frozen. Swirl in the jam mixture before placing into freezer.

Chianti Gelato *(Gelato di chianti)*

Chianti is a strong fruity Italian wine with notes of cherry, plum, almonds, tobacco, and vanilla. Adding the freshly ground pepper perfectly complements the wine while not overpowering it.

INGREDIENTS | YIELD: 1 QUART

2 cups whole milk

1 cup sugar

Pinch salt

1 teaspoon freshly ground black pepper

5 large egg yolks

1 cup heavy cream

1 cup good-quality Chianti

Chianti

Chianti wine comes from the Chianti region of Tuscany, Italy. Only wines from this region can properly be called Chianti, though there are other areas that use this name on their bottles as well. Chianti is produced to be used as a simple table wine. Often a basket encases the bottom of the bottle. It's a much sought-after, bold red wine, loved my many.

1. In a small saucepan, combine the milk, sugar, salt, and pepper. Stir over medium heat. Once simmering, remove from heat, cover, and allow to steep for 1 hour.

2. Reheat milk mixture over medium-low heat.

3. In a separate bowl, whisk egg yolks. Once milk mixture is hot, temper the yolks by adding half of the mixture into the eggs, whisking constantly. Return egg mixture to saucepan, and heat until thickened. Pour ½ cup of the heavy cream into a large mixing bowl over an ice bath. Strain custard into the cream. Add remaining ½ cup cream, and stir to combine.

4. Stir Chianti into gelato mixture. Refrigerate 8 hours to overnight.

5. Add to ice cream maker and follow manufacturer's instructions for freezing. Stop the churning as soon as the gelato is just frozen.

Toasted Coconut Gelato *(Gelato di noce di cocco tostata)*

*Coconuts have more than 100 uses. That's amazing stuff for one simple fruit!
The coconut tree has so many uses it is commonly called "the tree of life."*

INGREDIENTS | YIELD: 1 QUART

2 cups whole milk

1 vanilla bean, split

2 cups toasted coconut

1 cup desiccated coconut

1 cup sugar

Pinch salt

5 large egg yolks

1 (14-ounce) can coconut milk

1 cup heavy cream

2 teaspoons vanilla extract

1. In a medium saucepan, combine the milk, vanilla bean, toasted and desiccated coconut, sugar, and salt. Stir over medium heat. Bring just to a boil; remove from heat, cover, and allow to steep for 1–2 hours.

2. After steeping, strain the milk mixture. Reheat milk mixture over medium-low heat.

3. In a separate bowl, whisk egg yolks. Once milk mixture is hot, temper the yolks by adding half of the mixture into the eggs, whisking constantly. Add egg mixture to the saucepan, and heat until thickened. Pour coconut milk, heavy cream, and vanilla extract into a large mixing bowl over an ice bath. Strain custard into the cream.

4. Add to ice cream maker and follow manufacturer's instructions for freezing. Stop the churning as soon as the gelato is just frozen.

Cherry Limeade Gelato *(Gelato di bere ciliegia e calce)*

Cherry limeade is a popular summer drink. In this version of gelato you get the best of both worlds: refreshing cherry limeade and cool, creamy gelato.

INGREDIENTS | YIELD: 1 QUART

3 cups whole milk

1 vanilla bean, split and scraped

Zest of 2 limes, finely grated

⅔ cup sugar

Pinch salt

5 large egg yolks

1 cup heavy cream

2 teaspoons vanilla extract

4 tablespoons fresh lime juice

⅔ cup Cherry Compote (see Chapter 17)

Limeade

Limeade has been popular since the 1800s. Although it is not consumed extensively in the United States, limeade is actually one of the most popular drinks in India and Pakistan. There it is called *nimbu paani*.

1. In a small saucepan, combine the milk, vanilla seeds, empty bean pod, lime zest, sugar, and salt. Stir over medium heat. Once simmering, remove from heat, cover, and allow to steep for 1 hour.

2. After 1 hour, remove bean pod (save for later use). Reheat milk mixture over medium-low heat.

3. In a separate bowl, whisk egg yolks. Once milk mixture is hot, temper the yolks by adding half of the mixture into the eggs, whisking constantly. Return mixture to saucepan, and heat until thickened. Pour heavy cream and vanilla extract into a large mixing bowl over an ice bath. Strain custard into the cream.

4. Add lime juice to the prepared custard, whisking constantly. Place in refrigerator until thoroughly chilled, about 5 hours or overnight.

5. Add to ice cream maker and follow manufacturer's instructions for freezing. Stop the churning as soon as the gelato is just frozen. Swirl in the Cherry Compote before placing in the freezer.

Dark Chocolate Bourbon Gelato *(Gelato di cioccolato scuro borbone)*

*The dark, silky taste of chocolate and the smoky warmth of bourbon
come together in this perfect after-dinner treat.*

INGREDIENTS | YIELD: 1 QUART

3 cups whole milk

4 tablespoons dark cocoa powder

2 teaspoons espresso powder

1 cup sugar

Pinch salt

4 ounces bittersweet chocolate, chopped

5 large egg yolks

⅔ cup heavy cream

¼ cup good-quality bourbon

1 teaspoon vanilla extract

1. In a small saucepan, combine the milk, cocoa powder, espresso powder, sugar, and salt. Whisk vigorously over medium heat. Once at a high simmer, remove from heat and add chocolate. Whisk until smooth, then cover and allow flavors to meld for about 30 minutes.

2. Reheat milk mixture over medium-low heat.

3. In a separate bowl, whisk egg yolks. Once milk mixture is hot, temper the yolks by adding half of the mixture into the eggs, whisking constantly. Add egg mixture to the saucepan, and heat until thickened. Pour ½ cup of the heavy cream into a large mixing bowl over an ice bath. Strain custard into the cream.

4. Stir remaining cream, bourbon, and vanilla extract into gelato mixture. Refrigerate 4 hours to overnight.

5. Add to ice cream maker and follow manufacturer's instructions for freezing. Stop the churning as soon as the gelato is just frozen.

Blood Orange Gelato *(Gelato di arancia rosso)*

Blood oranges are less acidic than other oranges and carry undertones of strawberries or raspberries. Choose a heavy specimen to ensure a quality fruit for your gelato.

INGREDIENTS | YIELD: 1 QUART

1¾ cups sugar

1½ cups water

2¼ cups fresh blood orange juice

½ cup heavy cream

1 teaspoon vanilla

1. Place the sugar and water in a small saucepan, and stir over medium heat until all of the sugar is dissolved. Allow to cool, then combine with the orange juice. Cover and refrigerate until cool, approximately 2 hours or more.

2. In a separate bowl, whip the cream and vanilla to stiff peaks, then fold into the orange mixture.

3. Add to ice cream maker and follow manufacturer's instructions for freezing. Stop the churning as soon as the gelato is just frozen.

CHAPTER 4

Frozen Yogurt

Vanilla Frozen Yogurt
62

Strawberry Frozen Yogurt
62

Raspberry Frozen Yogurt
63

Blueberry Frozen Yogurt
63

Blackberry Lime Frozen Yogurt
64

Zesty Lemon Frozen Yogurt
64

Orange Frozen Yogurt
65

Lime Frozen Yogurt
65

Chocolate Frozen Yogurt
66

Rich Chocolate and Raspberry
Frozen Yogurt
66

Cream Cheese Frozen Yogurt
67

Peanut Butter Frozen Yogurt
68

Peach Pie Frozen Yogurt
68

Chocolate Cherry Frozen Yogurt
69

Espresso Frozen Yogurt
70

Banana Frozen Yogurt
70

Cucumber Mint Frozen Yogurt
71

Vanilla Frozen Yogurt

Want more vanilla flavor? Scrape the seeds from half a vanilla bean into the mixture with the rest of the ingredients. It won't be steeped, but it will offer a subtle flavor pop and increased aroma.

INGREDIENTS | YIELD: 1 QUART

2 cups Greek yogurt
2 cups plain whole-milk yogurt
½ cup sugar
¼ cup light corn syrup
1 teaspoon vanilla extract

1. Place all ingredients in a blender or food processor, and blend until smooth.

2. Add to ice cream maker and follow manufacturer's instructions for freezing.

Vanilla Beans

Vanilla beans are native to Mexico and South America, and are part of the orchid family, Orchidaceae. While Mexican vanilla is still widely popular, the most common is bourbon vanilla, also labeled as Madagascar vanilla, grown along the Indian Ocean.

Strawberry Frozen Yogurt

The addition of a little lemon juice here creates a playful tang that delights the taste buds. If you prefer more zip, use the zest and juice of one or more lemons.

INGREDIENTS | YIELD: 1 QUART

4 cups strawberries
Juice and zest of ½ lemon
1 cup sugar
1 cup Greek yogurt
1 teaspoon vanilla extract

1. In a small bowl, combine the strawberries, lemon juice and zest, and sugar. Stir and allow to macerate at room temperature for 1–2 hours.

2. After strawberries are ready, place all ingredients in a blender or food processor, and blend until smooth.

3. Add to ice cream maker and follow manufacturer's instructions for freezing.

Raspberry Frozen Yogurt

No oranges? No problem. Substitute an equal amount of commercial orange juice for the fresh squeezed.

INGREDIENTS | YIELD: 1 QUART

4 cups raspberries
3 tablespoons orange juice
1 cup sugar
1 cup Greek yogurt
1 teaspoon vanilla extract

Mix It Up

There are numerous varieties of raspberries, and any would be delicious here. Try golden raspberries for an unusual look, or black, red, or even white. All will be superb.

1. In a small bowl, combine the raspberries, orange juice, and sugar. Stir and allow to macerate at room temperature for 1–2 hours.

2. After raspberries are ready, place all ingredients in a blender or food processor, and blend until smooth.

3. Add to ice cream maker and follow manufacturer's instructions for freezing.

Blueberry Frozen Yogurt

This Blueberry Frozen Yogurt is sweet and tangy, and would look amazing served in a chocolate or white chocolate bowl. Add a few fresh berries and a mint sprig, and you'll deliver an impressive looking and tasting dessert.

INGREDIENTS | YIELD: 1 QUART

4 cups blueberries
Juice and zest of ½ lemon
¾ cup sugar
1 cup Greek yogurt
1 teaspoon vanilla extract

1. In a small bowl, combine the blueberries, lemon juice and zest, and sugar. Stir and allow to macerate at room temperature for 1–2 hours.

2. After blueberries are ready, place all ingredients in a blender or food processor, and blend until smooth.

3. Add to ice cream maker and follow manufacturer's instructions for freezing.

Blackberry Lime Frozen Yogurt

Blackberry and lime is a very popular combination, and you'll find it in recipes for everything from tarts to cheesecakes to muffins. The flavors complement each other wonderfully!

INGREDIENTS | YIELD: 1 QUART

4 cups blackberries
Juice and zest of 1 lime
1¼ cups sugar
1 cup Greek yogurt
1 teaspoon vanilla extract

1. In a small bowl, combine the blackberries, lime juice and zest, and sugar. Stir and allow to macerate at room temperature for 1–2 hours.

2. After blackberries are ready, place all ingredients in a blender or food processor, and blend until smooth.

3. Add to ice cream maker and follow manufacturer's instructions for freezing.

Zesty Lemon Frozen Yogurt

Did you know that lemons weren't originally grown for eating? It's true. They were seen as ornamental plants, used for decoration.

INGREDIENTS | YIELD: 1 QUART

2 cups Greek yogurt
2 cups plain whole-milk yogurt
¾ cup sugar
½ cup light corn syrup
¼ cup fresh lemon juice
2 tablespoons lemon zest

1. Place all ingredients in a blender or food processor, and blend until smooth.

2. Add to ice cream maker and follow manufacturer's instructions for freezing.

Orange Frozen Yogurt

You won't find the orange overwhelming in this yogurt recipe, but instead as a subtle undertone. Try pairing it with a drizzle of chocolate syrup or candied orange peel.

INGREDIENTS | YIELD: 1 QUART

1½ cups Greek yogurt
2½ cups plain whole-milk yogurt
⅔ cup sugar
½ cup light corn syrup
⅓ cup fresh orange juice
1 tablespoon orange zest
1 teaspoon vanilla extract

1. Place all ingredients in a blender or food processor, and blend until smooth.

2. Add to ice cream maker and follow manufacturer's instructions for freezing.

All Grown Up

Want to dress up this recipe? Pour a shot of Grand Marnier over a scoop of this yogurt and enjoy a grown-up float. The orange-flavored liqueur complements the subtle flavors of the yogurt perfectly.

Lime Frozen Yogurt

Lime isn't a flavor that everyone loves, but those who do love it really love it. Substitute key limes for the standard limes if you like.

INGREDIENTS | YIELD: 1 QUART

2 cups Greek yogurt
2 cups plain whole-milk yogurt
¾ cup sugar
½ cup light corn syrup
⅓ cup fresh lime juice
1 tablespoon lime zest

1. Place all ingredients in a blender or food processor, and blend until smooth.

2. Add to ice cream maker and follow manufacturer's instructions for freezing.

Chocolate Frozen Yogurt

The combination of different chocolates used here makes for a nice flavor, but feel free to choose all dark or all milk, or any variation to suit your own taste.

INGREDIENTS | YIELD: 1 QUART

3 cups Greek yogurt

1 cup plain whole-milk yogurt

8 ounces milk chocolate chips, melted

8 ounces semisweet chocolate chips, melted

¼ cup light corn syrup

1 teaspoon vanilla extract

1. Place all ingredients in a blender or food processor, and blend until smooth.

2. Add to ice cream maker and follow manufacturer's instructions for freezing.

Be Mine?

February isn't only the month of love, it's also the official Chocolate Appreciation Month. Share this recipe with those you love for a special Valentine's Day treat!

Rich Chocolate and Raspberry Frozen Yogurt

The tang of fresh berries is intensified by the darker flavors of the chocolate used in this recipe. Garnish with a few fresh berries, Raspberry Sauce (see Chapter 17), and chocolate curls to really impress.

INGREDIENTS | YIELD: 1 QUART

3 cups Greek yogurt

1 cup plain whole-milk yogurt

8 ounces bittersweet chocolate chips, melted

8 ounces semisweet chocolate chips, melted

⅓ cup light corn syrup

1 cup fresh red raspberries

1 teaspoon vanilla extract

1. Place all ingredients in a blender or food processor, and blend until smooth.

2. Add to ice cream maker and follow manufacturer's instructions for freezing.

Cream Cheese Frozen Yogurt

This yogurt is as close to baked cheesecake as you're going to get without turning on the oven! Serve with your favorite cheesecake topping, such as chocolate syrup, Dulce de Leche (see Chapter 17), or a fruit sauce. You can't go wrong!

INGREDIENTS | YIELD: 1 QUART

2 cups Greek yogurt

1 cup plain whole-milk yogurt

8 ounces cream cheese, softened

⅔ cup sugar

¼ cup light corn syrup

2 teaspoons vanilla extract

1. Place all ingredients in a blender or food processor, and blend until smooth.

2. Add to ice cream maker and follow manufacturer's instructions for freezing.

Dessert of Champions?

Historians believe that cheesecake may hail from ancient Greece, and was even served to Olympians at the first Olympic Games in Greece in 776 B.C. Today, July 30 is celebrated in America as National Cheesecake Day. Many towns across the country celebrate cheesecake on this day with a festival of their own, including Chicago's Eli's Cheesecake Festival.

Peanut Butter Frozen Yogurt

Trivia time! Did you know it takes roughly 540 peanuts to create one 12-ounce jar of peanut butter? You'll agree that it's worth it once you taste this recipe.

INGREDIENTS | YIELD: 1 QUART

1½ cups Greek yogurt

2 cups plain whole-milk yogurt

½ cup sugar

1 cup peanut butter

2 teaspoons vanilla extract

1. Place all ingredients in a blender or food processor, and blend until smooth.

2. Add to ice cream maker and follow manufacturer's instructions for freezing.

Peach Pie Frozen Yogurt

The only way to make this frozen yogurt any better is to serve it alongside a piping hot piece of peach pie. Indulge!

INGREDIENTS | YIELD: 1 QUART

4 cups fresh or frozen peaches, peeled and chopped

⅔ cup sugar

1 cup Greek yogurt

1 teaspoon ginger

2 teaspoons cinnamon

2 teaspoons vanilla extract

1. In small bowl, combine the peaches and sugar. Stir and allow to macerate at room temperature for 1–2 hours.

2. After peaches are ready, place all ingredients in a blender or food processor, and blend until smooth.

3. Add to ice cream maker and follow manufacturer's instructions for freezing.

Chocolate Cherry Frozen Yogurt

This very flavorful, very rich yogurt will conjure up the taste of cherry cordials, and rightly so.

INGREDIENTS | YIELD: 1 QUART

3 cups Greek yogurt

1 cup plain whole-milk yogurt

8 ounces bittersweet chocolate chips, melted

8 ounces semisweet chocolate chips, melted

1 cup cherry pie filling

1 teaspoon vanilla extract

1. Place yogurts and chocolates in a blender or food processor, and blend until smooth.

2. Stir in pie filling and vanilla until well combined.

3. Add to ice cream maker and follow manufacturer's instructions for freezing.

Being Cordial

Cherry cordials are the most widely known type of cordial, but in reality, a cordial is any fruit filling encased in a chocolate coating. Cherry cordials are especially popular during the holiday season, so popular, in fact, that Hershey's Kisses have developed a Holiday Edition Cherry Cordial Kiss.

Espresso Frozen Yogurt

Although developed in Italy over 100 years ago, espresso didn't gain popularity in the United States until the 1990s, when chain coffeehouses such as Starbucks introduced the very flavorful drink to the masses.

INGREDIENTS | YIELD: 1 QUART

1 cup heavy whipping cream
3 cups plain whole-milk yogurt
⅓ cup sugar
¼ cup light corn syrup
1 teaspoon vanilla extract
½ cup brewed strong espresso coffee

1. Place all ingredients in a blender or food processor, and blend until smooth.

2. Add to ice cream maker and follow manufacturer's instructions for freezing.

Smart Thinking

The creator of espresso developed the powerful drink to reduce the amount of time his employees spent on their coffee breaks. Espresso is made by forcing pressurized hot water through finely ground coffee.

Banana Frozen Yogurt

Did you know that bananas were first mentioned in Buddhist writings around 600 B.C.? This tropical fruit is not only healthy but has withstood the test of time!

INGREDIENTS | YIELD: 1 QUART

3 large ripe bananas, smashed
3 cups plain whole-milk yogurt
¼ cup light corn syrup
2 teaspoons vanilla extract
2 teaspoons lemon juice

1. Place all ingredients in a blender or food processor, and blend until smooth.

2. Add to ice cream maker and follow manufacturer's instructions for freezing.

Cucumber Mint Frozen Yogurt

Cucumbers and mint are a classic, refreshing combination for those sweltering days. Though not your average frozen dessert, this cool, creamy treat deserves some recognition.

INGREDIENTS | **YIELD: 1 QUART**

6 cucumbers, peeled, seeded, and chopped

⅓ cup fresh mint leaves

½ cup honey

8 ounces plain Greek yogurt (full fat)

Pinch salt

Juice of 1 lime

1 tablespoon gin or vanilla extract

1. Purée cucumbers in a blender until liquefied. Strain over large bowl to remove the pulp. Discard pulp.

2. Combine cucumber juice and remaining ingredients in the blender until mint leaves are chopped into very small pieces. Refrigerate overnight.

3. Add to ice cream maker and follow manufacturer's instructions for freezing.

Cucumbers

Cucumbers contain most of the vitamins you need every day. Just one cucumber contains vitamins B1, B2, B3, B5, and B6, folic acid, vitamin C, calcium, iron, magnesium, phosphorus, potassium, and zinc.

CHAPTER 5

Fanciful Flavors

Chocolate Chipotle Ice Cream
74

Raspberry Dark Chocolate Swirl
Ice Cream
75

Not-Too-Hot Red Hots Ice Cream
76

Lavender Honey Ice Cream
77

Lime and Coconut Ice Cream
78

Gimme S'More Ice Cream
79

Apple Pie Ice Cream
80

Bubble Gum Ice Cream
81

Cake Batter Ice Cream
82

Better Than Breakfast Cereal
Ice Cream
82

Caramel Pecan Ice Cream
83

Dulce de Leche Ice Cream
84

Double Brownie Blast Ice Cream
84

Concord Grape Ice Cream
85

Dragonfruit Mint Ice Cream
85

Caramelized Banana Rum Ice Cream
86

Red Velvet Cake Ice Cream
87

Kit Kat Ice Cream
88

Mascarpone Ice Cream
89

3 Musketeers Candy Bar Ice Cream
90

Pumpkin Cream Cheese Ice Cream
91

White Chocolate Pretzel Ice Cream
92

Super Double Dark Chocolate Ice Cream
93

Vanilla Brown Butter Ice Cream
94

Toasted Coconut Ice Cream
95

Peanut Butter Butterfinger Ice Cream
96

Lemon Cream Ice Cream
97

Chocolate Chipotle Ice Cream

Chocolate ice cream on its own is ever so satisfying. But when you pair it with the slow smoky heat of chipotles, you have an amazingly addictive treat you will dream about later.

INGREDIENTS | YIELD: 1 QUART

1 cup whole milk

4 ounces dark chocolate, chopped into ¼" pieces

½ teaspoon chipotle chili powder

¾ cup sugar

Pinch salt

3 tablespoons dark unsweetened cocoa powder

3 large egg yolks

2 cups heavy cream

2 teaspoons vanilla extract

Chipotle Chiles

Chipotle chiles are smoked and dried jalapeño peppers. They can be found in many forms, including whole dried, in cans of adobo sauce, or as a powder (like in this recipe). They are known to lend a smoky, earthy undertone to Mexican dishes, but recently have been found in more and more sweet and savory dishes.

1. In a small saucepan, combine the milk, chocolate, chipotle powder, sugar, salt, and cocoa powder. Stir over medium heat. Once simmering, remove from heat; cover.

2. Reheat milk mixture over medium-low heat.

3. In a separate bowl, whisk egg yolks. Once milk mixture is hot, temper the yolks by adding half of the mixture into the eggs, whisking constantly. Add egg mixture to the saucepan, and heat until thickened.

4. Pour heavy cream into a large mixing bowl over an ice bath. Strain custard into the cream, stirring until cooled. Add vanilla extract, stir, and place in refrigerator until thoroughly chilled, about 5 hours or overnight.

5. Once chilled, add to ice cream maker and follow manufacturer's instructions for freezing.

Raspberry Dark Chocolate Swirl Ice Cream

One of the most romantic and heavenly duos is raspberry and chocolate. In this ice cream, raspberry is swirled with rich Dark Chocolate Fudge Sauce (see Chapter 17) for just the right balance of rich chocolate and floral raspberries.

INGREDIENTS | YIELD: 1 QUART

1 cup half and half

1 cup sugar

Pinch salt

4 large egg yolks

½ cup heavy cream

1¾ cups raspberry purée, seeds strained out

2 teaspoons vanilla extract

Generous squeeze fresh lemon juice

1½ cups Dark Chocolate Fudge Sauce (see Chapter 17)

Raspberries

Did you know that a raspberry isn't one single fruit but many fruits all jumbled together? They are an excellent source of fiber and antioxidants—just a few more reasons to make this delicious, heavenly ice cream.

1. In a small saucepan, combine the half and half, sugar, and salt. Stir over medium heat. Once simmering, remove from heat and set aside.

2. In a separate bowl, whisk egg yolks. If needed, reheat milk mixture until hot, and temper the yolks by adding half of the mixture into the eggs, whisking constantly. Add egg mixture to the saucepan, and heat until thickened.

3. Pour heavy cream into a large mixing bowl over an ice bath. Strain custard into the cream, stirring until cooled. Add raspberry purée, vanilla extract, and lemon juice. Stir, and place in refrigerator until thoroughly chilled, about 5 hours or overnight.

4. Once chilled, add to ice cream maker and follow manufacturer's instructions for freezing. Just before storing in the freezer, quickly and loosely swirl in the Dark Chocolate Fudge Sauce.

Not-Too-Hot Red Hots Ice Cream

Red Hots, also known as Cinnamon Imperials, are fiery, sweet, and delectable candies. Some people shy away from this candy because it is too spicy, but this recipe is tempered quite a bit by the cream. You'll love the color, too.

INGREDIENTS | YIELD: 1 QUART

1 cup half and half

¾ cup Red Hots candies

½ cup sugar

Pinch salt

4 large egg yolks

2 cups heavy cream

2 teaspoons vanilla extract

Red Hots or Cinnamon Imperials

Red Hots Cinnamon-Flavored Candies were created in the 1930s by Ferrara Pan Candy Company. Other companies that made similar candies call them Cinnamon Imperials. No matter what you call them, they are delicious.

1. In a small saucepan, combine the half and half, Red Hots candies, sugar, and salt. Stir over medium heat until most of the Red Hots are dissolved. Once they are almost all dissolved, remove from heat, cover, and allow to sit for about 30 minutes or more. Stir again to ensure all the candies are dissolved.

2. Reheat milk mixture over medium-low heat.

3. In a separate bowl, whisk egg yolks. Once milk mixture is hot, temper the yolks by adding half of the mixture into the eggs, whisking constantly. Add egg mixture to the saucepan, and heat until thickened.

4. Pour heavy cream into a large mixing bowl over an ice bath. Strain custard into the cream, stirring until cooled. Add vanilla extract; stir, and place in refrigerator until thoroughly chilled, about 5 hours or overnight.

5. Once chilled, add to ice cream maker and follow manufacturer's instructions for freezing.

Lavender Honey Ice Cream

Rich and creamy with floral notes, this ice cream soothes the senses and indulges the taste buds.

INGREDIENTS | YIELD: 1 QUART

1 cup whole milk

1¼ cups honey

3 tablespoons lavender buds (dried or fresh)

½ cup sugar

Pinch salt

4 large egg yolks

2 cups heavy cream

2 teaspoons vanilla extract

Lavender

Lavender is an exceptionally versatile flower, utilized in everything from balms, lotions, and cosmetics to teas, savory meals, and of course desserts. It is known for its soothing and relaxing properties in aromatherapy.

1. In a small saucepan, combine the milk, honey, lavender buds, sugar, and salt. Stir over medium heat. Once simmering, remove from heat, cover, and allow to steep for 1 hour.

2. After 1 hour, strain milk mixture into a large measuring cup. Discard used buds and pour milk mixture back into pan. Reheat milk mixture over medium-low heat.

3. In a separate bowl, whisk egg yolks. Once milk mixture is hot, temper the yolks by adding half of the mixture into the eggs, whisking constantly. Add egg mixture to the saucepan, and heat until thickened.

4. Pour heavy cream into a large mixing bowl over an ice bath. Strain custard into the cream, stirring until cooled. Add vanilla extract; stir, and place in refrigerator until thoroughly chilled, about 5 hours or overnight.

5. Once chilled, add to ice cream maker and follow manufacturer's instructions for freezing.

Lime and Coconut Ice Cream

Tart limes and creamy coconut complement each other beautifully; when combined in an ice cream you have an explosion of refreshment.

INGREDIENTS | YIELD: 1 QUART

1½ cups whole milk

1 cup sweetened shredded coconut

¼ cup sugar

Pinch salt

4 large egg yolks

1 (14-ounce) can sweetened condensed milk

½ cup fresh lime juice

1 tablespoon lime zest, finely chopped

1 teaspoon coconut extract

Limes

Commercially, there are two main varieties of limes: Persian and key. You may use either variety, though many find it much easier and quicker to juice and zest a Persian lime than a key lime. Persian limes are typically less expensive as well.

1. In a small saucepan, combine the milk, coconut, sugar, and salt; stir over medium heat. Continue simmering until mixture has reduced by a quarter. Cover and allow to steep for 1 hour.

2. After 1 hour, strain coconut-milk mixture into a measuring cup. Reheat milk mixture over medium-low heat.

3. In a separate bowl, whisk egg yolks. Once milk mixture is hot, temper the yolks by adding half of the mixture into the eggs, whisking constantly. Add egg mixture to the saucepan, and heat until thickened.

4. Pour sweetened condensed milk, lime juice, and zest into a large mixing bowl over an ice bath. Strain custard into the cream, stirring until cooled. Add coconut extract; stir, and place in refrigerator until thoroughly chilled, about 5 hours or overnight.

5. Once chilled, add to ice cream maker and follow manufacturer's instructions for freezing.

Gimme S'More Ice Cream

When one thinks of summer, inevitably s'mores and ice cream come to mind. This recipe combines the two for a perfect summer treat, or just the thing to remind you of summers past.

INGREDIENTS | YIELD: 1 QUART

1 cup half and half
¼ cup dark brown sugar
½ cup sugar
Pinch salt
4 large egg yolks
2 cups heavy cream
2 teaspoons vanilla extract
⅛ teaspoon liquid smoke
½ cup finely crushed graham crackers
½ cup miniature marshmallows
½ cup Milk Chocolate Ganache (see Chapter 17)

S'mores

S'mores are said to have originated in the 1920s by the Campfire Girls. The name came from the delighted children chanting "Give me s'more! Give me s'more" when their treats had disappeared into their bellies. This ice cream will be drawing the same chants!

1. In a small saucepan, combine the half and half, sugars, and salt. Stir over medium heat. Once simmering, remove from heat, cover, and set aside.

2. Reheat half-and-half mixture over medium-low heat.

3. In a separate bowl, whisk egg yolks. Once half-and-half mixture is hot, temper the yolks by adding half of the mixture into the eggs, whisking constantly. Add egg mixture to saucepan, and heat until thickened.

4. Pour heavy cream into a large mixing bowl over an ice bath. Strain custard into the cream, stirring until cooled. Add vanilla extract and liquid smoke; stir, and place in refrigerator until thoroughly chilled, about 5 hours or overnight.

5. Once chilled, add to ice cream maker and follow manufacturer's instructions for freezing.

6. When ready to transfer to the freezer, quickly fold in the graham cracker crumbs, marshmallows, and Milk Chocolate Ganache. Cover tightly and transfer to freezer.

Apple Pie Ice Cream

This ice cream is an all-American classic: apple pie and ice cream rolled into one delectable treat!

INGREDIENTS | YIELD: 1 QUART

1 tablespoon unsalted butter
2 tart apples, peeled, cored, and cubed
3 tablespoons sugar
2 teaspoons Saigon cinnamon
3 cups heavy cream
1 cup half and half
½ cup Dulce de Leche (see Chapter 17)
½ cup brown sugar
6 large egg yolks
1 tablespoon vanilla extract
8 gingersnap cookies, crumbled

Apple Pie

Early English apple pies quite often had no sugar, due to its high cost. Sweet fruits, like figs, were added instead. Here, Dulce de Leche steps in as the main sweetener, offering a subtle caramel flavor.

1. In a medium saucepan, sauté butter, apples, sugar, and Saigon cinnamon together over medium heat until golden brown and tender. Set aside.

2. In a separate saucepan, heat cream, half and half, and Dulce de Leche to a steaming simmer. Remove from heat.

3. Whisk brown sugar and egg yolks in a large bowl. Slowly stream hot cream mixture into egg mixture until fully incorporated. Add egg mixture to heat and cook over medium heat until thick, being careful not to boil. Strain into a clean bowl and add vanilla extract. Refrigerate 4 hours to overnight.

4. Add to ice cream maker and follow manufacturer's instructions for freezing. Fold in apples and gingersnaps before placing in the freezer.

Bubble Gum Ice Cream

Yum! Bubble gum ice cream is like two treats in one. If you prefer not to mix in the gumball bits, feel free to omit them for a less chewy finish.

INGREDIENTS | YIELD: 1 QUART

4 ounces bubble gum

2 cups half and half

1¾ cups sugar

2 cups heavy cream

Pinch salt

1 tablespoon vanilla extract

⅓ cup small gumballs, roughly crushed

1. Heat bubble gum, half and half, and sugar in medium saucepan until just boiling. Remove from heat. Cover and let steep for 2 hours.

2. After 2 hours, remove bubble gum. Add cream, salt, and vanilla. Refrigerate 4 hours to overnight.

3. Add to ice cream maker and follow manufacturer's instructions for freezing. Just before storing, fold in gumballs.

Ancient Vending Machines

The first known vending machine was invented by the Greek engineer and mathematician Hero of Alexandria around 215 B.C. These first vending machines were located in Egyptian temples and dispensed holy water in exchange for coins. Times certainly have changed!

Cake Batter Ice Cream

Cake batter is a guilty pleasure. Now you can enjoy it with pride in this delicious ice cream.

INGREDIENTS | YIELD: 1 QUART

1 cup whole milk
¾ cup sugar
2 cups heavy cream
¾ cup yellow cake mix (or your favorite variety)
1 tablespoon vanilla extract

1. Place everything into a blender and process until completely smooth. Refrigerate for 4 hours.

2. Add to ice cream maker and follow manufacturer's instructions for freezing.

Cake Batter Ice Cream

Cake batter flavor for ice cream was originally produced by Cold Stone Creamery in early 2003. It has since become a wildly popular flavor nationwide.

Better Than Breakfast Cereal Ice Cream

Tomorrow morning, treat yourself to this for breakfast. Frosted corn flakes, crisp rice cereals, or other "kiddie" cereals deliver the best results here. If you love the flavor of the milk left in the bottom of your cereal bowl, you'll love this ice cream.

INGREDIENTS | YIELD: 1 QUART

½ cup heavy cream
1½ cups favorite breakfast cereal
2 cups half and half
½ cup sugar
Pinch salt

1. Bring heavy cream to a boil, then pour over cereal. Stir and allow to sit for 1 hour. Strain over a large bowl and discard cereal.

2. Add half and half, sugar, and salt. Stir and refrigerate until cold, at least 2 hours.

3. Add to ice cream maker and follow manufacturer's instructions for freezing.

Caramel Pecan Ice Cream

*Crunchy candied pecans and smooth cozy caramel ice cream will
please the pickiest of caramel pecan enthusiasts.*

INGREDIENTS | YIELD: 1 QUART

1 vanilla bean, split and seeded
1 cup sugar
¼ cup water
½ teaspoon cardamom
2 cups heavy cream
1 cup whole milk
Pinch salt
8 large egg yolks
½ cup Caramel Sauce (see Chapter 17)
1 cup Candied Pecans (see Chapter 17)

1. Add vanilla bean, sugar, and water to large saucepan. Stir over medium-high heat constantly until sugar is dissolved and boiling. Then allow mixture to boil without stirring until sugar is a deep amber color. Be careful when the color starts to change—it moves fast from caramel to burnt sugar. You want caramel. Remove from heat and add cardamom and cream. It will steam and bubble. Stir vigorously until mixture is completely combined and liquid again.

2. Add milk and salt; bring back to a simmer.

3. Whisk egg yolks in a large bowl; slowly stream caramel into the yolks, stirring constantly. Return custard to the saucepan and simmer to thicken, stirring constantly. Remove from heat and strain into a clean container. Refrigerate overnight.

4. Add to ice cream maker and follow manufacturer's instructions for freezing. Just before storing, fold in Caramel Sauce and Candied Pecans.

Dulce de Leche Ice Cream

The flavor of dulce de leche is very similar to caramel but with a bit more milk and a little less sugar. If you are lucky, you can find cans of dulce de leche on your supermarket shelf, often with sweetened condensed milks, or you can make your own; see the Dulce de Leche recipe in Chapter 17.

INGREDIENTS | YIELD: 1 QUART

2 cups whole milk

1 cup cream

2 (14-ounce) cans dulce de leche

1 teaspoon vanilla extract

1. In a medium saucepan, bring milk and cream to a boil. Remove from heat and whisk in dulce de leche and vanilla. Refrigerate for 4 hours.

2. Add to ice cream maker and follow manufacturer's instructions for freezing.

Dulce de Leche

Literally translated in Spanish, *dulce de leche* means "sweet of milk," or milk candy. It is prepared by slowly heating sweetened milk to create a product that is sweet and rich, and much like caramel. It is highly popular in Latin cultures. You can also make your own at home with very little effort; the recipe is found in Chapter 17.

Double Brownie Blast Ice Cream

You'll love this brownie-batter ice cream, crammed with chunks of moist fudgy brownies! Who can resist? Feel free to bake and freeze your own brownie recipe, or use Brownies for Breakfast Ice Cream Sandwiches (Chapter 11). You can also use store-bought brownies if you prefer.

INGREDIENTS | YIELD: 1 QUART

1 cup whole milk

¾ cup sugar

2 cups heavy cream

¾ cup brownie mix

1 tablespoon vanilla extract

½ cup frozen brownies, cut into ½" cubes

1. Place everything but the frozen brownies into a blender, and process until completely smooth. Refrigerate for 4 hours.

2. Add to ice cream maker and follow manufacturer's instructions for freezing. Just before storing, fold in the frozen brownie cubes.

Concord Grape Ice Cream

This will bring back memories of grape juice at snack time when you were a kid. Ah, the joys of childhood!

INGREDIENTS | YIELD: 1 QUART

2 cups heavy cream
1¼ cups 100% Concord grape juice
⅓ cup sugar
Pinch salt

1. Combine everything into a blender, and process for about 30 seconds. Refrigerate 4 hours to overnight.

2. Add to ice cream maker and follow manufacturer's instructions for freezing.

Concord Grapes

The Concord grape was created by Ephraim Wales Bull in 1849, through experimentation with native grape seeds. Growers cherish it for its robust and pleasing flavor. These grapes make a delicious juice, and many bakers are opting to use it as a base for the newly popular Concord grape pie.

Dragonfruit Mint Ice Cream

Dragonfruit is a delicate but vibrant fruit that combines perfectly with just a bit of mint. This recipe creates a beautiful and unique ice cream; it's even more beautiful when a red-fleshed dragonfruit is used.

INGREDIENTS | YIELD: 1 QUART

2 cups chopped dragonfruit
¼ cup fresh mint
1 cup mascarpone
1 cup heavy cream
⅓ cup honey

1. Place all ingredients into a blender, and process until smooth. Refrigerate 4 hours to overnight.

2. Add to ice cream maker and follow manufacturer's instructions for freezing.

Dragonfruit Tips

When buying dragonfruit, it should be blemish-free and bright pink in color. When you gently squeeze it, it should feel slightly soft.

Caramelized Banana Rum Ice Cream

This is a roasted banana and caramel ice cream with bits of toffee throughout. Go ahead and spoil yourself!

INGREDIENTS | YIELD: 1 QUART

4 very ripe bananas, unpeeled

1 vanilla bean, split and seeded

1 cup sugar

¼ cup water

2 cups heavy cream

1 cup whole milk

Pinch salt

8 large egg yolks

2 tablespoons dark rum

⅓ cup chocolate toffee bar, crushed (or use Toffee recipe in Chapter 17)

1. Preheat the oven to 350°F. Poke a few holes in the bananas and place on baking sheet lined with parchment paper. Roast for 45 minutes. Allow to cool and remove pulp from the peel. Discard peels.

2. Place vanilla bean, sugar, and water into large saucepan. Stir constantly over medium-high heat until sugar is dissolved and boiling. Then allow it to boil without stirring until sugar is a deep amber color. Be careful when the color starts to change—it moves fast from caramel to burnt sugar. You want caramel. Remove from heat and add cream. It will steam and bubble. Stir vigorously until the mixture is completely combined and liquid again.

3. Add milk and salt; bring back to a simmer.

4. In a large bowl, whisk egg yolks. Slowly stream caramel into the yolks, stirring constantly. Add custard to the saucepan and simmer to thicken, stirring constantly. Remove from heat and strain into a clean container.

5. Place bananas and rum in a blender, and process until smooth. Add to custard base. Refrigerate overnight.

6. Add to ice cream maker and follow manufacturer's instructions for freezing. Just before storing, fold in toffee bits.

Red Velvet Cake Ice Cream

This amazing ice cream is a white chocolate cream cheese ice cream with chunks of red velvet cake studded throughout. Red velvet cake is available in most grocery bake shops, or even in the frozen section. You can also use your own favorite recipe or the Red Velvet Cake recipe provided in Chapter 12.

INGREDIENTS | YIELD: 1 QUART

1 cup heavy cream

1 cup half and half

1 vanilla bean, split, seeded, and pod saved for another use

6 ounces white chocolate

¾ cup sugar

Pinch salt

4 egg yolks

12 ounces cream cheese, softened and cubed

1 tablespoon lemon juice

½ cup red velvet cake, cubed into ½" cubes and frozen solid

White Chocolate

Be sure to find white chocolate that is made with cocoa butter (not palm kernel oil); the flavor and texture will be much better with the cocoa butter. Scharffen Berger and Ghirardelli companies make very good white chocolates that would do very well in this recipe.

1. Bring cream, half and half, and vanilla seeds to a boil. Place white chocolate in a large bowl. Pour cream mixture over white chocolate. Allow to sit for 2 minutes, then stir until smooth.

2. Whisk sugar, salt, and egg yolks until thick and lighter in color.

3. Slowly stream hot cream mixture into egg mixture until fully incorporated. Add egg mixture to pan and cook over medium heat until thick, being careful not to boil. Strain into a clean bowl; stir in cream cheese until completely incorporated and smooth. Stir in lemon juice and refrigerate 4 hours to overnight.

4. Add to ice cream maker and follow manufacturer's instructions for freezing. Fold in frozen cake cubes before placing in the freezer.

Kit Kat Ice Cream

The addition of chunky Kit Kat pieces to ice cream just before storing in the freezer adds a nice crispy crunch that few people can resist. For a nice display, serve with two whole pieces of Kit Kat candy bar (one half of a standard candy bar).

INGREDIENTS | YIELD: 1 QUART

1 cup whole milk

¾ cup sugar

2 tablespoons Dutch-processed cocoa powder

¼ cup malted milk powder

Pinch salt

3 egg yolks

3 ounces milk- or semisweet chocolate, chopped

1 cup heavy cream

1 tablespoon vanilla extract

3 full-size Kit Kat bars, chopped

Malted Milk Powder

Malted milk powder can be found in most grocery stores, typically in the cocoa aisle. Do not confuse Ovaltine for malt powder, as the two are not interchangeable.

1. Combine the milk, sugar, cocoa powder, malted milk powder, and salt in a saucepan over medium heat. Stir to combine. Do not bring to a boil, only simmer until sugars and cocoa are dissolved.

2. Beat the egg yolks in a medium mixing bowl.

3. Drizzle half of the cocoa mixture into the eggs to temper, whisking constantly. Add egg mixture to saucepan, and heat until thickened.

4. Remove from heat. Add in chopped chocolate, heavy cream, and vanilla, and stir until chocolate is melted. Chill in refrigerator, stirring occasionally, until completely cooled.

5. Add to ice cream maker and follow manufacturer's instructions for freezing. Once the cycle is complete, stir in the chopped Kit Kat bars. Freeze as directed.

Mascarpone Ice Cream

Thick, creamy, with just the slightest hint of tang, mascarpone is similar in taste and texture to cream cheese, but you'll definitely note the difference once you've tried it yourself. If mascarpone is unavailable where you live, you can substitute cream cheese if necessary.

INGREDIENTS | YIELD: 1 QUART

1 cup whole milk

1½ cups heavy cream

4 large egg yolks

¾ cup sugar

Pinch salt

1 tablespoon limoncello

1 tablespoon candied lemon peel, minced (see Candied Citrus Peels, Chapter 17)

8 ounces mascarpone, softened

1. In a medium saucepan, bring milk and cream to a boil and set aside.

2. In a medium bowl, whisk together egg yolks, sugar, and salt until thick and lighter in color.

3. Slowly stream hot milk mixture into egg mixture until fully incorporated. Add egg mixture to saucepan and cook over medium heat until thick, being careful not to boil. Strain into a clean bowl; add limoncello, and refrigerate 4 hours to overnight.

4. Stir in mascarpone. Add to ice cream maker and follow manufacturer's instructions for freezing. Fold in minced candied lemon peel before placing in the freezer.

3 Musketeers Candy Bar Ice Cream

What starts with a simple chocolate ice cream base turns into a decadent treat with the addition of store-bought marshmallow creme. For extra wow, stir in some chocolate marshmallows and Hot Fudge Sauce (see Chapter 17) before freezing.

INGREDIENTS | YIELD: 1 QUART

3 cups heavy cream

1 cup whole milk

¾ cup sweetened cocoa powder

¾ cup sugar

Pinch salt

8 ounces marshmallow creme

1 tablespoon vanilla extract

3 regular-sized 3 Musketeers candy bars

1. In a large saucepan over medium heat, combine cream, milk, cocoa powder, sugar, and salt until sugar is dissolved. Remove from heat, and add marshmallow creme and vanilla. Stir to combine.

2. Allow to chill in refrigerator for 3–4 hours or overnight.

3. Once chilled, stir in chopped candy bar pieces and add to ice cream maker. Follow manufacturer's instructions for freezing.

Variations

Thanks to a fickle consumer base, 3 Musketeers has developed several new flavors, such as Mint Chocolate and Chocolate Truffle. Any flavor would be a wonderful addition to this recipe.

Pumpkin Cream Cheese Ice Cream

This recipe invokes falling leaves, brisk walks, and boisterous visits with loved ones. It is a perfect addition to any get-together.

INGREDIENTS | YIELD: 1 QUART

2 (8-ounce) blocks cream cheese

2 cups heavy cream

¾ cup sugar

1 cup half and half

1 tablespoon vanilla extract

Pinch salt

⅓ cup pumpkin purée

1 teaspoon cinnamon

¼ teaspoon fresh grated nutmeg

¼ cup brown sugar

Pinch ground ginger

1. Place cream cheese, cream, sugar, half and half, vanilla extract, and salt in a blender, and blend until smooth.

2. Divide mixture in half. Whisk pumpkin purée, cinnamon, nutmeg, brown sugar, and ginger into one half. Cover both halves and refrigerate until cold, 4 hours to overnight.

3. Add first half to ice cream maker and follow manufacturer's instructions for freezing. Place in freezer, then churn the other half. Before storing, swirl together both halves.

Pumpkin Purée

If you choose to use canned purée, be sure to choose 100 percent purée rather than pumpkin pie filling, which contains added spices and sugar. While great for making a pumpkin pie or other dessert, the added sugars of pumpkin pie filling are not appropriate for this recipe.

White Chocolate Pretzel Ice Cream

Pretzels and chocolate are a classic combination of sweet and salty taste. This takes it a notch up with the addition of sweet and creamy ice cream.

INGREDIENTS | YIELD: 1 QUART

1 cup half and half

4 egg yolks

12 ounces high-quality white chocolate, finely chopped

1½ cups heavy cream

1 tablespoon vanilla extract

1 cup white chocolate–covered pretzels, whole

Chocolate-Covered Pretzels

Be sure to keep the pretzels whole when folding them into the ice cream. The chocolate coating will ensure that the pretzels stay crispy in the ice cream.

1. Heat half and half in a small saucepan to a simmer.

2. Whisk the egg yolks in a medium bowl, then begin to slowly pour the half and half into the egg yolks to temper them. Return mixture to the pan and constantly stir over medium heat until thickened, being sure not to boil. Remove from heat and add the white chocolate. Stir until smooth.

3. Add cream and vanilla. Cover and refrigerate 4 hours to overnight.

4. Add to ice cream maker and follow manufacturer's instructions for freezing. Just before storing, carefully fold in the whole pretzels.

Super Double Dark Chocolate Ice Cream

This ice cream is the height of decadence with nothing but chocolate bliss.

INGREDIENTS | YIELD: 1 QUART

1½ cups heavy cream

6 ounces dark chocolate, finely chopped

1 cup whole milk

½ cup dark brown sugar

⅓ cup dark cocoa powder

1 teaspoon salt

4 egg yolks

⅓ cup dark chocolate chunks, about ¼" pieces

Chocolate

Switzerland is one of the top countries when it comes to chocolate consumption. The Swiss eat roughly 22 pounds of chocolate per person per year. U.S. citizens consume about 11 pounds per person each year.

1. Bring ¾ cup of the heavy cream to a boil in a small saucepan. Place chopped dark chocolate into a medium bowl, then pour heated cream over dark chocolate. Allow to sit for 2 minutes, then stir gently until silky and smooth. Set aside.

2. In a medium saucepan, bring remaining cream, milk, brown sugar, cocoa powder, and salt to a simmer. Remove from heat. Whisk egg yolks in a small bowl, and slowly add milk mixture, whisking all the while to temper the yolks. Return to heat, and stir constantly until steaming and thickened.

3. Slowly add the egg mixture to the chocolate mixture. Stir to combine. Refrigerate 4 hours to overnight.

4. Add to ice cream maker and follow manufacturer's instructions for freezing. Before storing, fold in chocolate chunks.

Vanilla Brown Butter Ice Cream

Adding browned butter is an unexpected and amazing addition to a standard vanilla ice cream recipe. You'll want to add it to everything!

INGREDIENTS | YIELD: 1 QUART

2 vanilla beans, split and scraped
1 cup unsalted butter

2 cups milk
¾ cup sugar
5 large egg yolks
1 cup cream
1 teaspoon vanilla extract
1 teaspoon salt

Brown Butter

When the butter is browning, first there will be big bubbles. Then, as the milk solids begin to sink to the bottom and brown, the bubbles will become very small and the butter will smell toasty and nutty. That is when you know it is ready.

1. Place vanilla beans and butter in a medium saucepan. Heat over medium heat, stirring constantly until the butter solids begin to turn a reddish brown. Scrape into a clean measuring cup, removing the vanilla pods.

2. In the same saucepan, add the milk and ½ cup of the sugar. Heat over medium-low heat until steaming.

3. Place eggs and remaining sugar in a blender, and process for 30 seconds. Slowly add the warm butter while blending. Add the warm milk. Return this whole mixture back into the saucepan and heat until thickened. Be sure not to boil it.

4. Strain into a clean container; stir in cream, vanilla, and salt. Refrigerate overnight.

5. Add to ice cream maker and follow manufacturer's instructions for freezing.

Toasted Coconut Ice Cream

*Warm and rich, toasted coconut ice cream makes a beautiful base
for so many desserts and is equally amazing on its own.*

INGREDIENTS | YIELD: 1 QUART

2 cups shredded coconut, toasted

2 cups heavy cream

1 cup half and half

¾ cup sugar

6 large egg yolks

2 tablespoons coconut-flavored rum

1 tablespoon vanilla extract

Toasted Coconut

This can be made just as easily with untoasted coconut, but toasting the coconut deepens the flavor, making for a richer experience. Toasting is as simple as placing coconut on a baking sheet and baking at 350°F until browned. Stir every few minutes to prevent burning.

1. Bring coconut and heavy cream to a boil in a large saucepan. Remove from heat and allow to steep for 2 hours. Process cream mixture in a blender until smooth. Return cream mixture to the pan.

2. Add half and half and sugar to the pan, and bring to a steaming simmer. Remove from heat.

3. In a large bowl, whisk eggs. Slowly stream hot cream mixture into eggs until fully incorporated. Return mixture to the pan and cook over medium heat until thick, being careful not to boil it. Strain into a clean bowl. Add rum and vanilla; stir until smooth. Refrigerate 4 hours to overnight.

4. Add to ice cream maker and follow manufacturer's instructions for freezing.

Peanut Butter Butterfinger Ice Cream

This is crispety crunchety peanut buttery goodness in ice cream form.

INGREDIENTS | YIELD: 1 QUART

1 vanilla bean, split and seeded

1¼ cup half and half

1¼ cups smooth peanut butter

¼ cup brown sugar

½ cup granulated sugar

2 cups heavy cream

Pinch salt

1 tablespoon vanilla extract

10 Butterfinger miniatures

1. Heat vanilla bean, half and half, peanut butter, and sugars in a medium saucepan until steaming with little bubbles around the edges. Remove from heat. Add heavy cream, salt, and vanilla. Cover and refrigerate overnight.

2. Add to ice cream maker and follow manufacturer's instructions for freezing. Just before storing, fold in whole Butterfinger miniatures; keeping them whole will prevent the crunchy center from softening or dissolving.

Butterfinger Candy

Butterfinger bars, currently made by Nestlé, were created by the Curtiss Candy Company in 1923. Butterfinger was the result of a contest to name this sweet and crunchy candy.

Lemon Cream Ice Cream

Tangy, tart, and oh so creamy, this is the ultimate summer treat. Allow the cream cheese to come to room temperature before using, as this makes it much easier to work with.

INGREDIENTS | YIELD: 1 QUART

2 (8-ounce) blocks cream cheese

2 cups heavy cream

¾ cup sugar

1 cup half and half

1 tablespoon vanilla extract

Pinch salt

Zest and juice from 3 large lemons

1. Place everything in a blender and blend until smooth.

2. Refrigerate until cold, 4 hours to overnight.

3. Add to ice cream maker and follow manufacturer's instructions for freezing.

CHAPTER 6

Sorbet

Lemon Lime Soda Sorbet
100

Lime Sorbet
100

Mango Sorbet
101

Lemonade Sorbet
101

Sparkling White Grape Sorbet
102

Ginger Pear Sorbet
102

Watermelon Sorbet
103

Cantaloupe Sorbet
104

Honeydew Sorbet
104

Bing Cherry Sorbet
105

Rhubarb Sorbet
105

Blackberry Sorbet
106

Blackberry Lime Sorbet
106

Strawberry Sorbet
107

Pineapple Coconut Sorbet
107

Raspberry Nectarine Sorbet
108

Strawberry Banana Sorbet
109

Tart Apple Sorbet
110

Kiwi Sorbet
110

Lemon Lime Soda Sorbet

Feel free to use your favorite lemon-lime soda here, even diet if you prefer. It won't save a lot of calories, but you can feel a little better about eating a second scoop.

INGREDIENTS | YIELD: 1 QUART

1 cup sugar
1 (12-ounce) can lemon-lime soda
1 cup lemon juice
1 cup lime juice

1. Place the sugar and soda in a small pot, and stir over medium heat until all of the sugar is dissolved. Allow to cool and combine with the lemon and lime juice. Cover and refrigerate until cool.

2. Add to ice cream maker and follow manufacturer's instructions for freezing.

Lemon-Lime Soda Trivia

The first lemon-lime soda was marketed in 1929, and it eventually became known as 7UP. It wasn't until years later, in 1965, that the first vending machine dispensed aluminum cans of the carbonated beverage.

Lime Sorbet

You'll find the pop of citrus in this sorbet the perfect pick-me-up after a hot day or as a welcome treat to end a summer barbecue.

INGREDIENTS | YIELD: 1 QUART

1 cup sugar
2 cups water
¾ cup freshly squeezed lime juice

1. Place the sugar and 1 cup of the water in a small pot, and stir over medium heat until all of the sugar is dissolved. Allow to cool; combine with the lime juice and remaining 1 cup of water. Cover and refrigerate until cool.

2. Add to ice cream maker and follow manufacturer's instructions for freezing.

Mango Sorbet

Delicious in both flavor and color, mango sorbet steps in and satisfies the need for a taste of the tropics when pineapple or coconut just won't do. If you are looking for a sweet accompaniment, coconut ice cream is a wonderful choice.

INGREDIENTS | YIELD: 1 QUART

¾ cup sugar

⅔ cup water

2 tablespoons lime juice

2 pounds fresh mangos

1 teaspoon vanilla extract

Mango

In India, the mango tree is considered to be a symbol of love and is believed to even grant wishes. Some residents hang mango leaves outside the door of their home as a blessing on the house.

1. Place the sugar and water in a small saucepan, and stir over medium heat until all of the sugar is dissolved. Allow to cool, and combine with the lime juice. Cover and refrigerate until cool.

2. Peel and chop the mangos. Purée the mangos in a food processor until smooth. Combine with the chilled syrup and vanilla.

3. Add to ice cream maker and follow manufacturer's instructions for freezing.

Lemonade Sorbet

One bite of this refreshing sorbet will have you reminiscing about the days of backyard ballgames and sidewalk lemonade stands. Enjoy!

INGREDIENTS | YIELD: 1 QUART

1 cup sugar

1 cup water

1 cup prepared lemonade

¾ cup freshly squeezed lemon juice

Lemonade Stands

While most commonly associated with school children, the first lemonade stand was set up by a shopkeeper in New York City in 1879. It was so popular that the police had to intervene when it thwarted sidewalk traffic.

1. Place the sugar and water in a small saucepan, and stir over medium heat until all of the sugar is dissolved. Allow to cool; combine with the lemonade and lemon juice. Cover and refrigerate until cool.

2. Add to ice cream maker and follow manufacturer's instructions for freezing.

Sparkling White Grape Sorbet

Try serving this decadent sorbet in a wine glass, topped with equal parts white wine. You'll be the hit of any social event!

INGREDIENTS | YIELD: 1 QUART

4 pounds white grapes
¼ cup water
¼ cup corn syrup
¼ cup sparking white grape juice

Sparkling Grape Juice

Experiment! Instead of adding plain water to your homemade grape juice concentrate, consider using sparkling water. The fizz is intoxicating and fun!

1. Wash and halve the grapes, and combine with the water in large pot over medium heat.

2. Stirring occasionally, cook the grapes until soft and liquidized. Remove from heat.

3. Press the grapes through a mesh strainer to remove the seeds and skins.

4. Add the corn syrup and sparkling juice to the grape mixture, and chill in the refrigerator until cool.

5. Add to ice cream maker and follow manufacturer's instructions for freezing.

Ginger Pear Sorbet

The hint of ginger in this refreshing sorbet kicks it up a notch, taking the sweetness of the pear to a new level of delicious. If ginger isn't your thing, you can simply omit it.

INGREDIENTS | YIELD: 1 QUART

3 pounds ripe pears
1 cup water
¼ teaspoon dried ginger
1 tablespoon lemon juice
¾ cup sugar

1. Peel, core, and chop the pears; place with ½ cup of the water and the ginger in a medium-sized covered saucepan. Heat over medium heat, stirring occasionally, for 15–20 minutes, or until very tender.

2. Remove pears from heat and add remaining water, lemon juice, and sugar in a food processor and process until smooth. Refrigerate until thoroughly chilled.

3. Add to ice cream maker and follow manufacturer's instructions for freezing.

Watermelon Sorbet

As its name indicates, watermelon is full of liquid, and thus, it freezes quite solidly. Therefore, it is best to remove frozen sorbet from the freezer 10–15 minutes before serving.

INGREDIENTS | YIELD: 1 QUART

3 cups watermelon juice

⅔ cup sugar

¼ teaspoon salt

1 tablespoon freshly squeezed lemon juice

¼ cup mini chocolate chips (for "seeds")

Serving Suggestion

When removing the flesh of the melon, take extra care and make a large "bowl" out of one half of the rind. Once the sorbet has gone through the churn cycle, pour it into the watermelon bowl to freeze. Your guests will be impressed!

1. Remove the watermelon flesh from the rind, taking care to discard seeds. Purée in food processor or blender until smooth to make 3 cups of watermelon juice.

2. Place the sugar, salt, and 1 cup of watermelon juice in a small saucepan; stir over medium heat until all of the sugar is dissolved. Allow to cool; combine with the lemon juice and remaining watermelon juice. Cover and refrigerate until cool.

3. Add to ice cream maker and follow manufacturer's instructions for freezing. Add in chocolate chips toward the end of freezing.

Cantaloupe Sorbet

This gorgeously colored sorbet is a true crowd pleaser, especially when served in cantaloupe bowls. Halve each melon, remove the flesh, and freeze the rind until serving time. A garnish of fresh mint finishes it beautifully!

INGREDIENTS | YIELD: 1 QUART

1 large, ripe cantaloupe (2–2½ pounds)
⅔ cup sugar
¼ teaspoon salt
1 teaspoon freshly squeezed lemon juice

1. Remove the flesh from the rind of the cantaloupe, taking care to discard seeds and any green flesh. Purée in a food processor or blender until smooth.

2. Add the remaining ingredients and purée until well combined. Cover and refrigerate until cool.

3. Add to ice cream maker and follow manufacturer's instructions for freezing.

Choosing a Cantaloupe

The old wives' tale about choosing a perfect melon is to "thump" it. That may be true, but it is much easier and reliable to go by the smell. If it smells sweet, it probably is! Tightly woven rind netting is also a good indication of ripeness.

Honeydew Sorbet

Similar in texture to the cantaloupe, the honeydew melon has its origins in France and is considered to be the sweetest variety of melon.

INGREDIENTS | YIELD: 1 QUART

1 large, ripe honeydew (2–2½ pounds)
½ cup sugar
Pinch salt
1 teaspoon freshly squeezed lime juice

1. Remove the flesh from the rind of the melon, taking care to discard seeds and any unripe flesh. Purée in a food processor or blender until smooth.

2. Add the remaining ingredients, and purée until well combined. Cover and refrigerate until cool.

3. Add to ice cream maker and follow manufacturer's instructions for freezing.

Choosing a Honeydew

The best honeydews will weigh around 5 pounds and will feel slightly waxy and have a yellowish color. Avoid those that appear green. Unripe melons can be kept at room temperature for a couple of days to further ripen, if necessary.

Bing Cherry Sorbet

Although there are easily more than 1,000 varieties of cherries, only about 10 percent are commercially grown. Of these, the Bing is considered to be one of the sweetest and most enjoyable.

INGREDIENTS | YIELD: 1 QUART

2½ pounds Bing cherries
¾ cup water
1 cup sugar
2 teaspoons lemon juice
½ teaspoon vanilla extract

1. Wash, pit, and halve the cherries, and combine with the water, sugar, and lemon juice in a large saucepan over medium heat.

2. Stirring occasionally, cook the cherries until soft and liquidized, about 15 minutes. Remove from heat, and cool to room temperature.

3. Place cherries and vanilla in blender or food processor, and purée until smooth. Refrigerate until thoroughly chilled.

4. Add to ice cream maker and follow manufacturer's instructions for freezing.

Rhubarb Sorbet

Rhubarb is pleasingly sour, and is a wonderful ingredient in many desserts. Though perfectly civil, its name actually means "root of the barbarian." Look for redder stalks when shopping; the redder that rhubarb is, the sweeter it should be.

INGREDIENTS | YIELD: 1 QUART

1½ pounds rhubarb, cleaned and chopped
⅔ cup water
¾ cup sugar
1 teaspoon fresh lemon juice

1. Wash, trim, and chop the rhubarb; combine with the water and sugar in large saucepan over medium heat.

2. Stirring occasionally, cook until tender, about 7 minutes. Remove from heat, and cool to room temperature.

3. Place cooled rhubarb in a blender or food processor. Add lemon juice and purée until smooth. Refrigerate until thoroughly chilled.

4. Add to ice cream maker and follow manufacturer's instructions for freezing.

Blackberry Sorbet

Need a reason to eat more of this mouthwatering sorbet? Consider that blackberries are high in fiber and are believed to remedy many stomach ailments. They also contain vitamin E, which helps promote a healthy heart.

INGREDIENTS | YIELD: 1 QUART

4 cups fresh blackberries
¾ cup water
¾ cup sugar
1 tablespoon lemon juice

1. Wash the berries and combine with the water, sugar, and lemon juice in large saucepan over medium heat.

2. Stirring occasionally, cook the berries until soft and liquidized, about 10 minutes. Remove from heat, and cool to room temperature.

3. Place berries in blender or food processor, and purée until smooth. Press through a strainer to remove seeds, if desired. Refrigerate until thoroughly chilled.

4. Add to ice cream maker and follow manufacturer's instructions for freezing.

Blackberry Lime Sorbet

Blackberry and lime reunite once again to delight the taste buds in this refreshing (and refreshingly easy) sorbet.

INGREDIENTS | YIELD: 1 QUART

4 cups fresh blackberries
1 cup water
1 cup sugar
⅔ cup lime juice

Try a Pretty Little Lime Bowl

This tangy sorbet and its beautiful blackberry color make it perfect to serve in hollowed lime peels. Simply remove the insides of the lime, cut a small end off the bottom to level it, and freeze until ready to serve. The sorbet can then be spooned or piped into the frozen peels.

1. Wash the berries and combine with the water and sugar in a large saucepan over medium heat.

2. Stirring occasionally, cook the berries until soft and liquidized, about 10 minutes. Remove from heat and cool to room temperature.

3. Place berries in blender or food processor and add lime juice. Purée until smooth. Press through strainer to remove seeds, if desired. Refrigerate until thoroughly chilled.

4. Add to ice cream maker and follow manufacturer's instructions for freezing.

Strawberry Sorbet

Who knew that three simple ingredients could deliver such a powerful punch? You'll soon be in strawberry heaven after a bite or two of this mouthwatering sorbet.

INGREDIENTS | YIELD: 1 QUART

1 cup sugar
1½ pounds fresh strawberries
1 tablespoon lemon juice

1. Place the sugar and strawberries in a medium bowl and stir until the sugar dissolves. Cover and refrigerate until cool.

2. Purée the strawberry mixture in a food processor or blender with the lemon juice until smooth.

3. Add to ice cream maker and follow manufacturer's instructions for freezing.

Pineapple Coconut Sorbet

The availability of canned pineapple makes this sorbet delightfully easy, and it's downright delicious. What more could you ask for?

INGREDIENTS | YIELD: 1 QUART

3 cups canned pineapple
½ cup pineapple juice, drained from can
¾ cup sugar
¼ cup sweetened coconut flake

1. Remove pineapple from can, reserving ½ cup of the juice. Purée in food processor or blender until smooth.

2. Add the juice and sugar, and purée until well combined. Cover and refrigerate until cool.

3. Stir in coconut. Add to ice cream maker and follow manufacturer's instructions for freezing.

The Pineapple King

James Drummond Dole, "the Pineapple King," began his first pineapple plantation in 1900 in Hawaii. One year later, he opened his first cannery. At that time, all fruit was hand picked, peeled, and cored, making it a slow process. Thirteen years later, an invention relieved the manual labor needed, and the canned pineapple industry began booming.

Raspberry Nectarine Sorbet

The gentle tang of the nectarines in this recipe plays perfectly with either black or red raspberries. If you can find them, golden raspberries are a delicious variety, and their sweetness is unrivaled when it comes to berries.

INGREDIENTS | YIELD: 1 QUART

1 pound nectarines

1 cup water

¾ cup fresh raspberries

1 tablespoon lemon juice

⅔ cup sugar

1 tablespoon brown sugar

Nectarines

The peak harvest season for nectarines is in July and August, when brilliantly hued fruit is ripe for picking. If your fruit seems a bit unready, leave it at room temperature for a few days to ripen.

1. Peel, core, and chop the nectarines. Place in a medium saucepan, add water, and cover. Heat over medium heat, stirring occasionally, for 8–10 minutes or until very tender.

2. Remove from heat and add raspberries, lemon juice, and sugars, stirring to combine. Let cool to room temperature.

3. Once cooled, purée mixture in a food processor or blender until smooth. Press through a metal strainer to remove seeds, if desired. Refrigerate mixture until thoroughly chilled.

4. Add to ice cream maker and follow manufacturer's instructions for freezing.

Strawberry Banana Sorbet

While great served straight from a bowl or cone on its own, this creamy combination can be stepped up a notch or two by adding dried strawberries into the freeze cycle, or by adding caramelized bananas to the dish just before serving.

INGREDIENTS | YIELD: 1 QUART

1 banana, peeled and chopped

2½ cups strawberries, hulled and chopped

½ cup sugar

½ cup water

1 tablespoon fresh lemon juice

1. Purée all of the ingredients in a food processor or blender until very smooth.

2. Cover and refrigerate until thoroughly chilled.

3. Add to ice cream maker and follow manufacturer's instructions for freezing.

Caramelizing Bananas

Nothing is simpler than caramelizing bananas, though few people think to do it! Simply peel your banana, halve it both lengthwise and widthwise, and lay the four segments on a baking sheet. Top with a healthy sprinkling of sugar, then place under your oven broiler or burn with a kitchen torch.

Tart Apple Sorbet

Prepare to pucker in the tastiest way with this incredible sorbet. You can opt to use the readily available Granny Smith apples, or any other apple that offers a tangy bite.

INGREDIENTS | YIELD: 1 QUART

⅔ cup sugar
1 tablespoon corn syrup
1 cup water
2 tart apples, peeled and cored
Juice of 1 lemon

1. Place the sugar, corn syrup, and water in a small saucepan; stir over medium heat until boiling. Allow to cool.

2. Slice the peeled and cored apples thinly, and drizzle the fresh lemon juice over them. Allow to rest, refrigerated, for up to 1 hour.

3. Place chilled apples and lemon juice (if any remains) in a food processor, and purée until smooth. Add in the sugar syrup and process until well combined.

4. Add to ice cream maker and follow manufacturer's instructions for freezing.

Kiwi Sorbet

Few fruits pack the punch of flavor that the kiwi does, which makes it the ideal fruit to turn into sorbet. Be sure to choose a kiwi that feels softer to the touch—a hard kiwi will be less juicy and less flavorful.

INGREDIENTS | YIELD: 1 QUART

1 cup sugar
1¼ cups water
Juice of ½ lemon
5 fresh kiwis, peeled

The Kiwi Fruit

An important export crop for New Zealand, the kiwi fruit was originally known as the Chinese gooseberry. The term *kiwi* was created as a marketing tool by New Zealand farmers, and the name caught on worldwide.

1. Place the sugar and water in a small saucepan; stir over medium heat until all of the sugar is dissolved. Allow to cool; combine with the lemon juice. Cover and refrigerate until cool.

2. Purée the kiwis in a food processor until smooth. Combine with the chilled syrup.

3. Strain mixture through a mesh strainer, if desired, to remove the seeds.

4. Add to ice cream maker and follow manufacturer's instructions for freezing.

CHAPTER 7

Sherbet

Lemon Sherbet
112

Lime Sherbet
112

Tangerine Sherbet
113

Blackberry Sherbet
114

Raspberry Sherbet
115

Blueberry Sherbet
116

Peach Sherbet
117

Mixed Berry Sherbet
118

Blueberry Peach Sherbet
119

Blackberry Lemon Tea Sherbet
120

Chocolate Sherbet
121

Chocolate Mint Sherbet
121

Chocolate Espresso Sherbet
122

Banana Sherbet
122

Strawberry Sherbet
123

Strawberry Banana Sherbet
124

Cocoa Banana Sherbet
125

Lemon Sherbet

Served after an evening meal, this sherbet is the perfect refreshing dessert. However, for fancier meals, should you serve them, this sherbet serves as a wonderful palate cleanser between courses.

INGREDIENTS | YIELD: 1 QUART

2 cups sugar

1¾ cups water

1½ cups fresh lemon juice

Zest of 1 lemon

⅓ cup heavy cream

Lemon Facts

While Italy is now known for its delicious lemons, the fruit is actually native to Asia. Another interesting fact? The lemon tree is an evergreen, keeping its leaves year-round.

1. Place the sugar and water in a small saucepan; stir over medium heat until all of the sugar is dissolved. Allow to cool, and combine with the lemon juice and zest. Cover and refrigerate until cool.

2. Once cooled, strain mixture through mesh strainer.

3. In separate bowl, whip the cream to stiff peaks, then fold into the lemon mixture.

4. Add to ice cream maker and follow manufacturer's instructions for freezing.

Lime Sherbet

This citrus-packed sorbet would be a delightful addition to many meals, especially after those that hail from South America. After a meal of zesty spice, the kick of lime would be just the thing to cool you down.

INGREDIENTS | YIELD: 1 QUART

1¾ cups sugar

2 cups water

1⅓ cups fresh lime juice

Zest of 2 limes

½ cup heavy cream

1. Place the sugar and water in a small saucepan; stir over medium heat until all of the sugar is dissolved. Allow to cool, and combine with the lime juice and zest. Cover and refrigerate until cool.

2. Once cooled, strain mixture through mesh strainer.

3. In separate bowl, whip the cream to stiff peaks, then fold into the lime mixture.

4. Add to ice cream maker and follow manufacturer's instructions for freezing.

Tangerine Sherbet

They may be small, but tangerines provide a powerful flavor, less tart than traditional oranges, and make for a delicious sherbet. For a dramatic twist, consider adding in a dash of fresh ground black pepper just before freezing.

INGREDIENTS | YIELD: 1 QUART

2 cups sugar

1½ cups water

2 cups fresh tangerine juice

Juice of 1 lemon

⅓ cup heavy cream

1 teaspoon vanilla

Oh My Darlin'

The clementine is a seedless tangerine, and both are variants of the mandarin orange family. Feel free to use clementines in this recipe to achieve very similar results. These smaller, thinly skinned oranges provide a punch of flavor typically not found in the larger varieties.

1. Place the sugar and water in a small saucepan; stir over medium heat until all of the sugar is dissolved. Allow to cool, and combine with tangerine and lemon juices. Cover and refrigerate until cool.

2. In a separate bowl, whip the cream and vanilla to stiff peaks, then fold into the orange mixture.

3. Add to ice cream maker and follow manufacturer's instructions for freezing.

Blackberry Sherbet

In late June and July, blackberries can be found growing wild along country roads, near fence posts, and lots of places in between. If you can't find them wild, blackberry farms are a great way to spend an early morning gathering a bounty with which to churn into this heavenly sherbet.

INGREDIENTS | YIELD: 1 QUART

2 cups fresh blackberries

Juice of 1 lemon

1 cup sugar

1 cup water

⅓ cup heavy cream

1. Rinse the blackberries, but do not dry. Drizzle with the lemon juice and 2 tablespoons of the sugar. Cover and set aside while making the syrup.

2. Place the remaining sugar and the water in a small saucepan; stir over medium heat until all of the sugar is dissolved. Allow to cool.

3. Place the blackberry mixture in a food processor, and purée until smooth. Press through a strainer to remove seeds, if desired. Stir into the sugar syrup.

4. In a separate bowl, whip the cream to stiff peaks, then fold into the blackberry mixture.

5. Add to ice cream maker and follow manufacturer's instructions for freezing.

Raspberry Sherbet

Deep, dark black raspberries would make a gorgeously colored sherbet, and a delicious one as well; however, any variety of raspberries or a combination thereof would be delightful.

INGREDIENTS | YIELD: 1 QUART

3 cups fresh raspberries

Juice of 1 lemon

1 cup sugar

1¼ cups water

¼ cup heavy cream

1. Rinse the raspberries, but do not dry. Drizzle with the lemon juice and 2 tablespoons of the sugar. Cover and set aside while making the syrup.

2. Place the remaining sugar and the water in a small saucepan; stir over medium heat until all of the sugar is dissolved. Allow to cool.

3. Place the raspberry mixture in a food processor, and purée until smooth. Press through a strainer to remove seeds, if desired. Stir into the sugar syrup.

4. In a separate bowl, whip the cream to stiff peaks, then fold into the raspberry mixture.

5. Add to ice cream maker and follow manufacturer's instructions for freezing.

Blueberry Sherbet

Blueberry sherbet isn't terribly popular, especially in commercial markets . . . but it should be! Luckily, it's a breeze to make yourself, and takes only moments to throw together.

INGREDIENTS | YIELD: 1 QUART

2½ cups fresh blueberries

Juice of 1 lemon

1 cup sugar

1 cup water

⅓ cup heavy cream

1. Rinse the blueberries, but do not dry. Drizzle with the lemon juice and 2 tablespoons of the sugar. Cover and set aside while making the syrup.

2. Place the remaining sugar and the water in a small saucepan; stir over medium heat until all of the sugar is dissolved. Allow to cool.

3. Place the blueberry mixture in a food processor, and purée until smooth. Press through a strainer. Stir into the sugar syrup.

4. In a separate bowl, whip the cream to stiff peaks, then fold into the blueberry mixture.

5. Add to ice cream maker and follow manufacturer's instructions for freezing.

Peach Sherbet

Peaches are grown in several states. While Georgia claims that it has the tastiest fruit, California can factually claim that it grows the greatest percentage of peaches: Over 60 percent of the national crop hails from California.

INGREDIENTS | YIELD: 1 QUART

2 cups fresh peaches

Juice of 1 lemon

¾ cup sugar

1 cup water

⅓ cup heavy cream

Extremes

The places that are suitable for peach trees to thrive in are fairly limited, as these trees are somewhat fickle. They require a chilling winter period, and a hot summer to mature the ripening plants. Southern states, such as the Carolinas and Georgia, have ideal climates for peaches due to their distinctive seasons.

1. Peel, pit, and chop the peaches. Drizzle with the lemon juice and 2 tablespoons of the sugar. Cover and set aside while making the syrup.

2. Place the remaining sugar and water in a small saucepan; stir over medium heat until all of the sugar is dissolved. Allow to cool.

3. Place the peach mixture in a food processor, and purée until smooth. Press through a strainer, if desired. Stir into the sugar syrup.

4. In a separate bowl, whip the cream to stiff peaks, then fold into the peach mixture.

5. Add to ice cream maker and follow manufacturer's instructions for freezing.

Mixed Berry Sherbet

Berries abound in the heart of summer, and combine deliciously in this mixed berry sherbet. If you have more or less of one variety, just use what you have. The results will be just as incredible.

INGREDIENTS | YIELD: 1 QUART

¾ cup fresh blackberries
⅔ cup fresh blueberries
⅔ cup fresh raspberries
Juice of 1 lemon
1 cup sugar
1 cup water
¼ cup heavy cream

1. Rinse the berries, but do not dry. Drizzle with the lemon juice and 2 tablespoons of the sugar. Cover and set aside while making the syrup.

2. Place the remaining sugar and water in a small saucepan; stir over medium heat until all of the sugar is dissolved. Allow to cool.

3. Place the berry mixture in a food processor, and purée until smooth. Press through a strainer to remove seeds, if desired. Stir into the sugar syrup.

4. In a separate bowl, whip the cream to stiff peaks, then fold into the berry mixture.

5. Add to ice cream maker and follow manufacturer's instructions for freezing.

Blueberry Peach Sherbet

The combination of blueberries and peaches makes one of the tastiest sherbets available. It screams of summer, but can be made in the dead of winter from frozen fruit, should you need a quick vacation!

INGREDIENTS | YIELD: 1 QUART

1 cup fresh blueberries
2 peaches, peeled, pitted, and chopped
Juice of 1 lemon
1¼ cups sugar
1 cup water
⅓ cup heavy cream

1. Rinse the blueberries, but do not dry. Add to a medium bowl with the chopped peaches. Drizzle with the lemon juice and 2 tablespoons of the sugar. Cover and set aside while making the syrup.

2. Place the remaining sugar and the water in a small saucepan; stir over medium heat until all of the sugar is dissolved. Allow to cool.

3. Place the blueberry-peach mixture in a food processor, and purée until smooth. Press through a strainer to remove seeds, if desired. Stir into the sugar syrup.

4. In a separate bowl, whip the cream to stiff peaks, then fold into the blueberry-peach mixture.

5. Add to ice cream maker and follow manufacturer's instructions for freezing.

Blackberry Lemon Tea Sherbet

Lemon tea can be found in practically every supermarket, especially in the summer months. Brew enough to enjoy over ice while making this sherbet; it's fantastic!

INGREDIENTS | YIELD: 1 QUART

2 cups fresh blackberries
Juice of 1 lemon
1¼ cups sugar
1 cup brewed lemon tea
⅓ cup heavy cream

In a Pinch?

If you prefer not to make your own tea, you can easily substitute a commercially brewed tea. Lemon teas have become staples in the soft drink aisles. Peach tea, Mandarin orange tea, or even a mild green tea would be a welcome substitution.

1. Rinse the blackberries, but do not dry. Drizzle with the lemon juice and 2 tablespoons of the sugar. Cover and set aside while making the syrup.

2. Place the remaining sugar and the brewed lemon tea in a small saucepan; stir over medium heat until all of the sugar is dissolved. Allow to cool.

3. Place the blackberry mixture in a food processor, and purée until smooth. Press through a strainer to remove seeds, if desired. Stir into the sugar syrup.

4. In a separate bowl, whip the cream to stiff peaks, then fold into the blackberry mixture.

5. Add to ice cream maker and follow manufacturer's instructions for freezing.

Chocolate Sherbet

Chocolate sherbet is a wonderful way to get a chocolate fix without the effort of making full-on ice cream. Just quickly combine and enjoy!

INGREDIENTS | YIELD: 1 QUART

1¼ cups sugar
1 cup water
½ cup heavy cream
¾ cup Dutch-processed cocoa powder
1 tablespoon vanilla extract

1. Combine all ingredients in food processor or blender, and purée until very smooth.

2. Refrigerate until thoroughly chilled.

3. Add to ice cream maker and follow manufacturer's instructions for freezing.

Chocolate Mint Sherbet

A touch of mint adds a cool zing to an already flavorful chocolate sherbet. Consider serving with chocolate crepes and a drizzle of chocolate syrup.

INGREDIENTS | YIELD: 1 QUART

1 cup sugar
¾ cup water
¾ cup heavy cream
¾ cup Dutch-processed cocoa powder
1 teaspoon mint extract

1. Combine all ingredients in food processor or blender, and purée until very smooth.

2. Refrigerate until thoroughly chilled.

3. Add to ice cream maker and follow manufacturer's instructions for freezing.

Chocolate Espresso Sherbet

*Chocolate and coffee are a classic combination, and this sherbet
marries the two in a satisfyingly delicious delight.*

INGREDIENTS | YIELD: 1 QUART

1¼ cups sugar

½ cup brewed espresso or strong coffee

1 cup heavy cream

¾ cup Dutch-processed cocoa powder

1 tablespoon Kahlua or coffee liqueur

1. Combine all ingredients in food processor or blender, and purée until very smooth.

2. Refrigerate until thoroughly chilled.

3. Add to ice cream maker and follow manufacturer's instructions for freezing.

An Espresso Warning

With the main ingredients containing a generous amount of caffeine, you should think twice before consuming this treat before bed. It may be a sleepless night!

Banana Sherbet

*As a banana ripens, the starches turn to sugar, resulting in added sweetness. Therefore, those
browning bananas on the counter would be well used in this banana sherbet.*

INGREDIENTS | YIELD: 1 QUART

1¼ cups sugar

1½ cups water

½ cup heavy cream

¼ cup lemon juice

½ cup orange juice

2 medium-large bananas, peeled and chopped

1. Heat sugar and water in small saucepan over medium heat until sugar is dissolved. Remove from heat.

2. Once cooled, combine all ingredients in food processor or blender, and purée until very smooth.

3. Refrigerate until thoroughly chilled.

4. Add to ice cream maker and follow manufacturer's instructions for freezing.

Strawberry Sherbet

Not only do strawberries have a unique flavor, but they are unique in design as well. They are the only fruit with their seeds on the outside.

INGREDIENTS | YIELD: 1 QUART

4 cups fresh strawberries, hulled

Juice of 1 lemon

1¼ cups sugar

1 cup water

¼ cup heavy cream

1. Chop the strawberries and place in a large bowl. Drizzle with the lemon juice and 2 tablespoons of the sugar. Cover and set aside while making the syrup.

2. Place the remaining sugar and the water in a small saucepan; stir over medium heat until all of the sugar is dissolved. Allow to cool.

3. Place the strawberry mixture in a food processor, and purée until smooth. Press through a strainer to remove seeds, if desired. Stir into the sugar syrup.

4. In a separate bowl, whip the cream to stiff peaks, then fold into the strawberry mixture.

5. Add to ice cream maker and follow manufacturer's instructions for freezing.

Strawberry Banana Sherbet

*What a pair! While bananas will continue to ripen after being picked,
a strawberry will only ripen on the vine. Don't pick too early!*

INGREDIENTS | YIELD: 1 QUART

3 cups fresh strawberries, hulled

1 medium-large banana

1 tablespoon lemon juice

1¼ cups sugar

1 cup water

2 teaspoons vanilla

¼ cup heavy cream

1. Chop the strawberries and banana; place in a mixing bowl. Drizzle with the lemon juice and 2 tablespoons of the sugar. Cover and set aside while making the syrup.

2. Place the remaining sugar and the water in a small saucepan; stir over medium heat until all of the sugar is dissolved. Allow to cool.

3. Place the strawberry-banana mixture with the vanilla in a food processor, and purée until smooth. Stir into the sugar syrup.

4. In separate bowl, whip the cream to stiff peaks, then fold into the strawberry-banana mixture.

5. Add to ice cream maker and follow manufacturer's instructions for freezing.

Cocoa Banana Sherbet

Cocoa and banana combine in this sherbet to offer a taste of the islands. Close your eyes and drink in the vacation!

INGREDIENTS | YIELD: 1 QUART

1½ cups sugar

1½ cups water

⅔ cup heavy cream

⅓ cup unsweetened cocoa powder

2 ripe medium-large bananas, peeled and chopped

1 tablespoon vanilla extract

1. Heat sugar and water in small saucepan over medium heat until sugar is dissolved. Remove from heat.

2. Once cooled, combine all ingredients in food processor or blender, and purée until very smooth.

3. Refrigerate until thoroughly chilled.

4. Add to ice cream maker and follow manufacturer's instructions for freezing.

CHAPTER 8

Granita

Lemon Granita
128

Cucumber Basil Granita
129

Orange Granita
130

Watermelon Granita
131

Lime Granita
132

Tart Apple Granita
133

Raspberry Granita
134

Pineapple Granita
135

Honeydew Melon Granita
136

Cantaloupe Granita
137

Cranberry Orange Granita
138

Strawberry Granita
139

Strawberry Kiwi Granita
140

Blueberry Granita
141

Pomegranate Granita
142

Blackberry Granita
143

Sparkling White Grape Granita
144

Pear Granita
145

Lemon Mint Granita
146

Pomegranate Orange Granita
147

Kiwi Granita
148

Lemon Granita

Light, tangy, and refreshing, lemon granita is an alluring summer treat and would be a wonderful accompaniment to strawberry sorbet. It's also great on its own with a dollop of sweetened whipped cream.

INGREDIENTS | YIELD: 1 QUART

2 tablespoons lemon zest

1¼ cups sugar

2¼ cups water

1¼ cups lemon juice

Lemon Zest

How many lemons will it take to produce 2 tablespoons of zest? On average, a medium-sized lemon will yield a single tablespoon of finely grated zest. Therefore, you'll need two lemons to make this particular recipe.

1. Combine the zest and sugar with your fingers, until the sugar is yellow and aromatic.

2. In a medium saucepan, combine ½ cup of the water with the zested sugar, and heat over medium heat until the sugar is completely dissolved.

3. Remove from heat and stir in the remaining water, then chill in the refrigerator.

4. Combine the lemon juice and chilled syrup. Pour into a covered container, and place in the freezer for 1 hour.

5. Remove mixture from the freezer, and stir the frozen crystals into the center of the container with a fork.

6. Return the container to the freezer, and repeat the process every 30–45 minutes, stirring carefully each time, until you have a fully frozen container of crystallized granita.

Pomegranate Granita • Chapter 8

Strawberry Sorbet • Chapter 6

Vegan Pineapple White Chocolate Macadamia Nut Ice Cream • Chapter 9

Brownies for Breakfast Ice Cream Sandwiches • Chapter 11

Bombé • Chapter 14

Fresh Fig Gelato • Chapter 3

Better Than Breakfast Cereal Ice Cream • Chapter 5

Frozen Bananas • Chapter 11

Good Morning Sunshine Smoothie • Chapter 16

Yogurt Fruit Pop • Chapter 11

Sorbet-Filled Frozen Oranges • Chapter 14

Cheesecake Milkshake • Chapter 15

Cantaloupe Sorbet • Chapter 6

Chocolate Chipwich • Chapter 11

Double Trouble Ice Cream Pops • Chapter 11

Waffle Cone • Chapter 11 with
Blackberry Lime Frozen Yogurt • Chapter 4

Cocoa Banana Sherbet • Chapter 7, **Honeydew Sorbet**
• Chapter 6, **Decadent Chocolate Ice Cream** • Chapter 2,
and **Strawberry Banana Sherbet** • Chapter 7

Tiramisu Ice Cream Cake Roll • Chapter 12

Cherry Limeade Gelato • Chapter 3

Watermelon Granita • Chapter 8

Espresso Gelato • Chapter 3

Cucumber Basil Granita

Cucumber and basil are a delightful pair. You'll enjoy the unusual combination in this cool, refreshing treat.

INGREDIENTS | YIELD: 1 QUART

4 large cucumbers
⅓ cup sugar
8 fresh basil leaves
Pinch salt

1. Remove the seeds and half of the peel from the cucumbers, and chop into chunks.

2. Combine all ingredients in a food processor or blender, and purée until very smooth.

3. Refrigerate until chilled.

4. Pour into a covered container and place in the freezer for 1 hour.

5. Remove from the freezer, and stir the frozen crystals into the center of the container with a fork.

6. Return container to the freezer, and repeat the process every 30–45 minutes, stirring carefully each time, until you have a fully frozen container of crystallized granita.

Orange Granita

Any variety of orange would be delightful in this recipe, from tangelo to navel.
Paired with a raspberry topping, you'll be in flavor heaven.

INGREDIENTS | YIELD: 1 QUART

2 tablespoons orange zest
1 cup sugar
4 cups freshly squeezed orange juice
1 teaspoon vanilla

1. Combine the zest and sugar with your fingers in a small bowl, until the sugar is pale orange and aromatic.

2. In a medium saucepan, combine 1 cup of juice with the zested sugar, and heat over medium heat until the sugar is completely dissolved.

3. Remove from heat and stir in the remaining juice and the vanilla, then chill in refrigerator.

4. Pour into a covered container and place in the freezer for 1 hour.

5. Remove from the freezer, and stir the frozen crystals into the center of the container with a fork.

6. Return the container to the freezer, and repeat the process every 30–45 minutes, stirring carefully each time, until you have a fully frozen container of crystallized granita.

Watermelon Granita

Few flavors evoke the feeling of summer like watermelon does.
Choose a fleshy, sweet melon for the best results.

INGREDIENTS | YIELD: 1 QUART

8 cups seeded and chunked watermelon
1 cup sugar
2 tablespoons lemon juice
Pinch salt

Say What?

While it may be a favorite fruit, the watermelon is actually a vegetable. Another tasty fact? Every part of the watermelon is edible, including the rind and the seeds.

1. Remove the seeds and rind from the melon, and chop the fruit into chunks.

2. Combine all ingredients in a food processor or blender, and purée until very smooth.

3. Refrigerate until chilled.

4. Pour into a covered container and place in the freezer for 1 hour.

5. Remove from the freezer, and stir the frozen crystals into the center of the container with a fork.

6. Return the container to the freezer, and repeat the process every 30–45 minutes, stirring carefully each time, until you have a fully frozen container of crystallized granita.

Lime Granita

Lime granita is a perfect end to a spicy dinner, as it plays well with the heat of the meal. Sweet and satisfying, it also is an excellent base for a splash of tequila, should you so desire.

INGREDIENTS | YIELD: 1 QUART

1 tablespoon lime zest
¾ cup sugar
2½ cups water
1½ cups freshly squeezed lime juice

1. Combine the zest and sugar with your fingers, until the sugar is pale green and aromatic.

2. In a medium saucepan, combine ½ cup of the water with the zested sugar, and heat over medium heat until the sugar is completely dissolved.

3. Remove from heat and stir in the lime juice and remaining water, then chill in refrigerator.

4. Pour into a covered container and place in the freezer for 1 hour.

5. Remove from freezer, and stir the frozen crystals into the center of the container with a fork.

6. Return the container to the freezer, and repeat the process every 30–45 minutes, stirring carefully each time, until you have a fully frozen container of crystallized granita.

Tart Apple Granita

There are many varieties of commercially grown apples, but stick with a very tart specimen for this recipe. Granny Smith apples work wonderfully.

INGREDIENTS | YIELD: 1 QUART

3–4 large ripe tart apples, peeled, cored, and chopped

2 cups sugar

1¾ cups water

1 teaspoon lemon juice

½ teaspoon ginger

Granny Smith

The Granny Smith apple was named for Mrs. Maria Smith, the woman who is responsible for nurturing the variety into existence. It is now the world's best-known green apple, available year-round in most every supermarket.

1. Combine the apples, sugar, and water in a saucepan over medium-low heat until sugar is completely dissolved and the apples are softened.

2. Remove from heat, and combine with the remaining ingredients. Purée in food processor or blender until smooth.

3. Refrigerate until chilled.

4. Pour into a covered container and place in the freezer for 1 hour.

5. Remove from freezer, and stir the frozen crystals into the center of the container with a fork.

6. Return the container to the freezer, and repeat the process every 30–45 minutes, stirring carefully each time, until you have a fully frozen container of crystallized granita.

Raspberry Granita

Absolutely delicious on its own, raspberry granita is also excellent when the zest of a lime is added to the sugar syrup. Serve in a chilled martini glass and garnish with a fresh berry or two and a lime wedge to impress your company.

INGREDIENTS | YIELD: 1 QUART

8 cups raspberries
1 teaspoon vanilla
1 cup sugar
2 cups water

1. Purée the berries in a food processor or blender with the vanilla. Press purée through a strainer to remove seeds.

2. Stir in the sugar and water until the sugar is completely dissolved.

3. Refrigerate until chilled.

4. Pour into a covered container and place in the freezer for 1 hour.

5. Remove from freezer, and stir the frozen crystals into the center of the container with a fork.

6. Return the container to the freezer, and repeat the process every 30–45 minutes, stirring carefully each time, until you have a fully frozen container of crystallized granita.

Pineapple Granita

For a taste of the tropics, look no further than Pineapple Granita. The citrus punch plays nicely with coconut, lime, or mango, so feel free to experiment at will.

INGREDIENTS | YIELD: 1 QUART

1½ cups cubed pineapple

1 cup pineapple juice

⅓ cup sugar

1 tablespoon light brown sugar

Topsy Turvy

Tired of waiting on your pineapple to ripen? Turn it upside down on its leaves and leave it to ripen more quickly. Simply watch for the golden color to move from the fruit until it is about halfway up the leaves. This will garner you a perfectly ripened pineapple!

1. Purée the pineapple in a food processor or blender with the juice. Press purée through a strainer, if desired.

2. Stir the sugars into the juice until the sugar is completely dissolved.

3. Refrigerate until chilled.

4. Pour into a covered container and place in the freezer for 1 hour.

5. Remove from freezer, and stir the frozen crystals into the center of the container with a fork.

6. Return the container to the freezer, and repeat the process every 30–45 minutes, stirring carefully each time, until you have a fully frozen container of crystallized granita.

Honeydew Melon Granita

Luscious and light, honeydew granita is excellent when made with a store-bought melon. But if you are lucky enough to get a melon from a farmers' market or garden, you are in for an amazing treat.

INGREDIENTS | **YIELD: 1 QUART**

1 medium-large honeydew melon (2½–3 pounds)
¾ cup sugar
¼ cup water
1 tablespoon lemon juice
Pinch salt

1. Remove the seeds and rind from the melon, and chop the fruit into chunks.

2. Combine all ingredients in a food processor or blender, and purée until very smooth.

3. Refrigerate until chilled.

4. Pour into a covered container and place in the freezer for 1 hour.

5. Remove from freezer, and stir the frozen crystals into the center of the container with a fork.

6. Return the container to the freezer, and repeat the process every 30–45 minutes, stirring carefully each time, until you have a fully frozen container of crystallized granita.

Cantaloupe Granita

The flavor of cantaloupe is heightened by the addition of pepper, resulting in a subtle yet very tasty granita.

INGREDIENTS | YIELD: 1 QUART

1 medium-large cantaloupe (2½–3 pounds)

¾ cup sugar

¼ cup water

1 tablespoon lime juice

Pinch salt

Dash black pepper

Cantaloupe

The orange fleshy melon known most commonly as cantaloupe also goes by the names muskmelon and rockmelon. To change things up from time to time, consider adding balsamic vinegar, lime, or even mint to your cantaloupe recipes for a refreshing twist.

1. Remove the seeds and rind from the melon, and chop the fruit into chunks.

2. Combine all ingredients in a food processor or blender, and purée until very smooth.

3. Refrigerate until chilled.

4. Pour into a covered container and place in the freezer for 1 hour.

5. Remove from freezer, and stir the frozen crystals into the center of the container with a fork.

6. Return the container to the freezer, and repeat the process every 30–45 minutes, stirring carefully each time, until you have a fully frozen container of crystallized granita.

Cranberry Orange Granita

Who says icy granitas have to be served only in the summer? The holidays are perfect for serving this festive granita, especially with a splash of celebratory champagne.

INGREDIENTS | YIELD: 1 QUART

2 tablespoons orange zest

1 cup sugar

3 cups frozen cranberries

1½ cups freshly squeezed orange juice

Growing Cranberries

Cranberries do not actually grow in water! Cranberries grow on bushes in sandy bogs that are flooded in the fall for ease of harvest. A mechanized harvester removes the ripened berries from the vine, which then float to the surface. The floating berries can then be easily corralled for transport. After the harvest, the bogs are again flooded to protect against a winter freeze.

1. Combine the zest and sugar with your fingers, until the sugar is pale orange and aromatic.

2. In a medium saucepan, combine remaining ingredients with the zested sugar, and heat over medium heat until the sugar is completely dissolved.

3. Remove from heat and allow to cool to room temperature.

4. Place mixture in food processor or blender, and purée until smooth. Press through strainer to remove any remaining solids.

5. Pour into a covered container and place in the freezer for 1 hour.

6. Remove from freezer, and stir the frozen crystals into the center of the container with a fork.

7. Return the container to the freezer, and repeat the process every 30–45 minutes, stirring carefully each time, until you have a fully frozen container of crystallized granita.

Strawberry Granita

Fresh strawberries are decadent, especially if picked at their brightest during peak season. However, this granita would be delicious made with frozen berries as well.

INGREDIENTS | YIELD: 1 QUART

2 pounds strawberries, chopped
1 teaspoon fresh lemon juice
1 teaspoon vanilla
⅓ cup sugar
1 cup water

1. Purée the berries in a food processor or blender with the lemon juice and vanilla. Press purée through a strainer to remove seeds.

2. Stir in the sugar and water, and allow to sit for 1 hour, stirring occasionally, until the sugar is completely dissolved.

3. Refrigerate until chilled.

4. Pour into a covered container and place in the freezer for 1 hour.

5. Remove from freezer, and stir the frozen crystals into the center of the container with a fork.

6. Return the container to the freezer, and repeat the process every 30–45 minutes, stirring carefully each time, until you have a fully frozen container of crystallized granita.

Strawberry Kiwi Granita

Strawberry and kiwi share a similar flavor and complement each other in a delightful way. Expect a powerful pop of taste in this refreshing recipe.

INGREDIENTS | YIELD: 1 QUART

1½ pounds strawberries, chopped

3 kiwis, chopped

1 tablespoon fresh lemon juice

½ cup sugar

1 cup water

Fuzzy

Whether it is the feel or the look of kiwis, most people opt to peel the skin off this fruit before eating it. No need! The skin is perfectly edible.

1. Purée the berries and kiwis in a food processor or blender with the lemon juice. Press purée through a strainer to remove seeds.

2. Stir in the sugar and water, and allow to sit for 1 hour, stirring occasionally, until the sugar is completely dissolved.

3. Refrigerate until chilled.

4. Pour into a covered container and place in the freezer for 1 hour.

5. Remove from freezer, and stir the frozen crystals into the center of the container with a fork.

6. Return the container to the freezer, and repeat the process every 30–45 minutes, stirring carefully each time, until you have a fully frozen container of crystallized granita.

Blueberry Granita

Blueberries are packed not only with loads of flavor, but with a multitude of beneficial vitamins, making them one of the famed "superfruits." This granita is another way to get more of that goodness into your diet.

INGREDIENTS | YIELD: 1 QUART

8 cups fresh blueberries
2 teaspoons fresh lemon juice
½ cup sugar
1 cup water

1. Purée the berries in a food processor or blender with the lemon juice. Press purée through a strainer to remove any solid bits.

2. Stir in the sugar and water, and allow to sit for 1 hour, stirring occasionally, until the sugar is completely dissolved.

3. Refrigerate until chilled.

4. Pour into a covered container and place in the freezer for 1 hour.

5. Remove from freezer, and stir the frozen crystals into the center of the container with a fork.

6. Return the container to the freezer, and repeat the process every 30–45 minutes, stirring carefully each time, until you have a fully frozen container of crystallized granita.

Pomegranate Granita

Thanks to companies like POM Wonderful, pomegranate juice has become an easily accessible fruit juice in supermarkets, and even in several gas station franchises and convenience stores.

INGREDIENTS | YIELD: 1 QUART

4 cups pomegranate juice
¾ cup sugar
1 tablespoon lemon juice

Biblical Proportions

The pomegranate derives its name from Old French, and means "seeded apple." Many scholars also believe that it was in fact the pomegranate, and not the apple, that was the forbidden fruit consumed by Adam and Eve in Genesis.

1. Combine the pomegranate juice and sugar over medium-low heat in a saucepan, and heat until sugar is completely dissolved.

2. Remove from heat and stir in the lemon juice.

3. Refrigerate until chilled.

4. Pour into a covered container and place in the freezer for 1 hour.

5. Remove from freezer, and stir the frozen crystals into the center of the container with a fork.

6. Return the container to the freezer, and repeat the process every 30–45 minutes, stirring carefully each time, until you have a fully frozen container of crystallized granita.

Blackberry Granita

The recipe calls for lemon juice, but you also could use either orange juice or lime juice for a nice variation. Whichever you have on hand will do just fine.

INGREDIENTS | YIELD: 1 QUART

8 cups blackberries
1 teaspoon lemon juice
1½ cups sugar
1½ cups water

1. Purée the berries in a food processor or blender with the lemon juice. Press purée through a strainer to remove seeds.

2. Stir in the sugar and water until the sugar is completely dissolved.

3. Refrigerate until chilled.

4. Pour into a covered container and place in the freezer for 1 hour.

5. Remove from freezer, and stir the frozen crystals into the center of the container with a fork.

6. Return the container to the freezer, and repeat the process every 30–45 minutes, stirring carefully each time, until you have a fully frozen container of crystallized granita.

Sparkling White Grape Granita

Sparkling white grape juice is readily available on supermarket shelves. For a quick change, sparkling red grape juice or even grape cider will be just as tasty.

INGREDIENTS | **YIELD: 1 QUART**

4 cups sparkling white grape juice

⅔ cup sugar

1 teaspoon lemon juice

1. Combine the white grape juice and sugar in a saucepan over medium-low heat until sugar is completely dissolved.

2. Remove from heat and stir in the lemon juice.

3. Refrigerate until chilled.

4. Pour into a covered container and place in the freezer for 1 hour.

5. Remove from freezer, and stir the frozen crystals into the center of the container with a fork.

6. Return the container to the freezer, and repeat the process every 30–45 minutes, stirring carefully each time, until you have a fully frozen container of crystallized granita.

Pear Granita

The gritty-textured pear makes it a perfect fruit for granita making, not only in terms of texture, but in subdued flavor as well.

INGREDIENTS | YIELD: 1 QUART

1¾ cups water

2 cups sugar

3–4 large very ripe pears, peeled and chopped

1 teaspoon lemon juice

1 teaspoon vanilla

Pears for Health

Pears are rich in fiber and a source of vitamin C, a proven antioxidant. They also contain potassium, and contain only around 100 calories. They're quite a healthy snack!

1. Combine the water and sugar in a saucepan over medium-low heat until sugar is completely dissolved.

2. Remove from heat, and combine with the remaining ingredients. Purée in food processor or blender until smooth.

3. Refrigerate until chilled.

4. Pour into a covered container and place in the freezer for 1 hour.

5. Remove from freezer, and stir the frozen crystals into the center of the container with a fork.

6. Return the container to the freezer, and repeat the process every 30–45 minutes, stirring carefully each time, until you have a fully frozen container of crystallized granita.

Lemon Mint Granita

Mint and lemon combine for a tart bite in this flavorful granita.

INGREDIENTS | YIELD: 1 QUART

2 tablespoons lemon zest

1¼ cups sugar

2¼ cups water

1½ cups lemon juice

25 fresh mint leaves, washed

1. Combine the zest and sugar with your fingers, until the sugar is yellow and aromatic.

2. In a medium saucepan, combine ½ cup of the water with the zested sugar, and heat over medium heat until the sugar is completely dissolved.

3. Remove from heat and stir in the remaining water, then chill in refrigerator.

4. Combine all ingredients in a food processor or blender, and purée until leaves are well chopped. Allow mixture to sit for 1 hour, refrigerated.

5. Pour into a covered container and place in the freezer for 1 hour.

6. Remove from freezer, and stir the frozen crystals into the center of the container with a fork.

7. Return the container to the freezer, and repeat the process every 30–45 minutes, stirring carefully each time, until you have a fully frozen container of crystallized granita.

Pomegranate Orange Granita

The sweetness of orange mellows the bitterness of the pomegranate juice in this refreshing granita.

INGREDIENTS | YIELD: 1 QUART

3 cups pomegranate juice
1 cup orange juice
⅔ cup sugar

Quite a Fruit

More scientific research is being done on the pomegranate than practically any other fruit, due to its incredible health benefits. Studies show the pomegranate has been found to reduce bad cholesterol, reduce heart disease, protect against some cancers, and aid in oral health.

1. Combine the juices and sugar in a saucepan over medium-low heat in a saucepan until sugar is completely dissolved. Remove from heat.

2. Refrigerate until chilled.

3. Pour into a covered container and place in the freezer for 1 hour.

4. Remove from freezer, and stir the frozen crystals into the center of the container with a fork.

5. Return the container to the freezer, and repeat the process every 30–45 minutes, stirring carefully each time, until you have a fully frozen container of crystallized granita.

Kiwi Granita

The tropical kiwi packs more punch per bite than most fruits, and thus makes an amazing granita. Consider serving with a drizzle of orange juice or Grand Marnier for an after-dinner treat.

INGREDIENTS | YIELD: 1 QUART

2 pounds kiwis, peeled and chopped
1¼ cups water
¾ cup sugar
1 tablespoon lemon juice

1. Combine all ingredients in a food processor or blender, and purée until very smooth.

2. Refrigerate until chilled.

3. Pour into a covered container and place in the freezer for 1 hour.

4. Remove from freezer, and stir the frozen crystals into the center of the container with a fork.

5. Return the container to the freezer, and repeat the process every 30–45 minutes, stirring carefully each time, until you have a fully frozen container of crystallized granita.

CHAPTER 9

Vegan Ice Cream

Vegan Strawberry Ice Cream
150

Vegan Caramelized Onion
Ice Cream
150

Vegan Almond Joy Swirl Ice
Cream
151

Vegan Vanilla Bean Ice Cream
152

Vegan White Chocolate
Ice Cream
153

Vegan Blueberry Lavender
Ice Cream
154

Vegan Rhubarb Cherry Swirl
Ice Cream
155

Vegan Raspberry Almond
Ice Cream
155

Vegan Cinnamon Cheesecake
Swirl Ice Cream
156

Vegan Choco-Avocado
Ice Cream
157

Vegan Cranberry White
Chocolate Chunk Ice Cream
157

Vegan Coffee Ice Cream
158

Vegan Pineapple White
Chocolate Macadamia Nut
Ice Cream
159

Vegan Lemon Poppy Seed
Ice Cream
160

Vegan Lemon-Infused Olive Oil
Ice Cream
161

Vegan Strawberry Ice Cream

There are few things better than sweet summer strawberries. This will give you that taste of summer you are looking for, or cool you off on a hot day.

INGREDIENTS | YIELD: 1 QUART

2 cups coconut milk

1 pound fresh strawberries, hulled and halved

⅓ cup agave nectar

2 teaspoons vanilla extract

Pinch salt

1. Blend everything together in a blender or food processor until completely liquefied. Refrigerate 4 hours to overnight.

2. Add to ice cream maker and follow manufacturer's instructions for freezing.

Vegan Caramelized Onion Ice Cream

You might not consider caramelized onions suitable for dessert, but they make a surprisingly deep, sweet, and complex treat.

INGREDIENTS | YIELD: 1 QUART

½ cup thinly sliced onions

1 tablespoon extra-virgin olive oil

½ cup unrefined sugar

⅔ cup shiraz wine

Juice and zest of 1 orange

12 ounces extra-firm tofu

1 cup coconut milk

Pinch salt

2 tablespoons aged balsamic vinegar or balsamic glaze

1. Add onions, olive oil, and sugar to a small sauté pan. Gently cook over low heat, stirring occasionally, until onions are deep brown in color, about 15–20 minutes. Be careful: Toward the end, the caramelization process turns quickly from caramel to burnt sugar.

2. Place onion mixture in a blender along with wine, orange juice and zest, tofu, coconut milk, and salt. Blend until smooth. Refrigerate overnight.

3. Add to ice cream maker and follow manufacturer's instructions for freezing. When ready to serve, drizzle with balsamic vinegar or glaze.

Vegan Almond Joy Swirl Ice Cream

Like the classic candy bar, this treat will satisfy your craving for crunchy, sweet, and creamy.

INGREDIENTS | YIELD: 1 QUART

3 cups coconut milk

1 cup unrefined sugar

1 cup shredded coconut

1 vanilla bean, split

Pinch salt

1 cup almond milk

¼ teaspoon almond extract

1 tablespoon vanilla extract

½ cup melted dark chocolate

½ cup toasted almonds, chopped

1. In a large saucepan, heat coconut milk, sugar, shredded coconut, vanilla bean, and salt to a high simmer. Remove from heat, cover, and allow to steep for 30 minutes to 1 hour.

2. Add almond milk and extracts; blend well. Refrigerate 4 hours to overnight.

3. Add to ice cream maker and follow manufacturer's instructions for freezing. Thirty seconds before the ice cream finishes churning, slowly drizzle in the melted chocolate. Before storing, fold in toasted almonds.

Almond Joy

Almond Joy candy bars were introduced by Peter Paul Candy Manufacturing Company in 1946 to replace the Dream Bar, which was coconut, chopped almonds, and chocolate. Almond Joys are not a vegan product, so you shouldn't add them in. If you do, the result will be vegetarian versus vegan.

Vegan Vanilla Bean Ice Cream

Ahh, the classic taste of vanilla ice cream. This version uses cashews, which happen to be a delicious and versatile replacement for dairy.

INGREDIENTS | YIELD: 1 QUART

1 cup cashews

I cup water

2 cups coconut milk

½ cup maple syrup

1 vanilla bean, split and seeded, pod saved for another use

Pinch salt

1 cup vanilla-flavored coconut milk creamer

1 tablespoon vanilla extract

1. Soak the cashews in water overnight. Drain.

2. Blend everything together in a blender or food processor until completely liquefied. Refrigerate 4 hours to overnight.

3. Add to ice cream maker and follow manufacturer's instructions for freezing.

Cashews

The "fruit" of the cashew nut is called the cashew apple. The cashew nut is the real fruit of the cashew tree, but the cashew apple is the swollen stalk of the nut. In some places around the world, the apple is used as a snack or distilled into liquor or wine.

Vegan White Chocolate Ice Cream

This homemade white chocolate ice cream not only makes a wonderful addition to your ice cream recipes, but it will also make a great topping for so many other treats.

INGREDIENTS | YIELD: 7 OUNCES

½ cup Superfine Sugar

Pinch salt

2 teaspoons soymilk powder

⅔ cup cocoa butter (found online or in health food stores)

1 teaspoon vanilla extract

1 vanilla bean, split and seeded, pod saved for another use

White Chocolate

White chocolate is not really chocolate at all but a confection made with cocoa butter, thereby making it acceptable in vegan and vegetarian recipes.

1. Sift together the sugar, salt, and soymilk powder; set aside.

2. Melt cocoa butter in double boiler until completely melted. Pour over sugar mixture and whisk until completely smooth. Add vanilla extract and vanilla bean seeds.

3. Blend everything together in a blender or food processor until completely liquefied. Refrigerate 4 hours to overnight.

4. Add to ice cream maker and follow manufacturer's instructions for freezing.

Vegan Blueberry Lavender Ice Cream

*Blueberries and lavender complement each other beautifully and
would make a great addition to afternoon tea.*

INGREDIENTS | YIELD: 1 QUART

1 cup cashews
1 cup water
½ cup extra-virgin coconut oil
1½ cups blueberry purée
½ cup agave nectar
2 teaspoons dried lavender flowers
Pinch salt
1 cup vanilla-flavored coconut milk creamer
1 tablespoon vanilla extract

1. Soak the cashews in water overnight. Drain.

2. Blend everything together in a blender or food processor until completely liquefied. Refrigerate 4 hours to overnight.

3. Add to ice cream maker and follow manufacturer's instructions for freezing.

Blueberry Road

Though New Jersey claims the blueberry as its state fruit, Maine is the blueberry production capital of North America and produces almost 100 percent of all berries harvested in the United States. The annual harvest of North American blueberries would cover a four-lane highway from Chicago to New York if spread out in a single layer.

Vegan Rhubarb Cherry Swirl Ice Cream

Tart rhubarb and cherries make a refreshing end to a meal.

INGREDIENTS | YIELD: 1 QUART

1 pound rhubarb, cut into 2" pieces

1 cup water

1 cup unrefined sugar

1 vanilla bean, split and seeded, pod saved for another use

Pinch salt

2 cups coconut milk

1 cup Cherry Compote (see Chapter 17)

1. Bring rhubarb, water, sugar, vanilla bean, and salt to a boil in a medium saucepan, stirring constantly. Continue to boil until the rhubarb is soft and has a bit of a thick consistency. Remove from heat, and cool to room temperature.

2. Purée rhubarb mixture in blender. Stir in coconut milk and refrigerate 4 hours to overnight.

3. Add to ice cream maker and follow manufacturer's instructions for freezing. Before storing in freezer, fold in Cherry Compote.

Vegan Raspberry Almond Ice Cream

Raspberries and almonds make a beautiful combination with their floral summery flavors. This is a lovely romantic dessert.

INGREDIENTS | YIELD: 1 QUART

1 cup marzipan or almond paste

2 cups coconut milk

½ cup honey

1 vanilla bean, split and seeded, pod saved for another use

Pinch salt

1 cup vanilla-flavored coconut milk creamer

1 teaspoon almond extract

½ cup seedless raspberry jam

1 cup frozen raspberries

1. Blend everything but the jam and raspberries together in a blender or food processor until completely liquefied. Refrigerate 4 hours to overnight.

2. Add to ice cream maker and follow manufacturer's instructions for freezing. Before storing, swirl in raspberry jam and frozen raspberries.

Vegan Cinnamon Cheesecake Swirl Ice Cream

This recipe is like a cinnamon roll, but in ice cream form. You won't be able to resist it!

INGREDIENTS | YIELD: 1 QUART

2 cups unrefined sugar

½ cup water

3 tablespoons cinnamon

16 ounces vegan cream cheese

2 cups coconut milk

1 cup agave nectar

1 cup vegan coconut coffee creamer

1 tablespoon lemon juice

Cinnamon

In the Middle Ages, cinnamon was only affordable for the wealthy elite of society. A person's social rank could be determined by the number of spices he could afford. Because cinnamon was one of the first spices sought by European explorers, many believe it actually led to the inadvertent discovery of America.

1. In a small saucepan, heat sugar, water, and cinnamon to a boil over medium heat. Stir until sugar is completely dissolved. Remove from heat and allow to cool.

2. Combine cream cheese, coconut milk, agave nectar, coconut creamer, and lemon juice in blender or food processor. Refrigerate 4 hours to overnight.

3. Add cream cheese mixture to ice cream maker and follow manufacturer's instructions for freezing. Before storing, swirl in cinnamon mixture.

Vegan Choco-Avocado Ice Cream

Avocado lends to the creaminess in this recipe, making for a strikingly rich dessert.

INGREDIENTS | YIELD: 1 QUART

4 ripe bananas
1 cup extra-virgin coconut oil
2 ripe avocados, peeled and pitted
¾ cup unrefined sugar
Pinch salt
1 tablespoon vanilla extract

1. Place bananas and coconut oil in a food processor or blender and blend well.

2. Add remaining ingredients and blend well. Refrigerate 4 hours to overnight.

3. Add to ice cream maker and follow manufacturer's instructions for freezing.

Avocados

In Indonesia, residents mix their avocados with milk, coffee, and rum to make a cold drink called *alpokat*. It is served as a sweet dessert, and is often served over ice cream, much like a milkshake.

Vegan Cranberry White Chocolate Chunk Ice Cream

The tartness of the cranberries makes a beautiful counterpoint to the sweetness of the white chocolate.

INGREDIENTS | YIELD: 1 QUART

6 ounces fresh cranberries
½ cup apple cider
½ cup unrefined sugar
1 vanilla bean, split and seeded, pod saved for another use
Pinch salt
2 cups coconut milk
1 cup vegan coconut creamer
½ cup vegan white chocolate chunks
½–1 cup dried cranberries

1. In a medium saucepan, bring cranberries, apple cider, sugar, vanilla bean, and salt to a boil, stirring constantly. Continue to boil until cranberries start to burst and the mixture has a bit of a thick consistency. Remove from heat, and cool to room temperature.

2. Purée cranberry mixture in a blender. Stir in coconut milk and creamer. Refrigerate 4 hours to overnight.

3. Add to ice cream maker and follow manufacturer's instructions for freezing. Before storing in freezer, fold in white chocolate and dried cranberries.

Vegan Coffee Ice Cream

This would be a great way to wake up in the morning! Or serve this treat with a slice of vegan apple pie.

INGREDIENTS | YIELD: 1 QUART

1 cup cashews

1 cup water

2 cups coconut milk

2 teaspoons instant espresso powder

½ cup maple syrup

1 vanilla bean, split and seeded, pod saved for another use

Pinch salt

1 cup vanilla-flavored coconut milk creamer

1 tablespoon vanilla extract

1. Soak the cashews in water overnight. Drain.

2. Blend everything together in a blender or food processor until completely liquefied. Refrigerate 4 hours to overnight.

3. Add to ice cream maker and follow manufacturer's instructions for freezing.

Coffee

Originally, coffee was eaten rather than consumed in liquid form. African tribes would mix the coffee berries with fat to make a powerful energy booster.

Vegan Pineapple White Chocolate Macadamia Nut Ice Cream

This recipe is truly tropical bliss in an ice cream treat. It's an explosion of island flavor!

INGREDIENTS | YIELD: 1 QUART

1⅓ cups full-fat coconut milk

7 ounces vegan white chocolate, chopped

2 pounds soft tofu

1⅓ cups extra-virgin coconut oil

2 tablespoons lemon juice

½ vanilla bean, split and seeded, pod saved for another use

1½ cups unrefined sugar

Pinch salt

2 (20-ounce) cans crushed pineapple, ⅔ cup drained and set aside

⅓ cup roughly chopped macadamia nuts

1. Heat coconut milk to a simmer and pour over white chocolate. Stir until smooth.

2. Blend everything except the ⅔ cup drained pineapple and macadamia nuts until smooth. You may have to do this in batches because of the quantity.

3. Cover and refrigerate overnight.

4. Add to ice cream maker and follow manufacturer's instructions for freezing. Before storing, fold in reserved pineapple and macadamia nuts.

Pineapple

A ripe pineapple will be a deep golden yellow at the bottom that will continue to the top. The higher the yellow color is up the side of the pineapple, the riper the fruit is. A ripe pineapple should also smell sweet; if it smells sweet, it's ready.

Vegan Lemon Poppy Seed Ice Cream

Lemons and poppy seeds make a classic and comforting combination in this delicious ice cream treat.

INGREDIENTS | YIELD: 1 QUART

1 cup coconut creamer

½ cup coconut milk, full fat

1¾ cups soymilk

2½ tablespoons vegan butter

Juice and zest of 4 lemons

½ vanilla bean, split and seeded, pod reserved for another use

⅓ cup unrefined sugar

¼ teaspoon xanthan gum plus 2 tablespoons sugar, mixed

1¼ teaspoons arrowroot

1 tablespoon agave nectar

2 tablespoons poppy seeds

1. Combine creamer, milks, butter, lemon zest and juice, vanilla beans, and sugar in heavy bottomed pot. Cook just until you achieve steam.

2. Reduce heat to low and slowly add xanthan gum–sugar mixture, whisking carefully but thoroughly.

3. Combine arrowroot and agave nectar thoroughly. Set aside. Bring lemon mixture back up to a light simmer; stir in arrowroot mixture and remove from heat. Cover and refrigerate overnight.

4. Add to ice cream maker and follow manufacturer's instructions for freezing. Add poppy seeds just before you stop churning the ice cream.

Vegan Lemon-Infused Olive Oil Ice Cream

*Lemon and olive oil make a classic combination in the Mediterranean,
and can make a surprisingly delicious ice cream as well.*

INGREDIENTS | YIELD: 1 QUART

12 ounces extra-firm tofu

½ cup extra-virgin olive oil

½ cup coconut milk

2 teaspoons fresh lemon zest

Pinch salt

¼ cup maple syrup

1. Blend all ingredients in a blender until smooth. Refrigerate 4 hours to overnight.

2. Add to ice cream maker and follow manufacturer's instructions for freezing.

Tofu

During the second century B.C. in China, someone discovered tofu when he accidentally dropped some nigari into a pot of simmering soybean milk. Just as acidic substances like lemon curdle cows' milk, the nigari curdled the soymilk. Voilà! Tofu was born and became popular throughout Asia.

CHAPTER 10

Sugar-Free Ice Cream

Sugar-Free Vanilla Caramel Swirl
Ice Cream
165

Sugar-Free Turtle Ice Cream
166

Sugar-Free Strawberry Ice Cream
167

Sugar-Free Dark Chocolate
Orange Ice Cream
168

Sugar-Free Coffee Chip
Ice Cream
169

Vanilla Bean Agave Ice Cream
170

Sugar-Free Dreamy Orange
Cream Ice Cream
170

Sugar-Free Chocolate Ice Cream
171

Sugar-Free Peanut Butter and
Jelly Ice Cream
172

Sugar-Free Decadent Dark
Chocolate Raspberry Ice Cream
173

Sugar-Free Mint Chip Ice Cream
174

Sugar-Free Piña Colada Ice
Cream
175

Sugar-Free Mango Ice Cream
176

Agave, Splenda, honey, and stevia are all sweeteners used in some recipes for special diets. If you are comfortable using another artificial or natural sweetener, experiment as you see fit. While a few of the recipes included in this chapter do not contain refined sugars, please note, agave nectar, fruits, and honey still contain sugar. They make for a healthier substitute for sugar, as they are natural, but if you're on a restricted diet, you should consult with your doctor before adding such ingredients to your own diet.

Sugar-Free Vanilla Caramel Swirl Ice Cream

Vanilla and caramel go hand in hand—both are creamy, rich, and sweet.
Here they play together to delight your taste buds.

INGREDIENTS | YIELD: 1 QUART

3 cups heavy cream

1 cup Splenda

1 vanilla bean, split

Pinch salt

4 large egg yolks

1 cup half and half

1 tablespoon vanilla extract

½ cup sugar-free caramel syrup

1. Combine heavy cream, Splenda, vanilla bean, and salt in a medium saucepan. Bring to a light simmer over medium-low heat. Remove from heat and allow to steep for 30 minutes. Remove vanilla bean, rinse, and save for another use.

2. In a separate bowl, whisk egg yolks. Reheat cream mixture until hot, then temper the yolks by adding half of the mixture into the eggs, whisking constantly. Add egg mixture to the saucepan, and heat until thickened.

3. Add half and half and vanilla extract. Refrigerate 4 hours to overnight.

4. Add to ice cream maker and follow manufacturer's instructions for freezing. Before storing in freezer, swirl in caramel sauce.

Sugar-Free Turtle Ice Cream

Chocolate, caramel, and toasty pecans are a beautiful combination just meant to be enjoyed.

INGREDIENTS | YIELD: 1 QUART

3 cups heavy cream

1 cup agave nectar

Generous pinch of salt

4 large egg yolks

½ cup half and half

1 tablespoon vanilla extract

½ cup melted sugar-free chocolate chips

½ cup pecans, toasted and chopped

½ cup sugar-free caramel sauce

Turtles

The famous chocolate, caramel, and pecan candy is called a turtle because the arrangement of the nuts sticking out from under the chocolate makes people think of a turtle. The four legs are the nuts, while the head and tail are formed by extra chocolate runoff.

1. Combine heavy cream, agave nectar, and salt in a medium saucepan. Bring to a light simmer. Remove from heat.

2. In a separate bowl, whisk egg yolks. While cream mixture is hot, temper the yolks by adding half of the mixture into the eggs, whisking constantly. Add egg mixture to the saucepan, and heat until thickened.

3. Add half and half and vanilla extract. Refrigerate 4 hours to overnight.

4. Add to ice cream maker and follow manufacturer's instructions for freezing. In the last 30 seconds of churning, slowly drizzle melted chocolate into the churning ice cream. Before storing, fold in pecans and caramel sauce.

Sugar-Free Strawberry Ice Cream

Mmm, strawberries and cream. This is a sweet, cool treat that brings a taste of summer to any time of the year.

INGREDIENTS | YIELD: 1 QUART

3 cups heavy cream

1 cup Splenda

Pinch salt

4 large egg yolks

1 cup strawberry purée

1 tablespoon vanilla extract

1 cup roughly mashed fresh strawberries

Replacing Sugar with Splenda

Replacing sugar in ice cream recipes can be tricky, as sugar is a big part of the texture. But using all cream in the recipe instead of part cream and part milk will help to ensure that the texture stays creamy and doesn't freeze rock hard.

1. Combine heavy cream, Splenda, and salt in a medium saucepan. Bring to a light simmer. Remove from heat.

2. In a separate bowl, whisk egg yolks. While cream mixture is hot, temper the yolks by adding half of the mixture into the eggs, whisking constantly. Add egg mixture to the saucepan, and heat until thickened.

3. Add strawberry purée and vanilla extract. Refrigerate 4 hours to overnight.

4. Add to ice cream maker and follow manufacturer's instructions for freezing. Before storing in freezer, fold in the mashed strawberries.

Sugar-Free Dark Chocolate Orange Ice Cream

*If you want an elegant, decadent dessert, this is it! Dark chocolate
and orange make a perfect, smooth, silky combination.*

INGREDIENTS | YIELD: 1 QUART

3 cups heavy cream

1 cup Splenda

⅓ cup Dutch-processed cocoa powder

Zest from 2 oranges

Pinch salt

8 large egg yolks

7 ounces sugar-free dark chocolate, roughly chopped

¼ cup fresh-squeezed orange juice

½ cup sugar-free dark chocolate, chopped

Orange Differences

Florida oranges may be greener than California oranges because the night temperatures in Florida are warmer, which causes more chlorophyll to migrate into the peel. They might appear green, but they are still ripe and sweet.

1. Whisk heavy cream, Splenda, cocoa powder, orange zest, and salt in a medium saucepan. Bring to a boil. Remove from heat and steep for 30 minutes to 1 hour.

2. In a separate bowl, whisk egg yolks. Reheat cream mixture until hot, then temper the yolks by adding half of the mixture into the eggs, whisking constantly. Return mixture to saucepan, and heat until thickened. Strain custard over chopped chocolate, and stir until smooth.

3. Add orange juice and stir. Refrigerate 4 hours to overnight.

4. Add to ice cream maker and follow manufacturer's instructions for freezing. Fold in chopped chocolate before storing.

Sugar-Free Coffee Chip Ice Cream

This coffee ice cream is delicious on its own, but the added bite from the chocolate chips mixed in is a real delight. Feel free to omit the chips, if you wish.

INGREDIENTS | YIELD: 1 QUART

3 cups heavy cream

½ cup Splenda

2 tablespoons instant coffee

Pinch salt

4 large egg yolks

½ cup sugar-free flavored creamer of choice

1 tablespoon vanilla extract

½ cup sugar-free chocolate chips, roughly chopped

1. Combine heavy cream, Splenda, instant coffee, and salt in a medium saucepan. Bring to a light simmer. Remove from heat.

2. In a separate bowl, whisk egg yolks. While cream mixture is hot, temper the yolks by adding half of the mixture into the eggs, whisking constantly. Add egg mixture to the saucepan, and heat until thickened.

3. Add sugar-free creamer and vanilla extract. Refrigerate 4 hours to overnight.

4. Add to ice cream maker and follow manufacturer's instructions for freezing. Before storing in freezer, fold in the chopped chocolate.

Vanilla Bean Agave Ice Cream

There is nothing "just plain vanilla" about this delicious, sugar-free treat.
The vanilla bean and vanilla extract together give it a warm, rich note.

INGREDIENTS | YIELD: 1 QUART

1 cup whole milk
½ cup agave nectar
1 vanilla bean, split and seeded
Pinch salt
4 large egg yolks
2 cups heavy cream
1 tablespoon vanilla extract

1. Combine milk, agave nectar, vanilla bean, and salt in a medium saucepan. Bring to a light simmer. Remove from heat.

2. In a separate bowl, whisk egg yolks. While milk mixture is hot, temper the yolks by adding half of the mixture into the eggs, whisking constantly. Add egg mixture to the saucepan, and heat until thickened.

3. Add cream and vanilla extract. Refrigerate 4 hours to overnight.

4. Add to ice cream maker and follow manufacturer's instructions for freezing.

Sugar-Free Dreamy Orange Cream Ice Cream

If you love Creamsicles, you will love this sugar-free version. It's citrusy, creamy, and oh-so-good.

INGREDIENTS | YIELD: 1 QUART

2 small packages sugar-free orange gelatin powder
2 cups boiling water
1 cup crushed ice
1 cup cream
¼ cup Splenda
1 tablespoon vanilla extract

1. Combine gelatin and boiling water until completely dissolved, about 2 minutes.

2. Stir in crushed ice to cool.

3. Stir in cream, Splenda, and vanilla extract.

4. Add to ice cream maker and follow manufacturer's instructions for freezing.

Sugar-Free Chocolate Ice Cream

Just because you need a sugar-free recipe doesn't mean you have to skimp in the flavor department. This recipe packs a surprising amount of flavor thanks to the cocoa powder.

INGREDIENTS | YIELD: 1 QUART

1 cup whole milk

4 cups heavy cream, divided use

1 teaspoon espresso powder

⅓ cup Dutch-processed cocoa powder

Pinch salt

1 teaspoon white stevia powder

4 large egg yolks

1 tablespoon vanilla extract

1. Combine milk, 2 cups of the heavy cream, espresso powder, cocoa powder, salt, and stevia powder in a medium saucepan. Bring to a light simmer. Remove from heat.

2. In a separate bowl, whisk egg yolks. While milk mixture is hot, temper the yolks by adding half of the mixture into the eggs, whisking constantly. Add egg mixture to the saucepan, and heat until thickened.

3. Add remaining 2 cups of heavy cream and the vanilla extract. Refrigerate 4 hours to overnight.

4. Add to ice cream maker and follow manufacturer's instructions for freezing.

Sugar-Free Peanut Butter and Jelly Ice Cream

A childhood favorite sandwich turns into a perfectly chilly treat in this recipe.

INGREDIENTS | YIELD: 1 QUART

3 cups heavy cream

1 cup sugar-free imitation honey

½ cup sugar-free peanut butter

Pinch salt

4 large egg yolks

½ cup half and half

1 tablespoon vanilla extract

½ cup sugar-free jelly, stirred to a thick, pourable consistency

PB and J

The world's largest peanut butter and jelly sandwich was created in Oklahoma City, Oklahoma, in 2002 by the Oklahoma Peanut Commission and the Oklahoma Wheat Commission. The PB and J sandwich weighed in at nearly 900 pounds and contained 350 pounds of peanut butter and 144 pounds of jelly. The amount of bread used to create the sandwich was equivalent to more than 400 (1-pound) loaves of bread.

1. Combine heavy cream, honey, peanut butter, and salt in a medium saucepan. Bring to a light simmer. Remove from heat.

2. In a separate bowl, whisk egg yolks. While cream mixture is hot, temper the yolks by adding half of the mixture into the eggs, whisking constantly. Add egg mixture to the saucepan, and heat until thickened.

3. Add half and half and vanilla extract. Refrigerate 4 hours to overnight.

4. Add to ice cream maker and follow manufacturer's instructions for freezing. Before storing in freezer, swirl in jelly.

Sugar-Free Decadent Dark Chocolate Raspberry Ice Cream

Dark chocolate and raspberries come together to make a sinful combination not so sinful. This one is sugar-free and so delicious.

INGREDIENTS | YIELD: 1 QUART

3 cups heavy cream

1 cup Splenda

⅓ cup Dutch-processed cocoa powder

Pinch salt

8 large egg yolks

7 ounces sugar-free dark chocolate, roughly chopped

1 cup raspberry purée

1 tablespoon vanilla extract

¼ teaspoon almond extract

½ cup fresh raspberries

1. Whisk heavy cream, Splenda, cocoa powder, and salt in a medium saucepan. Bring to a light simmer. Remove from heat.

2. In a separate bowl, whisk egg yolks. While cream mixture is hot, temper the yolks by adding half of the mixture into the eggs, whisking constantly. Add egg mixture to the saucepan, and heat until thickened. Strain custard over chopped chocolate, and stir until smooth.

3. Add raspberry purée, vanilla extract, and almond extract. Refrigerate 4 hours to overnight.

4. Add to ice cream maker and follow manufacturer's instructions for freezing. Before storing in freezer, fold in fresh raspberries.

Sugar-Free Mint Chip Ice Cream

Mint offers enough bite to counteract the sugar-free flavor. You'll find this dessert rich and satisfying, and incredibly delicious.

INGREDIENTS | YIELD: 1 QUART

3 cups heavy cream

1¼ cup Splenda

Pinch salt

4 large egg yolks

1 cup half and half

1 tablespoon vanilla extract

½ teaspoon peppermint oil

1 cup sugar-free chocolate chips, chopped into smaller chips

Peppermint

The name "peppermint" came from the mythological Greek nymph Mintha, who was turned into the flavorful plant and trod underfoot by the jealous goddess Persephone. Mintha (or Minthe) had fallen in love with Persephone's husband, Hades, god of the underworld.

1. Combine heavy cream, Splenda, and salt in a medium saucepan. Bring to a light simmer. Remove from heat.

2. In a separate bowl, whisk egg yolks. While cream mixture is hot, temper the yolks by adding half of the mixture into the eggs, whisking constantly. Add egg mixture to saucepan, and heat until thickened.

3. Add half and half, vanilla extract, and peppermint oil. Refrigerate 4 hours to overnight.

4. Add to ice cream maker and follow manufacturer's instructions for freezing. Before storing in freezer, fold in chocolate chips.

Sugar-Free Piña Colada Ice Cream

This ice cream is tropical bliss. The creamy coconut partnered with sweet and tangy pineapple will transport you to a quiet warm beach with a cool breeze.

INGREDIENTS | YIELD: 1 QUART

2 (15-ounce) cans coconut milk

1 vanilla bean, split

¼ cup agave nectar

Pinch salt

1 cup unsweetened shredded coconut

1 (8-ounce) can crushed pineapple

1 tablespoon vanilla extract

The Piña Colada

It is said the piña colada was created by a bartender in 1954 upon request by his employer at a Hilton bar in Puerto Rico. However, the earliest story found with this particular combination dates back to the 1800s when a ship's captain combined coconut, pineapple, and white rum to boost his crew's morale.

1. Bring coconut milk, vanilla bean, agave nectar, salt, and shredded coconut to a boil in a large saucepan. Immediately remove from heat; cover and allow to steep for 1 hour.

2. Strain milk mixture, then stir in crushed pineapple with juices and vanilla extract. Refrigerate 4 hours to overnight.

3. Add to ice cream maker and follow manufacturer's instructions for freezing.

Sugar-Free Mango Ice Cream

Tropical, sweet, with just a hint of pepper, this is one delicious ice cream!

INGREDIENTS | YIELD: 1 QUART

3 cups heavy cream

1 cup Splenda

Pinch salt

4 large egg yolks

1 cup mango purée

1 tablespoon vanilla extract

1 cup diced fresh mango

Selecting Mangos

When choosing mangos, don't judge by color but rather by firmness. Mangos that are ripe will give slightly to gentle pressure, very similar to an avocado or a peach.

1. Combine heavy cream, Splenda, and salt in a medium saucepan. Bring to a light simmer. Remove from heat.

2. In a separate bowl, whisk egg yolks. While cream mixture is hot, temper the yolks by adding half of the mixture into the eggs, whisking constantly. Add egg mixture to the saucepan, and heat until thickened.

3. Add mango purée and vanilla extract. Refrigerate 4 hours to overnight.

4. Add to ice cream maker and follow manufacturer's instructions for freezing. Before storing in freezer, fold in the diced mangos.

CHAPTER 11

For the Kids

Homemade Chocolate
Magic Shell
178

Popsicles
178

Nutty Buddies
179

Ice Cream Cupcakes
180

Waffle Cones
181

Yogurt Fruit Pops
181

Frozen Bananas
182

Double Trouble Ice Cream Pops
183

Sugar Cookie Cups
184

Chocolate Ice Cream
Sandwiches
185

Chocolate Chipwiches
186

Peanut Butter and Jelly Ice
Cream Sandwiches
187

Oatmeal Raisin
Ice Cream Sandwiches
188

Brownies for Breakfast Ice
Cream Sandwiches
189

Frozen Cheesecake Pops
190

Homemade Chocolate Magic Shell

Kids will love helping make this incredibly easy ice cream topping. It's just two simple ingredients that go from soft to hard in a flash . . . like magic!

INGREDIENTS | SERVES 4

4 tablespoons butter

6 ounces semisweet chocolate chips

Storage

Let's keep it simple! Prepare the ingredients in a wide-mouthed Mason jar. Feel free to double the recipe, and keep any leftovers in the same jar. No need to refrigerate! Whenever you get the craving, rewarm in 20-second increments until ready. Easy!

1. Heat chocolate and butter for 30 seconds in a microwave. Stir. Repeat in 20-second increments.

2. When soft and pourable, add to your favorite ice cream and watch the magic happen!

Popsicles

It's the simplest of concepts, but never fails to impress the youngsters! Many chain stores sell popsicle molds, but you can easily make them in small paper cups with craft sticks or plastic spoons as handles.

INGREDIENTS | SERVES 6

24 ounces fruit juice, lemonade, or punch

Additions

Chopped up bits of fresh fruit make a great addition to the standard pop. Try a few bits of strawberry to a lemonade pop for a good-looking and wonderful-tasting treat!

Pour juice into popsicle molds and freeze until set. (If using a vessel other than a commercial popsicle mold, cover each vessel with plastic wrap, and insert a popsicle stick through the wrap before freezing.)

Nutty Buddies

Kids and adults alike will love making the homemade version of this popular treat. Feel free to use your choice of ice creams; the fun is in adding all of your favorite flavors!

INGREDIENTS | SERVES 6

½ cup chopped peanuts

1 recipe Homemade Chocolate Magic Shell (see recipe in this chapter)

6 sugar cones, store-bought or homemade

4 cups Simple Vanilla Ice Cream, softened (see Chapter 2)

6 caramel candies, unwrapped

Having a Party?

Double the recipe! A standard muffin tin has twelve cups, perfect for making a big batch of these. When it's time for dessert, just pull out the prepared pan and prepare for happy squeals.

1. Place 6 parchment squares or nonstick cupcake liners in a muffin tin. Sprinkle chopped nuts onto each liner.

2. Spoon a small bit of magic shell into each sugar cone. Add equal amount of ice cream to each cone, and push one caramel square into the center of the ice cream.

3. When all cones have been filled, pour desired amount of magic shell over the nuts in the muffin tin. Quickly turn the filled cones upside down into the tins.

4. Freeze entire pan for 1–2 hours. If not consuming within 24 hours, cover entire cone in plastic wrap after 2 hours.

Ice Cream Cupcakes

Tired of scooping the ice cream alongside the birthday cake? Try this ingenious solution!
With this recipe you'll get cake and ice cream in one serving—no muss, no fuss!

INGREDIENTS | SERVES 36

1 recipe cake batter, using your favorite cake recipe or boxed cake mix

1 gallon ice cream

1 recipe Sweetened Whipped Cream (see Chapter 17)

36 maraschino cherries, if desired

1. Preheat oven to 350°F. Prepare three 12-serving disposable muffin tins with cupcake liners. Set aside.

2. Fill each tin with cake batter, roughly a quarter full. Bake for 10–12 minutes, or until set. Allow to cool completely.

3. Allow ice cream to soften slightly, then scoop and press into each tin, on top of the baked cupcakes. Cover tins with plastic wrap. Freeze until set.

4. When ready to serve, remove cupcakes from freezer and peel off plastic wrap. Top each with dollop or piped swirl of whipped cream, and garnish with cherry, if desired.

Waffle Cones

Making waffle cones is one of those things you simply must have the right equipment for. There are many different waffle cone machines on the market, from standard waffle to mini. A pizzelle maker works just as well.

INGREDIENTS | SERVES 12

1 cup heavy cream
2 teaspoons vanilla
1½ cups powdered sugar
1½ cups all-purpose flour
1 tablespoon cornstarch

1. Whip cream and vanilla in medium bowl with a whisk by hand, to almost soft peaks.

2. In a separate bowl, sift together the sugar, flour, and cornstarch. Add mixture to cream, and stir until combined.

3. Chill for 30 minutes to 1 hour, then prepare on waffle iron according to manufacturer's instructions. While still hot, wrap each waffle around a coning cool, shape by hand, or press into a bowl for an alternate vessel shape.

Yogurt Fruit Pops

Yogurt and kids don't always go hand in hand, but with the yogurt hidden in this healthy pop, the kids will never know it's good for them!

INGREDIENTS | SERVES 6

8 ounces plain low-fat yogurt
2 cups chopped fresh fruit, such as berries and peaches

1. In food processor or blender, purée the yogurt and fruit until smooth.

2. Pour evenly into molds or cups. Freeze until set.

Why Didn't I Think of That?

It is common to find kid-branded yogurts sold in tear-off tube packages in supermarkets. While these products are great served as is, you can also freeze them, creating a healthy frozen snack that's both easy and delicious.

Frozen Bananas

Why pay $3 or more each when you can make a half-dozen for less? Kids will love these "monkey tails," and you'll love how easy they are to prepare.

INGREDIENTS | SERVES 6

3 large or 6 small just-ripe bananas

12 ounces chocolate chips

1 tablespoon shortening

Fun Treats in Small Packages

For a fun twist, make smaller, decorated versions of these banana treats. Cut the bananas into 2" lengths, insert stick, dip about three-quarters into the melted chocolate, and then add sprinkles for a bit of color!

1. Peel bananas. If using large bananas, cut in half. Insert craft sticks into each banana or half. Refrigerate while preparing the chocolate.

2. Prepare a small baking sheet with parchment paper. Pan must fit easily into your freezer.

3. Melt chocolate and shortening in microwave, heating in 30-second increments. Stir after each heating. When smooth and liquid in texture, dip prepared bananas into chocolate, then place on parchment-lined pan.

4. Freeze 1–2 hours, then wrap in plastic, or carefully place all in a large zipper-top freezer bag.

Double Trouble Ice Cream Pops

While these treats can just as quickly be made in purchased freezer-pop molds, they are actually perfect for paper cups. The striping really makes an impact when peeling off those cups!

INGREDIENTS | SERVES 12

¾ cup milk, divided

4 cups light-colored ice cream, softened

2 cups dark-colored ice cream, softened

Fun Combinations

Chocolate and vanilla stripes aren't the only option! Try lemon and blackberry, coconut and pineapple, or orange and blueberry, just to name a few! For the adult variety, consider coffee and chocolate, and add a few chocolate-covered coffee beans for a surprise bite.

1. Stir ½ cup of the milk into the light-colored ice cream, and remaining ¼ cup milk into the dark.

2. Starting with the light ice cream, begin filling the paper cups about a third full. Place cup in freezer and freeze for 45 minutes. Keep unused ice cream chilled for 30 minutes in freezer, then in refrigerator for 15 minutes.

3. Remove cups from freezer, and add craft stick to center of each cup. Proceed to fill with dark ice cream (about a third of the cup). Top with light ice cream. Return to freezer until set.

4. To store pops not consumed within 24 hours, place a piece of plastic wrap over each cup, pulling it over the stick.

Sugar Cookie Cups

*Cones are fun, but how about an edible bowl? An edible bowl is a great
and tasty treat for containing a sundae or banana split.*

INGREDIENTS | SERVES 12

2¾ cups all-purpose flour
¾ teaspoon salt
1 cup butter, softened
1½ cups sugar
1 egg
1 tablespoon vanilla

1. Preheat oven to 350°F. Spray a cookie bowl pan, king-sized muffin tin, or the underside of several large cups with cooking spray. Set aside.

2. Combine flour and salt in small mixing bowl. In the bowl of a stand mixer, beat the butter and sugar until light and fluffy. Add in egg and vanilla; beat for 1 minute. Add in the flour in three additions, until combined. Chill dough for 20 minutes.

3. Roll out the chilled dough on a floured surface to roughly ⅛" thick. Using a large cookie cutter, cut into rounds large enough to drape over the prepared baking tins (around 4"–5" in diameter, depending on tin size).

4. Bake for 10–12 minutes, or until set. Remove from oven and allow to cool for 5 minutes. Wash pan and repeat until remaining dough is used.

Chocolate Ice Cream Sandwiches

More cake than cookie, these frozen snacks are a summertime staple. While not necessary, these chocolatey cookies can be baked in a specialty pan to give them the dimpled texture that store-bought ice cream sandwiches have. See Appendix B for details.

INGREDIENTS | SERVES 8

½ cup unsalted butter, melted

½ cup sugar

2 teaspoons vanilla

1 large egg, beaten

½ cup all-purpose flour

¼ cup unsweetened cocoa powder

Pinch salt

4 cups softened ice cream

Serving Suggestions

No one said vanilla ice cream must be used here. For a Neopolitan treat, spread equal parts strawberry, chocolate, and vanilla ice creams between the cake layers. Banana, peanut butter, or caramel ice creams or gelatos would also be incredible choices.

1. Preheat the oven to 350°F. Prepare a 10" × 15" rimmed baking sheet with parchment paper, leaving a 2" overhang on the short sides.

2. In a medium bowl or bowl of stand mixer, whisk butter, sugar, and vanilla. Add in egg and continue to whisk. Finally, whisk in flour, cocoa powder, and salt until well combined.

3. Spread batter onto the prepared baking sheet until even. Bake for 10 minutes, until set.

4. Remove from oven and allow to cool on a wire rack. Once cooled, remove the cake and parchment using the overhang. Cut the cake into two halves. Spread the softened ice cream over one half and top with the other cake half. Return the prepared dessert to the baking pan, wrap it tightly in plastic, and place in the freezer for 5 hours or overnight.

5. Before serving, remove from freezer and cut into 8 rectangles using a serrated knife. Serve immediately or wrap in squares of parchment paper and return to freezer.

Chocolate Chipwiches

Who wouldn't love classic chocolate chip cookies cradling their favorite ice cream? Delight your children with this delicious treat.

INGREDIENTS | SERVES 20

12 tablespoons unsalted butter (1½ sticks)

⅓ cup dark brown sugar

⅓ cup light brown sugar

⅔ cup granulated sugar

2 large eggs

1 tablespoon vanilla

2 generous cups flour

1 teaspoon sea salt

½ teaspoon baking soda

1 cup chocolate chips

1 quart of your favorite ice cream

Mini chocolate chips, sprinkles, or nuts

Chocolate Chip Cookies

Ruth Wakefield, owner of the Toll House Inn in Whitman, Massachusetts, invented the chocolate chip cookie in 1930. Nestlé obtained the recipe from Mrs. Wakefield in exchange for a lifetime supply of chocolate chips.

1. Preheat the oven to 350°F. Cream butter and all three sugars in a large mixing bowl until light and fluffy. Add eggs one at a time until fully incorporated. Mix in vanilla.

2. In a separate bowl, whisk together flour, sea salt, and baking soda. Slowly add to butter mixture until well combined. Then fold in chocolate chips.

3. Portion cookie dough in golf ball–sized mounds onto baking sheets lined with parchment.

4. Bake for 8–10 minutes.

5. When cookies have cooled, place in an airtight container and freeze solid. When frozen, place about ¼ cup of your favorite softened ice cream on the bottom of one cookie, then press the bottom of another cookie into the ice cream. Repeat until all of your sandwiches have been made. Roll the edges in your favorite toppings (mini chocolate chips, sprinkles, or nuts). Wrap in plastic wrap and store in the freezer.

Peanut Butter and Jelly Ice Cream Sandwiches

The kiddos will love this awesome twist on the classic peanut butter and jelly sandwich. Change it up by adding a dollop of marshmallow cream, or by swapping out your favorite ice cream flavor.

INGREDIENTS | SERVES 12

1 cup creamy or crunchy peanut butter

1 cup unsalted butter, softened

1 cup granulated sugar, plus more for rolling

1 cup packed light brown sugar

2 eggs

2½ cups flour

1 teaspoon salt

1 teaspoon baking powder

1½ teaspoons baking soda

3 cups Concord Grape Ice Cream (see Chapter 5) or your favorite flavor, softened

1. In the bowl of a stand mixer, cream peanut butter, butter, and sugars together until light and fluffy. Add eggs; beat until fully incorporated.

2. In a separate bowl, whisk together flour, salt, baking powder, and baking soda. Add to peanut butter mixture on low speed just until fully combined. Refrigerate for at least 1 hour.

3. Preheat the oven to 375°F. Roll walnut-sized balls of dough in sugar, then press onto a parchment-lined cookie sheet with a fork, making a criss-cross pattern. Bake for 10 minutes. Allow to cool, then freeze until firm.

4. When frozen, place about ¼ cup of ice cream on the bottom of one cookie, then press the bottom of another cookie into the ice cream. Repeat until all of your sandwiches have been made. Wrap in plastic wrap and store in the freezer.

Oatmeal Raisin Ice Cream Sandwiches

Be sure to use quick or instant oats for the cookies. These types of oats are thinner and have been slightly precooked for your convenience.

INGREDIENTS | SERVES 12

½ cup raisins

1 cup apple cider

1 cup unsalted butter, softened

1 cup packed dark brown sugar

2 eggs

1 teaspoon vanilla extract

½ teaspoon almond extract

2 cups flour

1 teaspoon salt

1 teaspoon baking soda

¼ teaspoon ground nutmeg

1½ teaspoons cinnamon

3 cups quick oats

3 cups Rum Raisin Ice Cream (see Chapter 2) or your favorite flavor, softened

1. Soak raisins in apple cider overnight. Drain and set aside.

2. Cream together butter and sugar until light and fluffy. Add eggs one at a time, incorporating fully before adding the next. Mix in vanilla and almond extracts.

3. In a separate bowl, combine flour, salt, baking soda, nutmeg, cinnamon, and oats. Add to butter mixture and mix slowly just until fully incorporated. Mix in raisins. Refrigerate for at least 1 hour.

4. Preheat the oven to 375°F. Roll dough into walnut-sized balls and place on a parchment-lined cookie sheet. Flatten each ball with a fork, making a criss-cross pattern. Bake for 8–10 minutes. Allow to cool, then freeze to firm up.

5. When frozen, place about ¼ cup of ice cream on the bottom of one cookie, then press the bottom of another cookie into the ice cream. Repeat until all of your sandwiches have been made. Wrap in plastic wrap and store in the freezer.

Brownies for Breakfast Ice Cream Sandwiches

This may be an extremely decadent breakfast, but there is cereal milk in the ice cream, after all. Enjoy!

INGREDIENTS | SERVES 4

⅓ cup dark cocoa powder

½ cup flour

1 teaspoon salt

¼ teaspoon baking powder

½ cup unsalted butter, cubed

1 cup granulated sugar

2 large eggs

1 tablespoon vanilla extract

4 cups Better than Breakfast Cereal Ice Cream (see Chapter 5)

1 cup complementary breakfast cereal

A Little Extra

Go beyond just the ice cream sandwich! Dip them in cooled but still melted chocolate, sprinkle with cereal, and then place in the freezer for a few moments to set. No one will be able to resist these treats!

1. Preheat the oven to 350°F. Lightly grease an 8" × 8" pan with butter.

2. Sift together cocoa powder, flour, salt, and baking powder. Set aside.

3. In a large saucepan, melt together butter and sugar. When butter is completely melted, remove from heat and add eggs and vanilla. Beat until thoroughly combined. Add cocoa mixture; stir until just combined. Spread into the prepared pan.

4. Bake for 25–30 minutes or until a toothpick inserted into the middle comes out with crumbs but is not gooey. Cool to room temperature, then freeze in the pan for 30 minutes. Once frozen, remove entire brownie in one piece.

5. Cut brownie in half, making two rectangles. Cover one half with ice cream, then top with the other half. Cut the filled brownie into 2" × 2" sections, totaling four squares, then dip each side into the cereal. Serve immediately, or wrap in parchment paper and refreeze for up to 2 weeks.

Frozen Cheesecake Pops

All kids like food on a stick. Cheesecake is no exception! While these are wonderful just out of the freezer, they are equally good simply refrigerated.

INGREDIENTS | SERVES 10–12

1 store-bought 8" plain cheesecake
1 cup chocolate or colored candy melts
10–12 lollipop sticks

Fancy!

Take this recipe even further by drizzling with white chocolate, or by dipping the still-melted chocolate coating in sprinkles for a festive look. You could also coat the pops in white candy melts and roll in toasted coconut for a tropical twist.

1. Freeze cheesecake until very firm. Using a spoon or ice cream scoop, scrape the cheesecake from the crust, and form into golf ball–sized balls using your hands. Place balls onto a parchment-lined pan, and place in the freezer after every two balls are made to prevent melting. If cheesecake begins to thaw too much before all of the balls can be made, return to freezer until set.

2. Once all balls are made, freeze uncovered for 1 hour. While freezing, microwave the candy melts at 30-second intervals until smooth and pourable.

3. Insert lollipop stick into each of the frozen balls, and dip one at a time into the candy melts. Decorate with sprinkles, if desired, while coating is still warm. Return to freezer.

4. To store for up to 1 week, place cheesecake pops in airtight freezer bags or container. Serve directly from freezer.

CHAPTER 12

Cakes, Ice Cream Cakes, Cupcakes, and Trifles

Vanilla Bean Butter Cake
192

Red Velvet Cake
193

Lemon Cake
194

Strawberry Cake
195

Chocolate Cake
196

Banana Coffee Toffee Ice Cream Cake Roll
197

Autumn Apple Ice Cream Cake
198

Blueberry Peach Ice Cream Cake
199

Chocolate Covered Banana Cake
200

Candy Ice Cream Cake
200

Chocolate Raspberry Ice Cream Cake
201

Red Velvet Lovers Ice Cream Cake
202

Turtle Ice Cream Cake
202

Triple Citrus Ice Cream Cake
203

Strawberry Lemonade Frozen Trifle
204

Strawberry Shortcake Ice Cream Cupcakes
205

Tiramisu Ice Cream Cake Roll
206

Lemon Cheesecake Ice Cream Cupcakes
207

Banana Split Trifle
208

Chocolate Caramel Ice Cream Cupcakes
209

Vanilla Bean Butter Cake

This is a delicious butter cake packed with vanilla specks and a rich vanilla aroma.

INGREDIENTS | YIELD: 2 (9") ROUND CAKES

12 tablespoons unsalted butter, softened (1½ sticks)

1½ cups granulated sugar

Seeds from 1 vanilla bean

2 large eggs

3 large egg yolks

3 cups flour

4 teaspoons baking powder

1 teaspoon fine sea salt

1 cup whole milk

1 tablespoon vanilla extract

Don't Over Mix

When making cake batters, you want to be sure not to overmix after you add the flour. As you beat the flour it adds more structure, and beating the mixture too much could end up making your cake tough and dry. Be sure to follow recipe instructions carefully!

1. Preheat the oven to 350°F.

2. Grease the bottoms of two 9" round cake pans. Line with parchment paper, then grease and flour the parchment paper.

3. Cream together butter, sugar, and vanilla bean until light and fluffy. Add eggs and egg yolks one at a time, combining well after each addition.

4. In a separate bowl, whisk together flour, baking powder, and salt. Turn mixer to low speed and alternately add flour mixture and milk, starting and ending with flour. Scrape down the sides, add vanilla, and beat for 20 seconds more on medium speed.

5. Portion batter into the prepared cake pans. Bake for 25–35 minutes until cakes are golden brown and spring back when lightly touched. Allow to cool in pan for 10 minutes, then remove to cooling rack until completely cooled.

Red Velvet Cake

Red velvet cake is a decadent buttermilk cake with just the slightest hint of cocoa and a rich red color.

INGREDIENTS | YIELD: 2 (9") ROUND CAKES

½ cup shortening
1½ cups granulated sugar
2 eggs
2 ounces red food coloring
2 tablespoons cocoa powder
2¼ cups flour
1 teaspoon salt
1 cup buttermilk
1 teaspoon baking soda
1 teaspoon white vinegar
1 tablespoon vanilla extract

Not Just Red Velvet

Instead of using red food coloring, try blue for a blue velvet cake or green for a green velvet cake. If you don't have food coloring, don't worry. Make the cake anyway, as it will be just as delicious no matter what the color.

1. Preheat the oven to 350°F.

2. Grease the bottoms of two 9" round cake pans, line with parchment paper, then grease and flour the parchment.

3. In the bowl of a stand mixer, cream together shortening, sugar, and eggs until light and fluffy. In a separate small bowl, mix 1 ounce of the red food coloring and the cocoa powder. Cream into shortening mixture. Add the remaining coloring.

4. In a medium bowl, whisk together the flour and salt. Turn mixer to low speed and alternately add flour mixture and buttermilk, starting and ending with flour. In a separate small bowl, mix baking soda and vinegar, then pour into the cake batter. Mix well. Mix in vanilla.

5. Portion batter into the prepared cake pans. Bake for 30–35 minutes until cakes spring back when lightly touched. Allow to cool in pan for 10 minutes, then remove to cooling rack until completely cooled.

Lemon Cake

Light and lemony, with just enough sweetness, this cake is a delicious base for multiple ice cream desserts.

INGREDIENTS | YIELD: 2 (9") ROUND CAKES

½ cup unsalted butter, softened

1¾ cups granulated sugar

Zest of 2 lemons

6 egg yolks

½ teaspoon lemon extract

½ teaspoon vanilla extract

2½ cups flour

2½ teaspoons baking powder

½ teaspoon salt

½ cup buttermilk

¼ cup fresh-squeezed lemon juice

3 tablespoons lemon yogurt

True Lemon Lovers

If you want even more lemon flavor, brush cakes with a simple lemon syrup. Heat ½ cup water, 1 cup sugar, and the zest of 1 lemon over medium heat until simmering and sugar is dissolved. Remove from heat, add the juice of ½ lemon, and allow to cool.

1. Preheat the oven to 350°F.

2. Grease the bottoms of two 9" round cake pans, line with parchment paper, then grease and flour the parchment paper.

3. In a large bowl, cream together butter, sugar, and zest until light and fluffy. Add egg yolks one at a time, combining well after each addition. Add lemon and vanilla extracts.

4. In a separate bowl, whisk together the flour, baking powder, and salt. In a separate pourable cup, mix buttermilk, lemon juice, and lemon yogurt. Turn mixer to low speed and alternately add flour mixture and milk mixture, starting and ending with flour mixture. Scrape down the sides. Beat for 20 seconds more on medium speed.

5. Portion batter into the prepared cake pans. Bake for 25–30 minutes until cakes are a golden brown and spring back when lightly touched. Allow to cool in pan for 10 minutes, then remove to cooling rack until completely cooled.

Strawberry Cake

If you have them, fresh strawberries can be substituted for the frozen berries this recipe calls for.

INGREDIENTS | YIELD: 2 (9") ROUND CAKES

4 large eggs

1½ cups frozen sugar-added strawberries, thawed and puréed

Juice of ½ lemon

¾ cup vegetable oil

1 tablespoon vanilla extract

3 cups self-rising flour

2 cups granulated sugar

1. Preheat the oven to 325°F.

2. Grease the bottoms of two 9" round cake pans, line with parchment paper, then grease and flour the parchment paper.

3. Beat the eggs in a large measuring cup or pourable bowl; whisk in puréed strawberries, lemon juice, oil, and vanilla extract.

4. In a separate large bowl, whisk together the flour and sugar. Whisk the liquids into the flour mixture until completely combined.

5. Portion batter into the prepared cake pans. Bake for 25–30 minutes until cakes spring back when lightly touched. Allow to cool in pan for 10 minutes, then remove to cooling rack until completely cooled.

Chocolate Cake

This chocolate cake will serve you well in so many ice cream cake applications. It is moist and incredibly delicious.

INGREDIENTS | YIELD: 2 (9") ROUND CAKES

⅔ cup dark cocoa powder
1 cup hot, strong coffee
1 cup unsalted butter, softened
1½ cups granulated sugar
1 vanilla bean, scraped
3 large eggs
1 tablespoon vanilla extract
2⅓ cups flour
1 tablespoon baking powder
1 teaspoon fine sea salt

Change It Up a Bit

Did you know you can change the flavor of the cake by changing the flavor of the coffee and/or extracts? Try hazelnut coffee double strength with Frangelico instead of vanilla extract. Kahlua coffee, espresso, or other flavorful coffee drinks would be a welcome change as well.

1. Preheat the oven to 350°F.

2. Grease the bottoms of two 9" round cake pans, line with parchment paper, then grease and flour the parchment paper.

3. Whisk together cocoa powder and hot coffee until combined. Set aside to cool.

4. In a large bowl, cream together butter, sugar, and scraped vanilla until light and fluffy. Add eggs one at a time, combining well after each addition. Add vanilla extract.

5. In a separate bowl, whisk together the flour, baking powder, and salt. Turn mixer to low speed and alternately add flour mixture and coffee mixture to the bowl with the butter and sugar, starting and ending with flour mixture. Scrape down the sides. Beat for 20 seconds more on medium speed.

6. Portion batter into the prepared cake pans. Bake for 25–35 minutes until cakes spring back when lightly touched.

Banana Coffee Toffee Ice Cream Cake Roll

Guests will love diving in to slices of this elegant cake, with its attractive spiral bands of ice cream and cake. Leftovers can be sliced and wrapped tightly for up to 2 weeks.

INGREDIENTS | YIELD: 1 (13") ROLL

1 cup sugar

½ cup water

1 tablespoon instant espresso powder

3 tablespoons Kahlua or other coffee-flavor liqueur

1 recipe Vanilla Bean Butter Cake batter (see recipe in this chapter)

Powdered sugar, as needed

1½ cups Toffee (see Chapter 17), crushed into bits

1 quart Caramelized Banana Rum Ice Cream (see Chapter 5), softened

1. To make the Kahlua-coffee simple syrup: Combine sugar, water, and espresso powder in a small saucepan. Bring to a boil, stirring to dissolve the sugar. Remove from heat and add Kahlua. Set aside to cool.

2. Preheat the oven to 325°F.

3. Grease the bottom of a jellyroll pan, line with parchment paper, then grease and flour the parchment paper.

4. Pour cake batter evenly into pan and bake only until lightly browned; *do not overcook*. While the cake bakes, prepare a long piece of aluminum foil, about 24" long. Sift powdered sugar over the entire sheet of foil.

5. As soon as the cake is done, loosen the sides of the cake, invert onto foil, peel off parchment, and brush with simple syrup. Spread the ice cream over all of the cake, and quickly sprinkle toffee bits on top of that. Roll tightly from the short end.

6. Use the aluminum foil to wrap the roll tightly. Place in the freezer for at least 2 hours. Garnish with chocolate-covered cocoa beans, toffee shards, and/or fresh bananas.

Autumn Apple Ice Cream Cake

Apple pie and ice cream are a beautiful pair. This brings them together in a whole new way.

INGREDIENTS | SERVES 12

1 tablespoon butter

2 cups apples, peeled, cored, and chopped

2 tablespoons dark brown sugar

1 teaspoon cinnamon

2 teaspoons lemon juice

2 (9") Vanilla Bean Butter Cakes (see recipe in this chapter)

1 quart Apple Pie Ice Cream (see Chapter 5)

1½ cups granola

½ cup Caramel Sauce (see Chapter 17)

1. Heat butter in a medium sauté pan over medium heat. Add apples, brown sugar, cinnamon, and lemon juice; cook until apples are softened. Set aside to cool slightly.

2. Place one cake round in the bottom of a 9" springform pan.

3. Spread half of the ice cream on cake round, then half of the apples and ½ cup of the granola. Top with the other cake round, the remainder of the sautéed apples, and the rest of the ice cream. Cover and freeze at least 2 hours.

4. When ready to serve, take out of the freezer and allow to soften 10 minutes before serving. Remove the sides of the pan, drizzle Caramel Sauce over the top, and sprinkle the remaining granola over the caramel. Garnish with fresh apple slices, if desired.

Blueberry Peach Ice Cream Cake

Wild blueberries are smaller and more flavorful than domestically grown blueberries. But if wild blueberries aren't available to you, feel free to substitute regular blueberries.

INGREDIENTS | SERVES 12

3 peaches, peeled, pitted, and diced

1½ tablespoons sugar

2 teaspoons lemon juice

2 (9") Lemon Cakes (see recipe in this chapter)

1 quart Blueberry Peach Sherbet (see Chapter 7)

1 pint fresh wild blueberries

½ cup White Chocolate Ganache (see sidebar recipe)

White Chocolate Ganache

In a small saucepan, bring ⅓ cup heavy cream to a simmer over medium heat. Remove from heat and stir in ¼ cup white chocolate chips. Allow to sit for 30 seconds, then stir until smooth. Use as needed.

1. In a medium bowl, stir peaches with sugar and lemon juice. Set aside.

2. Place one cake round in the bottom of a 9" springform pan.

3. Spread half of the sherbet on the cake round. Top with half of the blueberries and half of the peaches. Place the other cake round on top, sprinkle on the remainder of the berries and peaches, then spread the rest of the sherbet on top of that. Cover and freeze at least 2 hours.

4. When ready to serve, remove cake from freezer and allow to soften for 10 minutes before serving. Remove the sides of pan and drizzle White Chocolate Ganache over the cake. Garnish with fresh blueberries and fresh peach slices, as desired.

Chocolate Covered Banana Cake

This recipe is so simple and so elegant—it combines Chocolate Cake, fresh bananas, and Rich Vanilla Bean Ice Cream all drenched in a decadent Milk Chocolate Ganache.

INGREDIENTS | SERVES 12

2 (9") Chocolate Cakes (see recipe in this chapter)

1 quart Rich Vanilla Bean Ice Cream (see Chapter 2), softened

3 bananas, peeled and sliced

2 cups Milk Chocolate Ganache (see Chapter 17)

1. Place one cake round in the bottom of a 9" springform pan.

2. Spread half of the ice cream on the cake round. Top with half of the fresh bananas. Place the other cake round on top, then add remaining bananas and the rest of the ice cream. Cover and freeze at least 2 hours.

3. When ready to serve, take out of the freezer and remove the sides of the pan. Place over a jellyroll pan (or any other larger pan with a lip) and pour lukewarm ganache over the entire cake. Allow to set about 10 minutes.

Candy Ice Cream Cake

Candy, ice cream, and cake? It's a dream come true! This cake allows you to change out the flavor to suit your mood. Let the candy aisle be your guide!

INGREDIENTS | SERVES 12

2 (9") Chocolate Cakes (see recipe in this chapter)

2 cups Milk Chocolate Ganache (see Chapter 17)

3 cups chopped chocolate candy bars (any type)

1 quart Cake Batter Ice Cream (see Chapter 5), softened

1. Place one cake round in the bottom of a 9" springform pan.

2. Top the cake round with 1 cup chocolate ganache, then 1 cup chopped candy. Spread half of the ice cream over that. Top with the other cake round, then ganache, 1 cup candy, and remaining ice cream. Sprinkle remaining candy on top, cover, and freeze at least 2 hours.

3. When ready to serve, take out of the freezer and allow to soften about 10 minutes. Loosen and remove the sides of pan to serve.

Variations

Change out the candy for cookies or fresh fruit if you like. Strawberries or Oreo cookies would make wonderful substitutions in this decadent cake.

Chocolate Raspberry Ice Cream Cake

Rich chocolate cake and fresh floral raspberries make a perfectly romantic dessert for your sweetie, should you decide to share.

INGREDIENTS | SERVES 12

2 (9") Chocolate Cakes (see recipe in this chapter)

1 cup seedless raspberry jam

1 quart Raspberry Sherbet (see Chapter 7)

1½ pints fresh raspberries

1 cup Milk Chocolate Ganache (see Chapter 17)

Add a Little Kick for Adults

If you want to add just a little extra oomph, brush each cake round with a generous tablespoon of raspberry liqueur, and substitute dark chocolate ganache for the Milk Chocolate Ganache. Make it the exact same way as the milk chocolate version, but with dark chocolate.

1. Place one cake round in the bottom of a 9" springform pan.

2. Spread cake round with half of the jam, then half of the sherbet. Top with a handful of raspberries. Top with the other cake round, then the rest of the jam and another handful of raspberries, being sure to leave a generous amount for garnish. Top with the rest of the sherbet. Cover and freeze at least 2 hours.

3. When ready to serve, take out of freezer and allow to soften 10 minutes before serving. Remove the sides of the pan, drizzle the ganache over the top, then garnish with fresh raspberries.

Red Velvet Lovers Ice Cream Cake

This cake is for all those who dream about red velvet. The cake is equally delicious filled with Cream Cheese Frozen Yogurt (see Chapter 4), should the overabundance of red velvet not delight you.

INGREDIENTS | SERVES 12

2 (9") Red Velvet Cakes (see recipe in this chapter)

1 quart Red Velvet Cake Ice Cream (see Chapter 5), softened

A Pretty Garnish

Beat 1 softened 8-ounce block of cream cheese with 4 ounces cooled (but pour-able) melted white chocolate until smooth and creamy. Now you can pipe this onto your Red Velvet Lovers Ice Cream Cake to garnish!

1. Place one cake round in the bottom of a 9" springform pan.

2. Spread cake round with half of the ice cream. Top with the other cake round, then spread the remainder of the ice cream on top of the second cake round. Cover and freeze at least 2 hours.

3. When ready to serve, take out of the freezer and allow to soften 10 minutes before serving. Remove sides of pan to serve. For optional garnish, pipe with white chocolate cream cheese and decorate with a few fresh berries and mint leaves.

Turtle Ice Cream Cake

Chocolate cake, gooey butterscotch, crunchy pecans, and caramel pecan ice cream combine for an unforgettable treat. This recipe is every bit as good as the confection it is named for, if not better!

INGREDIENTS | SERVES 12

2 (9") Chocolate Cakes (see recipe in this chapter)

1 quart Caramel Pecan Ice Cream (see Chapter 5), softened

2¼ cups Butterscotch Sauce (see Chapter 17)

1½ cups Candied Pecans (see Chapter 17)

1. Place one cake round in the bottom of a 9" springform pan.

Spread cake round with half of the ice cream. Top with 1 cup of the Butterscotch Sauce and 1 cup of the candied pecans. Top with the other cake round, then 1 cup Butterscotch Sauce, 1 cup pecans, and the rest of the ice cream. Cover and freeze at least 2 hours.

2. When ready to serve, take out of the freezer and allow to soften 10 minutes before serving. Remove the sides of the pan, drizzle remaining Butterscotch Sauce on top, and then sprinkle with remaining pecans.

Triple Citrus Ice Cream Cake

Lemons, limes, and oranges come together in this tart treat. This dessert will be a hit at your next summertime dinner party!

INGREDIENTS | SERVES 12

2 (9") Lemon Cakes (see recipe in this chapter)

¼ cup Lemon Simple Syrup (see sidebar recipe)

½ quart Tangerine Sherbet (see Chapter 7)

½ quart Lime Sherbet (see Chapter 7)

¼ cup Candied Citrus Peels (see Chapter 17)

Lemon Simple Syrup

This flavorful syrup is wonderful mixed into tea, and is the perfect addition to this cake. To prepare the syrup, combine 1 cup of sugar and the zest of 1 lemon in a small saucepan over medium-high heat, stirring until sugar is dissolved. Bring to a boil, then remove from heat and allow to cool. Stir in the juice of 1 lemon. Leftover syrup can be covered and kept refrigerated for up to 1 month

1. Place one cake round in the bottom of a 9" springform pan.

2. Brush cake round with half the simple syrup. Spread with Tangerine Sherbet. Top with the other cake round, brush with remainder of simple syrup, and then spread the Lime Sherbet on top. Cover and freeze at least 2 hours.

3. When ready to serve, take out of freezer and allow to soften 10 minutes before serving. Remove the sides of the pan, and sprinkle Candied Citrus Peels over that. Garnish with fresh citrus slices.

Strawberry Lemonade Frozen Trifle

This trifle is a delicious alternative to the standard strawberry shortcake, and every bit as easy to make.

INGREDIENTS | SERVES 12

1 cup sugar

Zest of 1 lemon

Juice of 1 lemon

1 recipe Strawberry Cake batter (see recipe in this chapter)

Powdered sugar, as needed

1 quart Lemon Cream Ice Cream (see Chapter 5), softened

1 quart sliced fresh strawberries

3 cups Sweetened Whipped Cream (see Chapter 17)

1. Combine sugar and lemon zest in a small saucepan over medium-high heat, stirring until sugar is dissolved. Bring to a boil, then remove from heat and allow to cool. Stir in the lemon juice.

2. Preheat the oven to 325°F.

3. Grease the bottom of a jellyroll pan. Line with parchment paper, then grease and flour the parchment paper.

4. Pour cake batter evenly into pan and bake only until lightly browned; *do not overcook*. While the cake bakes, prepare a long piece of aluminum foil, about 24" long. Sift powdered sugar over entire sheet of foil.

5. As soon as the cake is done, loosen sides of the cake, invert onto foil, peel off parchment, and brush with simple syrup. Cut the cake into squares, and line the bottom of trifle dish. Top with ice cream, and half of the strawberries. Repeat layering, ending with a layer of strawberries. Pipe or spoon whipped cream onto the top of the trifle.

6. Place in the freezer for at least 1 hour. Remove 10 minutes before serving. Garnish with fresh whole berries, if desired.

Strawberry Shortcake Ice Cream Cupcakes

This is a fun treat for adults and children alike. The addition of macerated strawberries makes this a decadent and drool-worthy dessert.

INGREDIENTS | SERVES 24

1 quart fresh strawberries, hulled and quartered

1 teaspoon orange zest

Juice of ½ orange

¼ cup sugar

1 recipe Vanilla Bean Butter Cake batter (see recipe in this chapter)

2 quarts Simple Strawberry Ice Cream (see Chapter 2)

Fresh strawberries for garnish

1. In a medium bowl, mix strawberries, orange zest, orange juice, and sugar. Allow to rest 1 hour to meld flavors.

2. Preheat the oven to 350°F.

3. Line two 12-cup cupcake tins with paper liners. Pour batter into liners, filling only one-quarter of each cup. Bake until golden and a toothpick inserted into the cakes comes out clean. Cool completely.

4. Place one 3-ounce scoop of ice cream on each cupcake. Cover and freeze until ready to serve. When ready to serve, top with macerated strawberries and a fresh berry for garnish.

Tiramisu Ice Cream Cake Roll

Add a little pick-me-up to your dinner party with this fresh take on an Italian classic.

INGREDIENTS | YIELD: 1 (13") ROLL

1 cup sugar

½ cup water

1 tablespoon instant espresso powder

3 tablespoons Kahlua or other coffee-flavor liqueur

1 recipe Vanilla Bean Butter Cake batter (see recipe in this chapter)

Powdered sugar, as needed

1 quart Mascarpone Ice Cream (see Chapter 5), softened

1½ cups mini chocolate chips

1. To make Kahlua-coffee simple syrup: Combine sugar, water, and espresso powder in a small saucepan. Bring to a boil, stirring to dissolve the sugar. Remove from heat and add Kahlua. Set aside to cool.

2. Preheat the oven to 325°F.

3. Grease the bottom of a jellyroll pan, line with parchment paper, then grease and flour the parchment.

4. Pour cake batter evenly into the pan and bake only until lightly browned; *do not overcook*. While the cake bakes, prepare a long piece of aluminum foil, about 24" long. Sift powdered sugar over the entire sheet of foil. As soon as the cake is done, loosen sides of cake, invert onto foil, peel off parchment, and brush with simple syrup. Spread the ice cream over all of the cake and top with mini chocolate chips. Roll tightly from the short end.

5. Use the aluminum foil to wrap the roll tightly; place in the freezer for at least 2 hours. Garnish with a light dusting of sweetened cocoa powder if desired.

Lemon Cheesecake Ice Cream Cupcakes

These are tart and sweet—a perfect sunny treat. Even the adults will want in on these cupcakes!

INGREDIENTS | SERVES 24

1 recipe Lemon Cake batter (see recipe in this chapter)

2 quarts Cream Cheese Frozen Yogurt (see Chapter 4)

2 cups Lemon Curd (see Chapter 17)

Fresh strawberries for garnish

Make It a Strawberry Cheesecake

Instead of Lemon Curd, you can use macerated strawberries: Cut 1 quart fresh strawberries into quarters and combine with 1 teaspoon orange zest, the juice from half an orange, and ¼ cup sugar. Allow to rest 1 hour to meld flavors.

1. Preheat the oven to 350°F.

2. Line two 12-cup cupcake tins with paper liners. Pour batter into liners, filling only one-quarter of each cup.

3. Bake until golden and a toothpick inserted into the cakes comes out clean. Cool completely.

4. Place one 3-ounce scoop of frozen yogurt on each cupcake. Cover and freeze until ready to serve. When ready to serve, top with Lemon Curd and a fresh berry.

Banana Split Trifle

Because bananas become mushy and undesirable once they're peeled, wait and cut slices until just before serving. You'll have plenty of time as you wait on the trifle to warm a bit after its stint in the freezer.

INGREDIENTS | SERVES 12

1 recipe Vanilla Bean Butter Cake batter (see recipe in this chapter)

Powdered sugar, as needed

2 quarts Rich Vanilla Bean Ice Cream (see Chapter 2)

1 cup Butterscotch Sauce (see Chapter 17)

1 cup Strawberry Sauce (see Chapter 17)

Sweetened Whipped Cream (see Chapter 17), for garnish

1 cup Hot Fudge Sauce (see Chapter 17)

Maraschino cherries, for garnish

3 bananas, sliced

Variations

If you aren't a fan of butterscotch, no problem. Substitute Caramel Sauce or Blueberry Sauce (see recipes in Chapter 17), or any topping you prefer.

1. Preheat the oven to 325°F.

2. Grease the bottom of a jellyroll pan, line with parchment paper, then grease and flour the parchment paper.

3. Pour cake batter evenly into the pan and bake only until lightly browned; *do not overcook*. While the cake bakes, prepare a long piece of aluminum foil, about 24" long. Sift powdered sugar over the entire sheet of foil.

4. As soon as cake is done, loosen sides of the cake, invert onto foil, and peel off parchment. Cut cake into squares and line the bottom of a trifle dish. Top with one-third of the ice cream and Butterscotch Sauce. Repeat layering of cake and ice cream, topping with Strawberry Sauce. Add one last layer of cake and ice cream. Cover the trifle and freeze for 2 hours.

5. Ten minutes before serving, remove trifle from freezer. Pipe or spoon whipped cream to the top of the trifle, and drizzle with Hot Fudge Sauce. Garnish with cherries and slices of banana.

Chocolate Caramel Ice Cream Cupcakes

If you're more of a "Death by Chocolate" kind of person, you can substitute the Caramel Sauce with Hot Fudge Sauce, Milk Chocolate Ganache, or Dark Chocolate Fudge Sauce (see recipes in Chapter 17). Then top with mini chocolate chips or chocolate curls.

INGREDIENTS | SERVES 24

1 recipe Chocolate Cake batter (see recipe in this chapter)

2 quarts Double Brownie Blast Ice Cream (see Chapter 5)

1 cup Caramel Sauce (see Chapter 17)

Toffee (see Chapter 17) for garnish

1. Preheat the oven to 350°F.

2. Line two 12-cup cupcake tins with paper liners. Pour batter into liners, filling only one-quarter of each cup.

3. Bake until a toothpick inserted into the cakes comes out clean. Cool completely.

4. Place one 3-ounce scoop of ice cream on each cupcake. Cover and freeze until ready to serve. When ready to serve, drizzle generously with Caramel Sauce and top with Toffee.

CHAPTER 13

Ice Cream Pies

Sweet Dough Tart Crust
212

Chocolate Tart Crust
213

Gingersnap Tart Crust
214

Graham Cracker Crust
214

Vanilla Wafer Crust
215

Lime Ice Cream Pie
215

Banana Pudding Ice Cream Pie
216

Grasshopper Ice Cream Pie
217

Strawberry Cheesecake
Ice Cream Pie
218

Dreamsicle Heaven
Ice Cream Pie
219

Lemon Meringue Ice Cream Pie
219

Triple Chocolate Ice Cream Pie
220

Frozen Strawberry Lemonade
Ice Cream Pie
221

Dark Chocolate and Raspberry
Ice Cream Pie
222

Chocolate Covered Banana
Ice Cream Pie
222

Blueberry Muffin Ice Cream Pie
223

Florida Ice Cream Pie
224

Taste of the Tropics
Ice Cream Pie
225

Black Forest Ice Cream Pie
226

Piña Colada Ice Cream Pie
226

Pumpkin Cheesecake
Ice Cream Pie
227

Sweet Dough Tart Crust

This tart crust has just the right amount of sweet flavor, and is a wonderful base for a multitude of ice cream pies. Prepare the dough in advance and freeze it for up to 2 months so that you always have one at the ready when the urge for ice cream pie hits!

INGREDIENTS | YIELD: 1 (9") TART SHELL

1½ cups all-purpose flour

½ cup confectioner's sugar

Pinch salt

¼ teaspoon ground ginger

1 teaspoon lemon zest

9 tablespoons frozen butter, chopped (1⅛ sticks)

1 large egg

Puffing Crusts

Often, a pie crust will puff up during its initial bake. If you find this has happened when you remove the foil, don't worry! Simply take the backside of a spoon and lightly press the bubbles down. Voilà!

1. Place the flour, sugar, salt, ginger, and lemon zest in a food processor and pulse to combine. Scatter the pieces of butter over the mixture, and pulse to combine until dough is granular and clumpy, with some small bits and some about the size of peas.

2. Use a fork to break up the egg, then slowly pour into the dough, pulsing after each addition. Continue to pulse until the dough forms large clumps and holds together.

3. Remove dough from food processor and press into a buttered tart pan with a removable bottom. Wrap tightly in plastic and freeze for up to 2 months, or refrigerate for 2 hours or more.

4. To bake the crust, preheat the oven to 375°F. Butter a piece of foil, and press over the dough, butter side down. Bake for 22–25 minutes, remove the foil, and continue to bake for 10 more minutes, or until golden brown.

5. Remove from oven and allow to cool before using.

Chocolate Tart Crust

Ahh, chocolate! Nothing kicks an ice cream pie into high gear like a chocolate tart crust. It's excellent for frozen mousse, Peanut Butter Ice Cream (see Chapter 2), and especially Grasshopper Ice Cream Pie (see recipe in this chapter)!

INGREDIENTS | YIELD: 1 (9") TART SHELL

1 cup all-purpose flour

3 tablespoons Dutch-processed cocoa powder

3 tablespoons sugar

Pinch salt

½ cup frozen butter, chopped

1 large egg

1. Place the flour, cocoa, sugar, and salt in a food processor and pulse to combine. Scatter the pieces of butter over the mixture, and pulse to combine until dough is granular and clumpy, with some small bits and some about the size of peas.

2. Use a fork to break up the egg, then slowly pour into the dough, pulsing after each addition. Continue to pulse until the dough forms large clumps and holds together.

3. Remove dough from food processor, and press into a buttered tart pan with a removable bottom. Wrap tightly in plastic and freeze for up to 2 months, or refrigerate for 2 hours or more.

4. To bake the crust, preheat the oven to 375°F. Butter a piece of foil, and press it over the dough, butter side down. Bake for 22–25 minutes, remove the foil, and continue to bake for 10 more minutes, or until golden brown.

5. Remove from oven and allow to cool before using.

Gingersnap Tart Crust

The spice is nice! Gingersnap crusts are an amazing base for Lime Ice Cream Pie, Pumpkin Cheesecake Ice Cream Pie, and even Strawberry Cheesecake Ice Cream Pie (see recipes in this chapter). You'll find it to be one of those crusts you just can't get enough of.

INGREDIENTS | YIELD: 1 (9") PIE SHELL

1½ cups crushed gingersnaps (roughly 2 dozen cookies)

Pinch salt

¼ teaspoon ground ginger

¼ teaspoon cinnamon

⅓ cup melted butter

Did You Know?

Ginger is a natural antihistamine and decongestant. Not only that, ginger also increases blood circulation. And believe it or not, ginger even helps to counteract motion sickness, too!

1. Place the cookies in a food processor and pulse until finely ground. Add the spices and pulse to combine.

2. Remove from food processor and stir in the melted butter. Continue to mix until uniformly moistened.

3. Press into a 9" pie plate and up the sides, taking care to press evenly. Chill in the refrigerator for 30 minutes or more.

4. To bake the crust, preheat the oven to 350°F. Bake for 7 minutes or until crisp.

5. Remove from oven and allow to cool before using.

Graham Cracker Crust

Graham cracker crusts are a tried and true favorite. They are excellent for cheesecakes, blueberry pies, peanut butter pies, and of course, s'mores pies!

INGREDIENTS | YIELD: 1 (9") PIE SHELL

1½ cups finely ground graham cracker crumbs

⅓ cup sugar

⅓ cup melted butter

Pinch salt

¼ teaspoon cinnamon

1. Place all ingredients in a mixing bowl and stir to combine.

2. Continue to mix until uniformly moistened.

3. Press into a 9" pie plate and up the sides, taking care to press evenly. Chill in the refrigerator for 30 minutes or more.

4. To bake the crust, preheat the oven to 375°F. Bake for 7 minutes or lightly browned.

5. Remove from oven and allow to cool before using.

Vanilla Wafer Crust

You simply cannot have a Banana Pudding Ice Cream Pie (see recipe in this chapter) without a Vanilla Wafer Crust! This version is super simple to put together and quicker than running out to the grocery store to buy the premade version. It's more delicious, too!

INGREDIENTS | YIELD: 1 (9") PIE SHELL

1½ cups crushed vanilla wafer cookies (roughly 4 dozen)

Pinch salt

⅓ cup melted butter

1 teaspoon vanilla

1. Place the cookies in a food processor and pulse until finely ground. Add the salt and pulse to combine.

2. Remove from food processor and stir in the melted butter and vanilla. Continue to mix until uniformly moistened.

3. Press into a 9" pie plate and up the sides, taking care to press evenly. Chill in the refrigerator for 30 minutes or more.

4. To bake the crust, preheat the oven to 350°F. Bake for 7 minutes or until lightly browned.

5. Remove from oven and allow to cool before using.

Lime Ice Cream Pie

The first recipe for key lime pie hails from the 1930s and used sweetened condensed milk, as fresh milk was not common in the hot southern Florida Keys in the days before modern refrigeration. To turn this pie into key lime pie, substitute key limes in your sorbet or frozen yogurt recipes.

INGREDIENTS | SERVES 12

2 cups Lime Frozen Yogurt (see Chapter 4), slightly softened

1 baked Gingersnap Tart Crust (see recipe in this chapter)

2 cups Lime Sorbet (see Chapter 6), slightly softened

3 cups Marshmallow Meringue (see Chapter 17)

1. Spread the Lime Frozen Yogurt into the prepared pie shell. Top with the sorbet.

2. Allow to freeze for 30 minutes.

3. Add Marshmallow Meringue, piling high in the center. Quickly torch the meringue to brown, or place under your oven broiler.

4. Freeze until set. Remove from freezer 10 minutes before serving. Garnish with lime wedges, if desired.

Banana Pudding Ice Cream Pie

Banana pudding summons up thoughts of old-fashioned Sunday dinners and well-deserved afternoon naps. In ice cream form, you are in for a delicious spin on the original, sure to be requested time and time again.

INGREDIENTS | SERVES 12

2 cups Banana Frozen Yogurt (see Chapter 4), slightly softened

1 baked Vanilla Wafer Crust (see recipe in this chapter)

2 bananas, peeled and sliced

2 cups Simple Vanilla Ice Cream (see Chapter 2), slightly softened

3 cups Sweetened Whipped Cream (see Chapter 17)

6 vanilla wafer cookies, ground

12 vanilla wafer cookies, whole

1. Spread the Banana Frozen Yogurt into the prepared pie shell. Top with a layer of sliced bananas.

2. Spread the Simple Vanilla Ice Cream over the bananas. Allow to freeze for 30 minutes.

3. Remove from freezer and top with more banana slices. Add whipped cream, piling high in the center.

4. Sprinkle crushed cookies over the top, and garnish with whole wafer cookies. Freeze until set. Remove from freezer 10 minutes before serving.

A Reason to Celebrate

In 2010, Red Cross volunteers created the National Banana Pudding Festival just outside of Centerville, Tennessee, near the home of Sarah Cannon, more famously known as Minnie Pearl. Money is raised from the festival and cookoff to help fund victims of natural disasters.

Grasshopper Ice Cream Pie

Chocolaty, minty, and smooth—guests will swoon from the refreshing zip of this flavorful dessert.

INGREDIENTS | SERVES 12

1 cup Decadent Chocolate Ice Cream (see Chapter 2), slightly softened

1 baked Chocolate Tart Crust (see recipe in this chapter)

3 cups Mint Chocolate Chip Ice Cream (see Chapter 2), slightly softened

3 cups Chocolate Whipped Cream (see Chapter 17)

Origins

Grasshopper pie gets its name from a popular drink from the 1950s, made with crème de cacao and crème de menthe. The dessert really gained in popularity in the 1960s and has continued to please in the decades since.

1. Spread the Decadent Chocolate Ice Cream into the prepared pie shell. Top with the Mint Chocolate Chip Ice Cream.

2. Allow to freeze for 30 minutes.

3. Add Chocolate Whipped Cream, piling high in the center.

4. Freeze until set. Remove from freezer 10 minutes before serving. Garnish with mint leaves, halved Peppermint Patties, or Junior Mints, if desired.

Strawberry Cheesecake Ice Cream Pie

Strawberries and cheesecake just scream to go together. You'll be screaming for more!

INGREDIENTS | SERVES 12

1 cup Simple Strawberry Ice Cream (see Chapter 2), slightly softened

1 baked Graham Cracker Crust (see recipe in this chapter)

2 cups Cream Cheese Frozen Yogurt (see Chapter 4), slightly softened

1 cup Strawberry Sorbet (see Chapter 6), slightly softened

3 cups Sweetened Whipped Cream (see Chapter 17)

1 cup fresh strawberries, sliced

1. Spread the Strawberry Ice Cream into the prepared pie shell. Top with the Cream Cheese Frozen Yogurt and then the Strawberry Sorbet.

2. Allow to freeze for 30 minutes.

3. Add whipped cream, piling high in the center.

4. Freeze until set. Remove from freezer 10 minutes before serving. Garnish with fresh strawberries.

An American Influence

Original cheesecake recipes did not contain cream cheese. American chefs are responsible for omitting the standard ricotta cheese in favor of tangy cream cheese, which is now a staple in most recipes.

Dreamsicle Heaven Ice Cream Pie

So many flavors, all bursting in intensity! Cheesecake, orange, and vanilla beans combine to deliver deliciousness in this creamy dessert.

INGREDIENTS | SERVES 12

1 cup Rich Vanilla Bean Ice Cream (see Chapter 2), slightly softened

1 baked Vanilla Wafer Crust (see recipe in this chapter)

2 cups Tangerine Sherbet (see Chapter 7), slightly softened

1 cup Cream Cheese Frozen Yogurt (see Chapter 4), slightly softened

3 cups Sweetened Whipped Cream (see Chapter 17)

1. Spread the Rich Vanilla Bean Ice Cream into the prepared pie shell. Top with the Tangerine Sherbet and then the Cream Cheese Frozen Yogurt.

2. Allow to freeze for 30 minutes.

3. Add whipped cream, piling high in the center.

4. Freeze until set. Remove from freezer 10 minutes before serving. Garnish with candied orange slices, if desired.

Lemon Meringue Ice Cream Pie

This pie is the frozen version of the classic, and doubly refreshing on a hot summer day. Grab a fork and dig in!

INGREDIENTS | SERVES 12

2 cups Lemon Ice Cream (see Chapter 2), slightly softened

1 baked Sweet Dough Tart Crust (see recipe in this chapter)

1 cup Lemon Curd (see Chapter 17)

2 cups Lemon Sherbet (see Chapter 7), slightly softened

3 cups Marshmallow Meringue (see Chapter 17)

1. Spread the Lemon Ice Cream into the prepared Sweet Dough Tart Crust pie shell. Allow to freeze for 30 minutes.

2. Top with the Lemon Curd, followed by the Lemon Sherbet. Allow to freeze for 30 minutes.

3. Add Marshmallow Meringue, piling high in the center. Quickly torch the meringue to brown, or place under your oven broiler.

4. Freeze until set. Remove from freezer 10 minutes before serving. Garnish with lemon wedges, if desired.

Triple Chocolate Ice Cream Pie

Layers upon layers of chocolate meld to provide one heck of a rich delight.
You could never go wrong with a bit of chocolate syrup on the side.

INGREDIENTS | SERVES 12

¾ cup Milk Chocolate Ganache (see Chapter 17)

1 baked Chocolate Tart Crust (see recipe in this chapter)

1 cup Decadent Chocolate Ice Cream (see Chapter 2), slightly softened

2 cups Milk Chocolate Ice Cream (see Chapter 2), slightly softened

1 cup White Chocolate Ice Cream (see Chapter 2)

3 cups Sweetened Whipped Cream (see Chapter 17)

Chocolate curls, for garnish

1. Spread a layer of Milk Chocolate Ganache over the pie shell. Layer the Decadent Chocolate Ice Cream into the prepared pie shell. Top with the Milk Chocolate Ice Cream and then the White Chocolate Ice Cream.

2. Allow to freeze for 30 minutes.

3. Add whipped cream, piling high in the center.

4. Freeze until set. Remove from freezer 10 minutes before serving. Garnish with chocolate curls or chocolate shavings, if desired.

Chocolate Curls

Chocolate curls are easy to make. Simply melt about a cup of chocolate with a tablespoon of shortening, spread onto the back side of a baking pan, and allow to chill in the freezer for 1 minute. Remove and scrape into curls with a metal spatula or trowel.

Frozen Strawberry Lemonade Ice Cream Pie

Lemons. Strawberries. Tart, sweet, and delectable, this pie is perfect for summer picnics.

INGREDIENTS | SERVES 12

2 cups Lemonade Sorbet (see Chapter 6), slightly softened

1 baked Sweet Dough Tart Crust (see recipe in this chapter)

1 cup Lemon Curd (see Chapter 17)

2 cups Strawberry Sherbet (see Chapter 7), slightly softened

3 cups Sweetened Whipped Cream (see Chapter 17)

Pink Lemonade
Pink lemonade isn't pink just because of food colorants. Beet juice is often used as the sweetener and provides that delightful pink color.

1. Spread the Lemonade Sorbet into the prepared Sweet Dough Tart Crust pie shell. Allow to freeze for 30 minutes.

2. Top with the Lemon Curd, followed by the Strawberry Sherbet. Allow to freeze for 30 minutes.

3. Add whipped cream, piling high in the center.

4. Freeze until set. Remove from freezer 10 minutes before serving. Garnish with lemon wedges and whole strawberries, if desired.

Dark Chocolate and Raspberry Ice Cream Pie

There is a reason you see dark chocolate and raspberries paired time and time again. The flavors play off each other in wonderful ways, showcasing the other's best qualities.

INGREDIENTS | SERVES 12

2 cups Decadent Chocolate Ice Cream (see Chapter 2), slightly softened

1 baked Chocolate Tart Crust (see recipe in this chapter)

1 cup Raspberry Sauce (see Chapter 17)

2 cups Raspberry Sherbet (see Chapter 7)

3 cups Chocolate Whipped Cream (see Chapter 17)

1. Spread the Decadent Chocolate Ice Cream into the prepared Chocolate Tart Crust pie shell. Allow to freeze for 30 minutes.

2. Top with the Raspberry Sauce, followed by the Raspberry Sherbet. Allow to freeze for 30 minutes.

3. Add the Chocolate Whipped Cream, piling high in the center.

4. Freeze until set. Remove from freezer 10 minutes before serving. Garnish with chocolate curls and fresh raspberries, if desired.

Chocolate Covered Banana Ice Cream Pie

Did you buy your bananas still green in hopes of them keeping longer? Just know you should never refrigerate green bananas. A too-cold temperature will disturb the ripening process, and the bananas may not be able to continue ripening again even after they are removed from the refrigerator.

INGREDIENTS | SERVES 12

2 cups Banana Frozen Yogurt (see Chapter 4), slightly softened

1 baked Chocolate Tart Crust (see recipe in this chapter)

1 cup Milk Chocolate Ganache (see Chapter 17)

2 cups Milk Chocolate Ice Cream (see Chapter 2), slightly softened

3 cups Sweetened Whipped Cream (see Chapter 17)

2 bananas, sliced, for garnish

Chocolate curls, for garnish

1. Spread the Banana Frozen Yogurt into the prepared Chocolate Tart Crust pie shell. Allow to freeze for 30 minutes.

2. Top with the Milk Chocolate Ganache, followed by the Milk Chocolate Ice Cream. Allow to freeze for 30 minutes.

3. Add whipped cream, piling high in the center.

4. Freeze until set. Remove from freezer 10 minutes before serving. Garnish with sliced bananas and chocolate curls.

Blueberry Muffin Ice Cream Pie

Layers of flavor unite to bring the taste of blueberry muffins to this incredible pie. Serve it for breakfast; no one will mind!

INGREDIENTS | SERVES 12

1 cup Cake Batter Ice Cream (see Chapter 5), slightly softened

1 baked Gingersnap Tart Crust (see recipe in this chapter)

2 cups Blueberry Frozen Yogurt (see Chapter 4), slightly softened

1 cup Rich Vanilla Bean Ice Cream (see Chapter 2), slightly softened

3 cups Sweetened Whipped Cream (see Chapter 17)

1 cup fresh blueberries

1 cup Streusel Topping (see sidebar recipe)

1. Spread the Cake Batter Ice Cream into the prepared Gingersnap Tart Crust pie shell. Top with Blueberry Frozen Yogurt and then the Rich Vanilla Bean Ice Cream.

2. Allow to freeze for 30 minutes.

3. Add whipped cream, piling high in the center.

4. Freeze until set. Remove from freezer 10 minutes before serving. Garnish with fresh blueberries and Streusel Topping.

Streusel Topping

Streusel is a simple and delicious topping. To prepare, combine 5 tablespoons sugar, 3 tablespoons brown sugar, and 2 tablespoons flour by whisking in a small bowl. Add in ¼ cup melted butter and mix until fully incorporated. Texture will be grainy.

Florida Ice Cream Pie

Florida Ice Cream Pie is a tasty combination of two of the state's most flavorful treats: coconut and key lime. Great separately, they become an incredible pairing you'll come to crave on hot summer days.

INGREDIENTS | SERVES 12

2 cups Toasted Coconut Gelato (see Chapter 3), slightly softened

1 baked Sweet Dough Tart Crust (see recipe in this chapter)

2 cups Lime Sherbet (see Chapter 7), slightly softened

3 cups Marshmallow Meringue (see Chapter 17)

Lime wedges, for garnish

Coconut flakes, for garnish

1. Spread the gelato into the prepared Sweet Dough Tart Crust pie shell. Top with the Lime Sherbet.

2. Allow to freeze for 30 minutes.

3. Add Marshmallow Meringue, piling high in the center.

4. Freeze until set. Remove from freezer 10 minutes before serving. Garnish with lime wedges and coconut flakes, if desired.

Monkey Faces

The coconut derives its name from early Spanish sailors, who dubbed the hairy, brown facelike globes *coco*, meaning "monkey face." Later, "nut" was added to the end of coco, and thus, the coconut was born.

Taste of the Tropics Ice Cream Pie

Pineapple, lime, and mango deliver a fruity punch of flavor, cool and refreshing in this unusual pie.

INGREDIENTS | SERVES 12

1 baked Vanilla Wafer Crust (see recipe in this chapter)

1½ cups Pineapple Coconut Sorbet (see Chapter 6), slightly softened

1 cup Lime Curd (see Chapter 17)

1½ cups Mango Sorbet (see Chapter 6), slightly softened

3 cups Marshmallow Meringue (see Chapter 17)

1. Spread the Pineapple Coconut Sorbet into the prepared Vanilla Wafer Crust pie shell.

2. Allow to freeze for 30 minutes, then top with the Lime Curd.

3. Top with Mango Sorbet.

4. Add Marshmallow Meringue, piling high in the center.

5. Freeze until set. Remove from freezer 10 minutes before serving. Garnish with lime wedges, if desired.

Mango

Although not the most popular in America, more mangos are consumed every day in the world than any other fruit. Over 20 million metric tons of mangos are grown throughout the tropical and subtropical world. India is the leading producer. Mexico and China compete for second place, with Pakistan and Indonesia following.

Black Forest Ice Cream Pie

Black forest cake is a traditional dessert hailing from Germany and consists of layers of chocolate cake, whipped cream, and lots of cherries. This pie is a wonderful adaptation of the traditional gateau.

INGREDIENTS | SERVES 12

2 cups Decadent Chocolate Ice Cream (see Chapter 2), slightly softened

1 baked Chocolate Tart Crust (see recipe in this chapter)

1 cup Cherry Compote (see Chapter 17)

1 cup Cream Cheese Frozen Yogurt (see Chapter 4), slightly softened

1 cup Chocolate Cherry Frozen Yogurt (see Chapter 4), slightly softened

3 cups Sweetened Whipped Cream (see Chapter 17)

Chocolate curls, for garnish

Maraschino cherries, for garnish

1. Spread the Decadent Chocolate Ice Cream into the prepared Chocolate Tart Crust pie shell. Allow to freeze for 30 minutes.

2. Top with the Cherry Compote, followed by the Cream Cheese Frozen Yogurt. Allow to freeze for 30 minutes.

3. Top with Chocolate Cherry Frozen Yogurt. Add whipped cream, piling high in the center.

4. Freeze until set. Remove from freezer 10 minutes before serving. Garnish with chocolate curls and cherries.

Piña Colada Ice Cream Pie

Not a fan of meringue? That's okay. You can leave this pie unadorned, showing off the gorgeous color. Pipe circles of sweetened whipped cream around the edge of the pie instead, and garnish with lime wedges. Beautiful!

INGREDIENTS | SERVES 12

2 cups Toasted Coconut Gelato (see Chapter 3), slightly softened

1 baked Sweet Dough Tart Crust (see recipe in this chapter)

2 cups Pineapple Coconut Sorbet (see Chapter 6), slightly softened

3 cups Marshmallow Meringue (see Chapter 17)

Coconut flakes, for garnish

Pineapple wedges, for garnish

1. Spread the Toasted Coconut Gelato into the prepared Sweet Dough Tart Crust pie shell. Top with the sorbet.

2. Allow to freeze for 30 minutes.

3. Add Marshmallow Meringue, piling high in the center.

4. Freeze until set. Remove from freezer 10 minutes before serving. Garnish with coconut flake and fresh pineapple wedges, if desired.

Pumpkin Cheesecake Ice Cream Pie

Ahh, fall. Why not serve up this frosty delight at Thanksgiving versus the traditional pumpkin pie? It would be excellent fare while curled up fireside with friends and family to share.

INGREDIENTS | SERVES 12

2 cups Pumpkin Gelato (see Chapter 3), slightly softened

1 baked Gingersnap Tart Crust (see recipe in this chapter)

2 cups Cream Cheese Frozen Yogurt (see Chapter 4), slightly softened

3 cups Sweetened Whipped Cream (see Chapter 17)

1. Spread the Pumpkin Gelato into the prepared Gingersnap Tart Crust pie shell. Top with the Cream Cheese Frozen Yogurt.

2. Allow to freeze for 30 minutes.

3. Add whipped cream, piling high in the center.

4. Freeze until set. Remove from freezer 10 minutes before serving.

CHAPTER 14

Decadent Frozen Confections

Profiteroles
230

Crepes
231

Chocolate Crepes
232

White Chocolate Mousse Cake
233

Fried Ice Cream
234

Chocolate Bowls
235

Neapolitan Baked Alaska
236

Sorbet-Filled Frozen Oranges
237

French Twist
237

Bombe
238

Lemon Shortbread
Ice Cream Sandwiches
239

Frozen Red Velvet Whoopie Pies
240

Frozen Pumpkin Whoopie Pies
241

Profiteroles

Profiteroles are one of life's true delights. Made from pâte à choux *(the basis of cream puffs and eclairs) and your favorite ice cream, you'll revel in the applause of your unsuspecting dinner guests when they sample your deceptively difficult dessert. Shhh . . . it's really quite simple!*

INGREDIENTS | SERVES 18

1 cup water

½ cup unsalted butter, cut into pieces

2 teaspoons sugar

½ teaspoon salt

1 cup all-purpose flour

4 large eggs, room temperature

2 pints ice cream

Storage

Cream puffs, unfilled, are best consumed the day they are made; however, once they have cooled, they can be placed in a freezer bag and frozen for up to a month. To defrost, allow them to come to room temperature, then warm in a 200°F oven until crisp.

1. Preheat the oven to 400°F. Prepare two baking sheets with parchment paper or silicone mats. Set aside.

2. In a large saucepan over medium heat, combine water, butter, sugar, and salt; stir until butter is completely melted. Reduce heat and add in the flour all at once. Stir quickly to incorporate the flour until mixture is smooth and begins to pull away from the sides of the pan, about 3 minutes. Remove from heat.

3. Dump the mixture in the bowl of a stand mixer and beat on low speed for 5 minutes in order to cool before adding the eggs. Add eggs one at a time, beating for 1 minute between each. Dough will be smooth and shiny when ready.

4. Using a pastry bag or ice cream scoop, pipe or scoop rounds of dough onto the prepared baking sheets. Moisten your finger and smooth any rough edges or points on the mounds of dough before baking.

5. Bake the puffs for 30 minutes, or until puffed and browned. Turn off the oven and leave them inside for an additional 10 minutes. Remove from oven and allow to cool to room temperature.

6. Just before serving, cut puffs in half, fill with your favorite ice cream flavor, and, if desired, top with chocolate fudge or ganache.

Crepes

Crepes served with a nice dollop of ice cream and fresh fruit or sauce is an often-overlooked dessert option, although it shouldn't be! Crepes are prefect, especially for dinner parties, because they can be prepared ahead of time and then plated in a very short time. Bon appétit!

INGREDIENTS | SERVES 10

1 cup whole milk

3 tablespoons melted butter

1 teaspoon vanilla extract

2 teaspoons sugar

4 large eggs

¼ teaspoon salt

1 cup all-purpose flour

2 pints favorite ice cream

Decadence!

After cooking your crepe on one side and flipping it over, place a few fresh strawberries and a sprinkling of chocolate chips onto one half of the crepe. The chocolate will melt and become a wonderful gooey filling that will be fantastic with your ice cream!

1. Combine the milk, butter, vanilla, sugar, eggs, and salt in a blender for 1 minute. Add in the flour and blend until very smooth. Place blender bowl in the refrigerator for 1 hour or more.

2. When ready to fry, remove batter from refrigerator and bring to room temperature. Heat a large skillet or griddle over medium-high heat. Ladle ½–¾ cup batter onto pan and spread by tilting the pan or using a silicone scraper to even the crepe. Cook for 30–45 seconds, until edges start to brown, then flip and cook another 30–45 seconds. Repeat with remaining batter.

3. Refrigerate prepared crepes until ready to serve, or use immediately. Rewarm in microwave, if needed, then roll crepes into tubes and top with ice cream and other toppings, as desired.

Chocolate Crepes

These are a little richer than your average crepe, and oh, so delicious! Chocolate crepes are divine filled with fresh bananas and strawberries, and topped with Rich Vanilla Bean Ice Cream. Add a drizzle of hot fudge for an extra indulgence!

INGREDIENTS | SERVES 10

1 cup whole milk

2 ounces semisweet chocolate, chopped

½ cup heavy cream

2 teaspoons cocoa powder

2 large eggs

¼ teaspoon salt

1 cup all-purpose flour

2 pints Rich Vanilla Bean Ice Cream (see Chapter 2), or your favorite flavor ice cream

1. Heat the milk and chocolate in a small saucepan until chocolate is melted and smooth.

2. Combine mixture with the cream, cocoa, eggs, and salt in a blender for 1 minute. Add in flour and blend until very smooth. Place blender bowl in refrigerator for 1 hour or more.

3. When ready to fry, remove batter from refrigerator and bring to room temperature. Heat a large skillet or griddle over medium-high heat. Ladle ½–¾ cup batter onto pan and spread by tilting the pan or using a silicone scraper to even the crepe. Cook for 30–45 seconds, until edges start to brown, then flip and cook another 30–45 seconds. Repeat with remaining batter.

4. Refrigerate prepared crepes until ready to serve, or use immediately. Rewarm in microwave, if needed, then roll crepes into tubes and top with ice cream and other toppings, as desired.

White Chocolate Mousse Cake

This delicious concoction is a cross between a cake, a pie, and a cheesecake. It would be wonderful served with a drizzle of Strawberry Sauce, a layer of Milk Chocolate Ganache, or both!

INGREDIENTS | SERVES 12

INGREDIENTS | SERVES 12

1 recipe Sweet Dough Tart Crust (see Chapter 13), unbaked

2 cups heavy whipping cream

10 ounces white chocolate chips

1 tablespoon vanilla extract

¼ cup water

½ cup sugar

4 large egg whites, room temperature

Variations

Oh, the possibilities! Consider adding crème de cacao or crème de menthe along with the vanilla, or substituting Chocolate Tart Crust (see Chapter 13) for the Sweet Dough Tart Crust.

1. Preheat the oven to 325°F. Press prepared, unbaked tart crust into the bottom and part way up the sides of a greased 9" springform pan. Bake for 10–12 minutes. Allow to cool to room temperature.

2. In a small saucepan, bring ½ cup of the heavy cream to a simmer over medium heat. Remove from heat and immediately stir in white chocolate chips and vanilla until smooth. Allow to cool completely.

3. In a separate saucepan over medium heat, bring water and sugar to a boil for roughly 5 minutes, or until mixture reaches 240°F. While sugar mixture is cooking, beat egg whites to soft peaks. When sugar syrup is ready, add it slowly to the egg whites in a thin stream, continually beating. Bring to stiff peaks, then cool.

4. In a separate mixing bowl, beat 1½ cups heavy cream to stiff peaks. Fold white chocolate mixture into the cream carefully. Once incorporated, delicately fold in the egg whites, being careful not to deflate.

5. Pour mixture into the prepared crust. Freeze for 5 hours or overnight. Remove from freezer 3 hours before serving, and keep chilled in refrigerator. Top as desired.

Fried Ice Cream

If you've visited a Mexican restaurant, you know what a treat this dessert holds! Fried ice cream is a traditional delicacy in many establishments, and is often served with a smattering of chocolate syrup.

INGREDIENTS | SERVES 8–10

1 gallon Simple Vanilla Ice Cream (see Chapter 2)

4 egg whites, lightly beaten

4 cups crushed corn flake cereal

1 teaspoon cinnamon

Vegetable oil, as needed

Extra Crispy

If you'd like a little more crisp and crunch, feel free to do the dipping process twice. Just redip the egg and roll again in the cereal mixture. Freeze as directed.

1. Prepare a baking sheet with parchment paper. The pan must easily fit in your freezer. Scoop ice cream into 2" balls, and place each on the baking sheet. Freeze for a minimum of 2 hours.

2. Set up two dipping bowls, one with the egg whites, the other with the crushed cereal and cinnamon. Remove ice cream balls from freezer. Dip each in the egg whites, and then immediately into the cereal. Replace coated ice cream balls on baking sheet and freeze 4 hours or overnight.

3. Bring 4" or more of vegetable oil in a large, deep frying pan to 375°F. Fry the ice cream for roughly 1 minute. Repeat until all are fried. Serve immediately, garnished as desired.

Chocolate Bowls

This could have been included as a kids' recipe, because the little ones just love helping out with the preparation. However, the results are so decadent, it needs to be considered adult!

INGREDIENTS | YIELD: 5–6 BOWLS

1 cup semisweet chocolate chips
5–6 small round balloons, washed

Two Tone

For even more glam, melt half semisweet and half white chocolate in separate bowls. Dip the inflated balloon first in white chocolate on half of the balloon, and then in the semisweet for the other half. Voilà!

1. Prepare a baking sheet with parchment paper.

2. Place the chocolate in a medium bowl and place in the microwave. Melt chocolate by turning the microwave on high for 30-second intervals, stirring in between intervals, until chocolate is smooth and fluid, but not too hot.

3. Spoon a dollop of melted chocolate onto the prepared baking sheet. Spray the balloon with cooking spray, then dip the balloon into the bowl of melted chocolate, creating a bowl shape of chocolate. Place balloon upright on the baking sheet where you spooned the chocolate, which will hold the balloon in place. Repeat with remaining balloons.

4. Allow chocolate to cool. Baking sheet can be placed in refrigerator to speed up process if desired. When cool, carefully pop balloons. Fill chocolate bowls with favorite ice cream and garnish as desired.

Neapolitan Baked Alaska

To celebrate the acquisition of the Alaska Territory, Delmonico's Restaurant in New York City developed this meringue-covered ice cream and cake confection in 1867.

INGREDIENTS | SERVES 24

2 baked Vanilla Bean Butter Cakes (see Chapter 12)

4 cups any chocolate ice cream or frozen yogurt

4 cups any strawberry ice cream or frozen yogurt

5–6 cups Marshmallow Meringue (see Chapter 17)

Neapolitan?

The original Italian "Neapolitan" ice cream was actually called *spumoni* and consisted of chocolate, cherry, and pistachio layers. It is no longer a favorite in Italy, but the term Neapolitan remains here in the United States.

1. Lightly grease two round springform pans. Place one baked cake round in each pan. Top each with 2 cups of chocolate ice cream, followed by 2 cups of strawberry ice cream. Cover tightly with plastic wrap, and place in the freezer for 2 or more hours.

2. Just before serving, remove one pan at a time from the freezer and top immediately with meringue, swirling or piping it on. Quickly place under the broiler until lightly browned, or use a kitchen torch if you desire. Serve immediately.

Sorbet-Filled Frozen Oranges

Impress your guests with this simple yet elegant after-dinner treat. Hollowed-out oranges make the perfect vessels for a refreshing sorbet.

INGREDIENTS | SERVES 6

6 large oranges, uniform in size
4 cups any flavor sorbet (see Chapter 6)

So Easy

Oranges can be made and filled several days in advance, if needed, making them ideal for larger dinner parties. Just slip into the kitchen as your guests finish their entrées, pull the prepared fruits out of the freezer, and you'll be the star of the party with very little effort involved.

1. Remove and reserve the top third of the orange (opposite the stem). Using a grapefruit knife, remove the flesh and pulp from the center of the fruit, taking care not to puncture the rind. (You may choose to use this removed fruit to make your sorbet.)

2. Carefully level off the bottom of each orange using a sharp knife. Again, do not cut all the way through the orange, the "cup" needs to remain intact. This bottom cut will make the orange sit up straight and not fall over.

3. Fill each orange with sorbet, then replace the top. Wrap each in plastic and return to freezer. Remove 5 minutes before serving.

French Twist

It's hard to believe how incredible such a simple, rustic dessert can be. This French Twist uses store-bought croissants filled with ice cream and fruit, then topped with hot fudge. You'll agree: Easy doesn't have to mean boring.

INGREDIENTS | SERVES 2

2 store-bought croissants, halved
2 cups vanilla ice cream or frozen yogurt
1½ cups sliced strawberries
1 cup Hot Fudge Sauce (see Chapter 17)

1. Toast the halved croissants in the oven until slightly crisp and warmed.

2. Fill the bottom half of each with roughly 1 cup ice cream, followed by strawberries. Replace croissant top, and cover with Hot Fudge Sauce.

3. Garnish with fresh berries and whipped cream, if desired.

Bombe

"Impressive" is the right word for this gorgeous dessert. It features three layers of complementary ice creams, pressed into a bowl, then sliced and served. You'll be giving yourself a pat on the back for this one!

INGREDIENTS | SERVES 8–10

4 cups favorite sorbet

3 cups complementary sorbet

2 cups complementary ice cream or sorbet

Taste the Rainbow

The beauty of this dessert is that once you cut into it, you are presented with a striped, rainbow-like confection. Choose flavors and colors that will impress, such as strawberry, mango, and vanilla. The hues will delight even before the first bite!

1. Place a piece of plastic wrap on the inside of an 8"–9" bowl. Press 4 cups of chosen sorbet into the center and up the sides of the bowl, leaving a hollowed out space in the center. Place a slightly smaller bowl into the hollow, and freeze until set, roughly 30–45 minutes.

2. Remove bowls from freezer, and remove the smaller bowl from the center. Into the bowl-shaped hollow, add your second sorbet, spreading and pressing it just as you did the first. Again, fill the hollow with an even smaller bowl, and freeze for 30–45 minutes.

3. Take both bowls out of the freezer once again, remove center bowl, and fill with remaining ice cream or sorbet. Cover tightly in plastic, and return to freezer until ready to serve.

4. Just before serving, remove bowl from freezer, and turn out the frozen sorbet onto a plate, flat side down. Peel off the plastic, and cut into serving-sized wedges.

Lemon Shortbread Ice Cream Sandwiches

Tangy, tart, buttery, and crisp, these are beautiful cookies. They're divine when filled with Lemon Sherbet (see Chapter 7) or creamy Rich Vanilla Bean Ice Cream (see Chapter 2).

INGREDIENTS | SERVES 24

1 cup unsalted butter, softened

¾ cup light brown sugar

Zest of 3 lemons

1 tablespoon vanilla extract

Juice of 2 lemons

2 cups all-purpose flour

Favorite ice cream, as needed for filling

Shortbread History

In its early days, shortbread was quite expensive and considered a luxury, reserved for special occasions such as Christmas. Over time, it has become an everyday favorite and is now available as a popular treat all across the world.

1. Preheat the oven to 325°F.

2. Cream butter and brown sugar in mixer, scraping down sides of bowl occasionally.

3. Add lemon zest, vanilla, lemon juice, and flour. Mix on low until just combined.

4. Roll shortbread dough out flat to ⅓" thickness on a lightly floured surface. Cut into 2" circles and place on parchment-lined cookie sheets. Bake 15–18 minutes, until the cookies just begin to take on a golden hue. Cool cookies on a wire rack.

5. Spread ice cream on half of the cookies. Top with remaining cookies. Serve immediately.

Frozen Red Velvet Whoopie Pies

The typical red velvet cookie or cake is filled with cream cheese or vanilla frosting. These frozen treats will benefit immensely from their ice cream counterparts: Cream Cheese Frozen Yogurt (see Chapter 4) or Rich Vanilla Bean Ice Cream (see Chapter 2).

INGREDIENTS | SERVES 30

2 cups all-purpose flour
2 tablespoons cocoa powder
½ teaspoon baking powder
Pinch salt
½ cup unsalted butter, softened
1 cup light brown sugar, packed
1 large egg
2 teaspoons vanilla extract
½ cup buttermilk, at room temperature
Few drops red food coloring

1. Preheat oven to 375°F. Prepare multiple baking sheets with parchment paper and set aside.

2. Whisk together flour, cocoa, baking powder, and salt in a medium bowl and set aside.

3. In the bowl of a stand mixer, beat butter on medium-high speed until smooth. Add brown sugar and beat until light and fluffy, about 2–3 minutes. Add egg and beat for 2 minutes, then beat in vanilla. Alternate adding in flour mixture and buttermilk, starting and ending with buttermilk. Scrape bowl with a rubber spatula to incorporate any remaining flour. Stir in food coloring.

4. With a tablespoon, spoon batter onto prepared baking sheets, leaving roughly 1"–2" in between to allow for spreading. Bake for 8 minutes, or until set. Allow to cool on wire racks.

5. Once cooled, pipe or spread ice cream onto half of the cookies, and top with remaining cookies. Place all in a sealed container, layering with parchment paper if needed. Freeze 5 hours or overnight, until set. Serve immediately or wrap individually until ready to eat.

Frozen Pumpkin Whoopie Pies

This is a fun dessert option for your next fall family gathering. For even more fun, insert a craft stick into the ice cream center before freezing to create a frozen cookie pop!

INGREDIENTS | SERVES 18

2 cups packed dark brown sugar

1 cup vegetable oil

1½ cups pumpkin purée

1 tablespoon vanilla extract

2 large eggs

3 cups flour

1 teaspoon salt

1 teaspoon baking soda

1 teaspoon baking powder

2 tablespoons cinnamon

½ teaspoon cardamom

2 teaspoons ground cloves

2 teaspoons ground ginger

1 quart Caramel Pecan Ice Cream (see Chapter 5)

1. Preheat the oven to 350°F. Prepare two large baking sheets with parchment paper and set aside.

2. Cream sugar, oil, pumpkin purée, vanilla, and eggs in mixer, scraping down the sides of the bowl occasionally.

3. Add flour, salt, baking soda, baking powder, cinnamon, cardamom, ground cloves, and ginger. Mix on low until just combined.

4. Drop dough by heaping teaspoons on parchment-lined cookie sheets, spacing at least 2" apart. Bake 10–12 minutes.

5. Sandwich about ¼ cup softened ice cream in the middle of two cookies, and repeat with remaining ice cream.

Easier Filling

To make filling the soft, cakey whoopie pies easier, put them in the freezer for a few minutes to firm them up before filling them.

CHAPTER 15

Milkshakes

Peachy Keen Milkshake
244

Purple Cow Milkshake
244

Classic Vanilla Milkshake
245

Tropical Milkshake
245

Tiramisu Milkshake
246

Classic Strawberry Milkshake
246

Elvis Milkshake
247

Caramel DeLite Milkshake
247

Cheesecake Milkshake
248

Caramel Corn Milkshake
248

Classic Chocolate Milkshake
249

Deep Dark Chocolate
Depths Milkshake
249

Cherry Pie Milkshake
250

Coffee Caramel Milkshake
250

Chocolate Malted Milkshake
251

Cookies and Cream Milkshake
251

Dreamsicle Milkshake
252

Peachy Keen Milkshake

Peaches and cream make almost everything better. This milkshake is no exception.

INGREDIENTS | SERVES 2

4 scoops White Chocolate Ice Cream (see Chapter 2)

1 cup cold peach nectar or white grape juice

1 cup diced peaches, frozen and thawed or fresh

½ cup half and half

Place everything into a blender and process until smooth. Divide into two tall glasses to serve.

Purple Cow Milkshake

This is such a fun milkshake, combining grape and banana. It's a perfect treat for the little ones.

INGREDIENTS | SERVES 1

3 scoops Concord Grape Ice Cream (see Chapter 5)

1 cup whole milk

1 banana, peeled and sliced

Place everything into a blender and process until smooth. Pour into a tall glass to serve.

Even More Fun!

Though it may sound odd, a tablespoon of creamy peanut butter is a fun and welcome addition to this milkshake. Plus, it's added protein! You could also add a spoonful of grape jelly for a little added flavor.

Classic Vanilla Milkshake

You can never go wrong with a classic. This delicious shake is great as an afternoon pick-me-up or as a treat after your favorite meal.

INGREDIENTS | SERVES 2

3 scoops Simple Vanilla Ice Cream (see Chapter 2)

1 cup whole milk

½ cup half and half

1 tablespoon vanilla extract

1 tablespoon Caramel Sauce (see Chapter 17)

Place everything into a blender and process until smooth. Divide into two tall glasses to serve.

Tropical Milkshake

Coconut, pineapple, and mangos call you to the tropics in this refreshing drink.

INGREDIENTS | SERVES 2

4 scoops Toasted Coconut Ice Cream (see Chapter 5)

1 cup pineapple juice

¼ cup frozen mango

¼ cup fresh strawberries

1 fresh banana, peeled

½ cup coconut milk

Place everything into a blender and process until smooth. Divide into two tall glasses to serve.

Tropical Fruits

You can trade out other tropical fruits in this recipe if you'd like. For example, trade the mangos for papaya or the strawberries for lychee fruit. Or, use some star fruit and fresh pineapple.

Tiramisu Milkshake

Based on the famous Italian dessert, this milkshake contains mascarpone, espresso, and dark rum.

INGREDIENTS | SERVES 2

4 scoops Mascarpone Ice Cream (see Chapter 5)

1 cup light cream

¼ cup dark rum

¼ cup espresso, cooled

Vanilla wafers, crumbled, for garnish

Chocolate shavings, for garnish

Place Mascarpone Ice Cream, light cream, rum, and espresso into a blender and blend until smooth. Divide into two tall glasses. Garnish with crumbled vanilla wafers and chocolate shavings.

Classic Strawberry Milkshake

Sweet summer strawberries make for a perfectly delicious treat in this irresistible milkshake.

INGREDIENTS | SERVES 1

3 scoops Simple Strawberry Ice Cream (see Chapter 2)

1 cup whole milk

½ cup sliced strawberries

1 tablespoon vanilla extract

1 squeeze lemon juice

Place everything into a blender and process until smooth. Pour into a tall glass to serve.

Elvis Milkshake

Peanut butter, banana, and marshmallow cream come together in this homage to the King.

INGREDIENTS | SERVES 2

4 scoops Caramelized Banana Rum Ice Cream (see Chapter 5)

1 cup half and half

¼ cup smooth peanut butter

¼ cup Marshmallow Topping (see Chapter 17)

1. Place everything but the Marshmallow Topping into a blender and process until smooth.

2. Divide into two tall glasses and swirl in Marshmallow Topping.

Elvis

It is said that one of Elvis's favorite sandwiches was a fried peanut butter and banana sandwich with marshmallow fluff. If it's good enough for the King, it's bound to be delicious!

Caramel DeLite Milkshake

Named after that classic Girl Scout cookie, this milkshake has coconut, caramel, and chocolate to delight your senses.

INGREDIENTS | SERVES 2

4 scoops Toasted Coconut Ice Cream (see Chapter 5)

1 cup whole milk

¼ cup mini chocolate chips

¼ cup toasted coconut

½ cup Caramel Sauce (see Chapter 17)

Place everything into a blender and process until smooth. Pour into a tall glass to serve.

Girl Scout Cookies

The sale of cookies as a way to finance Girl Scout troop activities began in 1917, five years after Juliette Gordon Low started Girl Scouting in the United States. Today, an estimated 200 million boxes are sold per year!

Cheesecake Milkshake

Oh, the possibilities! Add in your favorite syrup or sauce and drink in the deliciousness!

INGREDIENTS | SERVES 2

4 scoops Cream Cheese Frozen Yogurt (see Chapter 4)

1 cup light cream

¼ cup graham cracker crumbs

¼ cup favorite syrup or sauce (see Chapter 17)

Place everything into a blender and blend until smooth. Divide into two tall glasses to serve.

Caramel Corn Milkshake

Caramel corn is delicious, but caramel corn milkshakes are amazing.

INGREDIENTS | SERVES 2

4 scoops Vanilla Brown Butter Ice Cream (see Chapter 5)

1 cup light cream

½ cup Caramel Sauce (see Chapter 17)

Caramel corn for garnish

1. Place Vanilla Brown Butter Ice Cream and light cream into a blender and blend until smooth.

2. Pour into a large glass and swirl in Caramel Sauce. Garnish with caramel corn.

Classic Chocolate Milkshake

Love sipping your milkshakes through a straw? Well, you have Joseph Friedman to thank for it. After watching his young daughter struggle with her milkshake, he invented the flexible straw and had it patented in 1937.

INGREDIENTS | SERVES 2

3 scoops Simple Chocolate Ice Cream (see Chapter 2)

1 cup whole milk

½ cup half and half

1 tablespoon Milk Chocolate Fudge Sauce (see Chapter 17)

1 teaspoon vanilla extract

Place everything into a blender and process until smooth. Divide into two tall glasses to serve.

Deep Dark Chocolate Depths Milkshake

This milkshake is for true chocolate lovers—three types of chocolate combine to deliver a sinfully sweet dessert.

INGREDIENTS | SERVES 2

4 scoops Double Brownie Blast Ice Cream (see Chapter 5)

1 cup light cream

½ cup Dark Chocolate Fudge Sauce (see Chapter 17)

¼ cup dark cocoa powder

Place everything into a blender and blend until smooth. Divide into two tall glasses to serve.

Cherry Pie Milkshake

You won't find a more hearty, more delicious, more intensely flavored milkshake anywhere. That is, unless you opt to substitute a slice of apple pie for the cherry pie!

INGREDIENTS | SERVES 2

4 scoops Rich Vanilla Bean Ice Cream (see Chapter 2)

1 cup light cream

1 slice baked cherry pie

Place everything into a blender and blend until smooth. Divide into two tall glasses to serve.

Coffee Caramel Milkshake

This milkshake features strong coffee flavor with sweet dulce de leche undertones. Delicious!

INGREDIENTS | SERVES 2

4 scoops Dulce de Leche Ice Cream (see Chapter 5)

½ cup light cream

½ cup very strong coffee or espresso, cooled

5–6 chocolate-covered espresso beans

Place everything into a blender and process until smooth. Divide into two tall glasses to serve.

Chocolate Malted Milkshake

This recipe is a classic throw back to simpler times. You'll love the distinct flavor combined with the creamy texture.

INGREDIENTS | SERVES 2

4 scoops Simple Chocolate Ice Cream (see Chapter 2)

1 cup light cream

¼ cup Milk or Dark Chocolate Fudge Sauce (see Chapter 17)

⅓ cup malted milk balls

¼ cup malted milk powder

Place everything into a blender and blend until smooth. Divide into two tall glasses to serve.

Cookies and Cream Milkshake

Who doesn't love an Oreo cookie? No matter how you eat one, you'll fall in love with this creamy milkshake. Substitute chocolate ice cream for the vanilla for even more chocolatey flavor!

INGREDIENTS | SERVES 2

4 scoops Rich Vanilla Bean Ice Cream (see Chapter 2)

1 cup light cream

4 Oreo cookies

2 tablespoons Milk Chocolate Fudge Sauce (see Chapter 17)

Place everything into a blender and blend until smooth. Divide into two tall glasses to serve.

Experiment with Your Cookies

Limited Edition Oreos are available in a variety of flavors throughout the year. Try experimenting with mint, peanut butter, or even the yellow Oreos for a new take on the original milkshake.

Dreamsicle Milkshake

Orange and vanilla make a smooth and refreshing treat.

INGREDIENTS | SERVES 2

4 scoops Simple Vanilla Ice Cream (see Chapter 2)

1 cup half and half

¼ cup orange juice concentrate

Zest of 1 orange

1 tablespoon vanilla extract

Place everything into a blender and process until smooth. Divide into two tall glasses to serve.

Orange or Lemon?

You can make this a delicious, creamy lemon shake by swapping out anything orange with lemon. For example, trade the orange juice concentrate with lemonade concentrate, and zest a lemon instead of an orange. You could also experiment with grapefruit flavors too, or mix and match your favorite citrus fruits for a delectable combination!

CHAPTER 16

Smoothies

Cherry Lime Smoothie
254

Caramel Apple Smoothie
254

Bloody Mary Smoothie
255

Blue Banana Smoothie
256

Blackberry Lemon Tea Smoothie
257

Banana Toffee Latté Smoothie
257

Orange Dream Smoothie
258

Mango White
Chocolate Smoothie
259

Great Grapes Smoothie
259

Peanut Butter Banana Smoothie
260

Cucumber Mint Smoothie
260

Strawberry Kiwi Smoothie
261

Watermelon Smoothie
261

Good Morning
Sunshine Smoothie
262

Strawberry Coconut Smoothie
262

Raspberry Lemonade Smoothie
263

Cherry Lime Smoothie

Cherry and limes are a delicious and refreshing combination—especially in smoothie form.

INGREDIENTS | SERVES 2

2 cups frozen sweet cherries

3 scoops Lemon Lime Soda Sorbet (see Chapter 6)

Juice of 2 limes

½ cup plain Greek yogurt, reduced or nonfat

½ cup crushed ice

½ cup lemon-lime soda

Place everything from cherries to crushed ice into a blender and blend until smooth. Slowly stir in the soda. Divide into two glasses to serve.

For the Adults

Liven up your smoothie by adding a few ounces of lime or cherry vodka. Serve in highball glasses, and garnish with a lime wedge and perfect cherry.

Caramel Apple Smoothie

This smoothie is sweet, tart, buttery, and delicious, just as its namesake describes. You won't miss the tacky fingers or the wooden stick.

INGREDIENTS | SERVES 2

4 scoops Tart Apple Sorbet (see Chapter 6)

½ cup apple cider, very cold

¼ cup Caramel Sauce (see Chapter 17)

½ cup crushed ice

¼ cup Toffee (see Chapter 17), crushed into bits

Place everything into a blender and blend until smooth. Divide into two tall glasses to serve.

Bloody Mary Smoothie

Searching for something savory, not sweet? This is the smoothie for you. Traditionally, Bloody Marys are made with vodka, but they are equally delicious without.

INGREDIENTS | SERVES 2

1 cup V8 juice, frozen into cubes
Pinch celery salt
½ teaspoon fresh ground pepper
½ cup crushed ice
1 teaspoon horseradish
4 dashes Worcestershire sauce
Juice of 1 lime
1 cup V8 juice, very cold

Place everything into a blender and blend until smooth. Divide into two tall glasses to serve.

Bloody Mary

There is a lot of speculation about the origin of the Bloody Mary. It seems that an original recipe of equal parts vodka and tomato juice, created by George Jessel, an entertainer and movie producer, was transformed into the drink we know today by one Fernand Petiot in the 1930s. Petiot was a bartender at Harry's New York Bar in Paris, a haunt for expats such as Ernest Hemingway.

Blue Banana Smoothie

A different take on a popular classic, you'll appreciate these sweet fruits when mixed with the subtle banana and tang of the yogurt and lemon. This would make a wonderful weekend breakfast drink.

INGREDIENTS | SERVES 2

2 ripe bananas, peeled, chopped, and frozen

¼ cup blueberries

2 scoops Blueberry Peach Sherbet (see Chapter 7)

½ cup plain Greek yogurt, reduced or nonfat

A squeeze fresh lemon

½ cup crushed ice

Place everything into a blender and blend until smooth. Divide into two tall glasses to serve.

Greek Yogurt

Greek yogurt is thicker and has more protein than what Americans know as "normal" yogurt. One reason for the richness is that Greek-style yogurt is strained, removing much of the liquid, resulting in extra creaminess. You can also strain plain yogurt through a cheesecloth in the fridge overnight to thicken it to a Greek yogurt consistency.

Blackberry Lemon Tea Smoothie

Most people know about the refreshing combination of lemon and iced tea, but this takes it to a whole new level. Consider adding a shot of limoncello for a welcome after-dinner treat.

INGREDIENTS | SERVES 2

1 cup strong black tea, chilled

⅓ cup frozen blackberries

3 scoops Blackberry Lemon Tea Sherbet (see Chapter 7)

¼ cup frozen lemonade concentrate

½ cup crushed ice

¼ cup honey

Place everything into a blender and blend until smooth. Divide into two tall glasses to serve.

Banana Toffee Latté Smoothie

When freezing bananas, cut them into about 8–10 pieces, then place them on a wax paper–lined cookie sheet. Freeze for 2 hours, then quickly place into a plastic bag to freeze until you need them. It's a great way to save bananas that are almost too old to enjoy.

INGREDIENTS | SERVES 2

4 bananas, chopped and frozen

½ cup Greek yogurt

½ cup espresso, chilled

½ cup crushed ice

¼ cup Dulce de Leche or Caramel Sauce (see Chapter 17)

Place everything into a blender and blend until smooth. Divide into two tall glasses to serve.

Orange Dream Smoothie

This is a modified take on a popular classic made famous by the company Orange Julius of America. You'll gladly forego the line at the mall after one sip of this version.

INGREDIENTS | SERVES 2

1 can frozen orange juice concentrate
¼ cup pasteurized egg white
¼ cup honey
2 cups crushed ice
Zest of 1 orange
1 tablespoon vanilla extract

Place everything into a blender and blend until smooth. Divide into two tall glasses to serve.

Orange Julius Drinks

Julius Freed and Bill Hamlin created the Orange Julius drink in 1928 as a way to draw more customers to their orange juice stand in Los Angeles, California. The name came from their regulars shouting "Give me an orange, Julius!"

Mango White Chocolate Smoothie

The sweetness of the white chocolate is the perfect complement to the peppery mango.

INGREDIENTS | SERVES 2

⅓ cup heavy cream

¼ cup white chocolate chips

4 scoops Mango Sorbet (see Chapter 6)

½ cup fresh mango, cubed

½ cup pineapple juice, very cold

½ cup crushed ice

Garnish!

You can garnish with white chocolate curls by running a vegetable peeler along the side of a slightly warmed white chocolate bar. Add a cube or two of fresh mango for a real wow factor.

1. In a small saucepan, bring heavy cream to a simmer over medium heat. Remove from heat and stir in white chocolate chips. Allow to sit for 30 seconds, then stir until smooth. Cool to room temperature.

2. Place white chocolate mixture and remaining ingredients into a blender and blend until smooth. Divide into two tall glasses to serve.

Great Grapes Smoothie

There are few things better than a big chilly glass of grapey goodness. You'll find that here!

INGREDIENTS | SERVES 2

1 cup Concord grape juice

3 scoops Concord Grape Ice Cream (see Chapter 5)

¼ cup honey

½ cup crushed ice

Place everything into a blender and blend until smooth. Divide into two tall glasses to serve.

Peanut Butter Banana Smoothie

This recipe is a little switch-up from the traditional fruity smoothie, and will add a good amount of protein to your diet, too. Drink it up!

INGREDIENTS | SERVES 2

4 bananas, cut up and frozen

¼ cup smooth peanut butter

½ cup milk, very cold

½ cup crushed ice

1 scoop Peanut Butter Frozen Yogurt (see Chapter 4)

Place everything into a blender and blend until smooth. Divide into two tall glasses to serve.

Protein Rich

Peanuts contain more plant protein than any other nut or legume—nearly 8 grams per 1 ounce serving! This high level of protein also aids in satiation, creating a feeling of fullness. Eat up!

Cucumber Mint Smoothie

Cucumber and mint are often found together in lotions and shampoos, but they also combine to make a very cool and delightful drink.

INGREDIENTS | SERVES 2

1 cup cucumber, peeled and diced

⅓ cup fresh mint

3 scoops Cucumber Mint Frozen Yogurt (see Chapter 4)

½ cup plain Greek yogurt, reduced or nonfat

½ cup crushed ice

Juice of 1 lime

Place everything into a blender and blend until smooth. Divide into two tall glasses to serve.

Stay Cool!

Did you know the internal temperature of a cucumber can be up to 20 degrees cooler than the outside? There's a reason for that old saying "as cool as a cucumber!"

Strawberry Kiwi Smoothie

No Kiwi Sorbet? No problem. Substitute Strawberry Sorbet (see Chapter 6)
for the kiwi, and frozen kiwifruit for the frozen berries.

INGREDIENTS | SERVES 2

4 scoops Kiwi Sorbet (see Chapter 6)
1 cup frozen strawberries
1 cup white grape juice, very cold
½ cup crushed ice
2 tablespoons honey

Place everything into a blender and blend until smooth. Divide into two tall glasses to serve.

Watermelon Smoothie

Light and refreshing, this will satisfy your thirst and cool you off on the hottest of days.

INGREDIENTS | SERVES 2

4 cups seedless watermelon, cubed and frozen
½ cup Greek yogurt, reduced or nonfat
½ cup fresh squeezed orange juice
½ cup crushed ice
¼ cup honey

Place everything into a blender and blend until smooth. Divide into two tall glasses to serve.

Good Morning Sunshine Smoothie

*The addition of a cooked egg adds valuable nutrients and protein, enough
to keep you full of energy as you tackle your hectic day.*

INGREDIENTS | SERVES 2

2 bananas, chopped and frozen

2 cups frozen raspberries

1 cooked egg, scrambled

½ cup Greek yogurt, reduced or nonfat

¼ cup orange juice

½ cup crushed ice

½ cup diet lemon-lime soda

Place everything into a blender and blend until smooth.
Divide into two tall glasses to serve.

Quick!

No time to stand over the stove and cook
your eggs? Scramble them in a microwave-
safe bowl and cook on medium-high heat
in 30-second increments until done.

Strawberry Coconut Smoothie

*Sweet and tart, creamy and smooth . . . strawberry and coconut
combine to make a very unusual and delicious treat.*

INGREDIENTS | SERVES 2

1¼ cups coconut milk, full fat

12–15 frozen whole strawberries

3 scoops Strawberry Sorbet (see
Chapter 6)

½ cup crushed ice

¼ cup honey

Place everything into a blender and blend until smooth.
Divide into two tall glasses to serve.

Add a Little Extra Coconut . . .

The addition of a few shots of coconut-
flavored rum to this drink will heighten the
tropical flavors. You may also use ½ teaspoon coconut extract if the kids are
involved.

Raspberry Lemonade Smoothie

If you have sweetened raspberry purée or Raspberry Sauce (see Chapter 17), you can swirl some in after you have portioned the smoothies into their glasses for garnish and a flavor boost.

4 scoops Lemonade Sorbet (see Chapter 6)

½ cup frozen lemonade concentrate

1 cup frozen raspberries

½ cup crushed ice

2 tablespoons honey

Place everything into a blender and blend until smooth. Divide into two tall glasses to serve.

Toppings and Mix-Ins

Sweetened Whipped Cream
266

Peanut Butter Whipped Cream
266

Chocolate Whipped Cream
267

Fruity Whipped Cream
267

Crunchy Caramelized Nuts
268

Walnuts in Syrup
269

Candied Pecans
269

Candied Citrus Peels
270

Dulce de Leche
271

Butterscotch Sauce
271

Caramel Sauce
272

Hot Fudge Sauce
272

Strawberry Sauce
273

Blueberry Sauce
273

Blackberry Sauce
274

Raspberry Sauce
274

Mixed Berry Sauce
275

Peach Compote
275

Lemon Curd
276

Lime Curd
277

Cherry Compote
278

Spiced Apple Compote
278

Milk Chocolate Fudge Sauce
279

Peanut Butter Topping
279

Dark Chocolate Fudge Sauce
280

Marshmallow Topping
280

Milk Chocolate Ganache
281

Toffee
282

Marshmallow Meringue
283

Sweetened Whipped Cream

No sundae will ever be complete without a dollop (or two!) of sweetened whipped cream.
It mellows out a rich flavor, or adds just the right amount of sweetness if needed.

INGREDIENTS | YIELD: 1 CUP

⅔ cup heavy cream
2 tablespoons confectioner's sugar
1 teaspoon vanilla extract

Piping Whipped Cream

Why not be fancy? Disposable plastic piping bags are available at most craft stores and many big-box stores. Simply buy a few of the bags and a metal star tip (also available with the bags). Insert the tip as directed, fill the bag with the cream, and pipe away!

1. Whip the cream to soft peaks.

2. Add in the confectioner's sugar and vanilla, and whip until well combined. Do not overbeat.

3. Add to sealed container (or piping bag). Keep refrigerated until needed.

Peanut Butter Whipped Cream

This whipped cream is glorious when paired with a rich chocolate ice cream or gelato.
It's even better when topped with a few dark chocolate chips!

INGREDIENTS | YIELD: 1 CUP

⅔ cup heavy cream
2 tablespoons confectioner's sugar
2 tablespoons creamy peanut butter
1 teaspoon vanilla extract

Quick Change

Not a fan of peanut butter? Try substituting Nutella tablespoon for tablespoon. The rich hazelnut-chocolate spread adds a wonderful dimension to a multitude of ice cream flavors when combined with the whipped cream.

1. Whip the cream to soft peaks.

2. Add in the confectioner's sugar, peanut butter, and vanilla, and whip until well combined. Do not overbeat.

3. Add to sealed container (or piping bag). Keep refrigerated until needed.

Chocolate Whipped Cream

This quick whipped cream is divine when paired with vanilla or coffee-flavored ice creams, but it also has the ability to stand on its own as a mousse filling. It's creamy and light, and just right for cake fillings or even as an icing.

INGREDIENTS | YIELD: 1 CUP

⅔ cup heavy cream
¼ cup chocolate chips, melted and cooled
2 tablespoons confectioner's sugar
1 teaspoon vanilla extract

1. Whip the cream to soft peaks.

2. Add in the melted chocolate by hand, stirring softly.

3. Add in the confectioner's sugar and vanilla, and whip until well combined. Do not overbeat.

4. Add to sealed container (or piping bag). Keep refrigerated until needed.

Melted Chocolate

The chocolate in this recipe needs to be melted until smooth, and then cooled. If it is too warm when combined with the cream, it will deflate the airiness of your efforts. If it is too cold, however, you may find that it starts to seize. Don't let this bother you; the flavor is still just as decadent!

Fruity Whipped Cream

Adding puréed fruit to whipped cream is an ingenious way to gain added flavor to a gorgeous sorbet or to use as a needed garnish on a fancier dessert plate. Use your imagination!

INGREDIENTS | YIELD: 1 CUP

⅔ cup heavy cream
¼ cup fresh berries, cherries, or soft fruit, puréed
2–3 tablespoons confectioner's sugar
1 teaspoon vanilla extract

1. Whip the cream to soft peaks.

2. Stir the puréed berries into the cream.

3. Add in the confectioner's sugar and vanilla, and whip until well combined. Do not overbeat.

4. Add to sealed container (or piping bag). Keep refrigerated until needed.

Proper Fruit Choices

Raspberries, blueberries, or blackberries are excellent choices for this recipe, as are cherries and peaches. Strawberries contain a lot of water, so if choosing to use them, first chop them and allow them to drain before using.

Crunchy Caramelized Nuts

Talk about crunch! No matter which variety of nuts you opt to incorporate into this simple recipe, you'll be rewarded with flavorful crunch in each and every bite.

INGREDIENTS | YIELD: 2 CUPS

1 cup sugar

Pinch salt

1½ cups toasted nuts

Adding Nuts to Caramel

Stirring the nuts into the hot caramel can be a bit arduous. Try adding them just after they have been toasted, while still warm. You'll find the process much easier.

1. Prepare a baking sheet with either a Silpat liner, parchment paper, or aluminum foil. Set aside.

2. Heat the sugar and salt in a saucepan over medium heat. Carefully stir the sugar after it begins to brown at the edges, taking care not to splash.

3. Once the caramel is liquid and uniform, add the nuts, and quickly stir to coat.

4. Remove from heat and pour onto the prepared baking sheet, spreading as evenly as possible.

5. Allow to cool completely, then break into small pieces by hand with a rolling pin or in a food processor. Store in an airtight container.

Walnuts in Syrup

You don't have to visit the old-fashioned ice cream shop to enjoy this taste of yesteryear. These sweet, gooey nuts are the perfect addition to hot fudge sundaes or banana splits. Indulge!

INGREDIENTS | YIELD: 1 CUP

⅓ cup maple syrup
1 cup chopped walnuts
Pinch salt

Nuts about Nuts

While walnuts are the most common nut to find drenched in syrup, feel free to substitute your favorite variety, such as pecans, almonds, or hazelnuts. For added flavor, take an extra 10 minutes and toast the nuts before preparing the recipe.

1. Bring the maple syrup to a boil in a saucepan, then stir in the walnuts.

2. Allow the syrup to return to a boil, then stir for about 10 seconds. Remove from heat and allow to cool.

3. Store refrigerated in a covered container. Reheat as needed in a microwave, if desired.

Candied Pecans

These little candies are deliciously addictive. You may substitute other nuts if you like.

INGREDIENTS | YIELD: 2 CUPS

½ cup water
2 cups white sugar, divided
1 tablespoon cinnamon
½ teaspoon fresh ground black pepper
2 cups pecans
2 teaspoons kosher salt

1. Combine water, 1 cup of the sugar, cinnamon, and black pepper in a saucepan over medium heat. Bring to a boil, then add the pecans.

2. Cook and stir the mixture until all the liquid has evaporated.

3. Pour the pecans onto a baking sheet lined with parchment paper. Allow pecans to cool for about 10 minutes, then pour remaining 1 cup sugar and the kosher salt over them. Toss to coat.

4. Store in an airtight container.

Candied Citrus Peels

These little candies are delicious on their own, served with ice cream, or dipped in chocolate. Use lemons, limes, or oranges—you won't be disappointed!

INGREDIENTS | YIELD: 1 CUP

3 large navel oranges or 5 large lemons
2¼ cups sugar, plus more for storage
¾ cup water

1. Cut the tops and bottoms off the citrus, then score into quarters, cutting only through the peels and not the fruit. Remove peels and save the fruit for another recipe. Or, eat it.

2. Cut peels into ¼" strips. Boil strips in water for 5 minutes. Drain, rinse, and repeat with fresh water two more times. Drain and set aside.

3. In a medium saucepan, bring sugar and water to a simmer, stirring until the sugar dissolves. Allow to simmer for about 10 minutes.

4. Add citrus peels to sugar syrup and keep at a low simmer for about 45 minutes, until the peels are translucent.

5. Strain out peels and roll them in a bowl of sugar. Lay out on parchment paper and allow them to dry for 4–5 hours, then store in an airtight container with more sugar.

Dulce de Leche

Dulce de leche is incredibly easy to make, and equally delicious. Enjoy it on many ice cream flavors, on cakes, or even in your morning coffee.

INGREDIENTS | YIELD: 14 OUNCES

1 (14-ounce) can of sweetened condensed milk

1. Remove paper from the can, place can in a large pot, and cover can with water at least 2 inches over top of can. Boil, covered, for 3–4 hours. Be sure to keep the can covered by boiling water the whole time.

2. Allow can to cool in the water overnight.

Butterscotch Sauce

This sauce is so deep and smooth and sweet, you may just want to drink it straight from the pot.

INGREDIENTS | YIELD: 3 CUPS

½ cup light cream
8 tablespoons unsalted butter (1 stick)
1 teaspoon sea salt
2 cups packed light brown sugar

Stir everything in a pot over low heat until sugar is completely dissolved and the sauce is smooth and creamy. Be sure not to boil, as it could curdle the cream.

Caramel Sauce

Making caramel seems intimidating, but don't be worried at all. After you've done it once, you'll see it's quite simple, and you'll never go back to store-bought sauce again.

INGREDIENTS | YIELD: 2 CUPS

5 tablespoons unsalted butter, cold

1⅓ cups sugar

1½ cups heavy cream

¼ teaspoon coarse sea salt

1 teaspoon vanilla extract

Caution!

When first adding the cream to the hot sugar, take care: The mixture will likely bubble up madly, and if not prepared, you may get burned. Wear an oven mitt, or arm yourself with a long-handled whisk to avoid the hot liquid. The sauce will stop bubbling as quickly as it began.

1. Cut the cold butter into pieces, then add to a saucepan with sugar and cook over medium low heat until sugar is a deep amber.

2. Remove from heat and quickly whisk in half of the cream. Once combined, add in the remaining cream, the sea salt, and vanilla, and whisk again until smooth.

3. If any lumps of caramel remain, place over low heat and stir until dissolved.

Hot Fudge Sauce

Smooth, shiny, and ever so delicious, this Hot Fudge Sauce will transport you back to a time when the world was a little slower and ice cream shops were the place to be on a hot summer day.

INGREDIENTS | YIELD: 2 CUPS

¼ cup salted butter, cold

⅔ cup heavy cream

1½ tablespoons corn syrup

½ cup sugar

6 ounces semisweet chocolate chips

1 teaspoon vanilla extract

Storing Hot Fudge Sauce

Kept covered, this Hot Fudge Sauce can be kept refrigerated for 2 weeks. It will thicken while cold, so rewarm it in a microwave for a few seconds before reusing.

1. Cut the cold butter into pieces, then add to a saucepan with the cream, corn syrup, and sugar. Bring to a boil over medium heat. Allow to boil for 2–3 minutes, stirring occasionally.

2. Remove from heat and stir in the chocolate chips until smooth.

3. Once chocolate sauce is smooth, stir in vanilla extract.

Strawberry Sauce

*Strawberry sauce is perfect over Simple Vanilla Ice Cream or Rich Vanilla Bean Ice Cream
(see Chapter 2), made into a banana split, or used to top a lemony sorbet.
It is equally good added into your morning oatmeal.*

INGREDIENTS | YIELD: 2 CUPS

1½ pounds fresh strawberries, hulled

⅓ cup sugar

1½ teaspoons fresh lemon juice

1. Place all ingredients in a food processor and purée until smooth.

2. Press through a mesh strainer to remove seeds, if desired.

3. Refrigerate, covered, until needed, up to 3 days.

Blueberry Sauce

*If you have access to them, wild blueberries are the perfect variety to use in this recipe,
but farmers' market fresh blueberries would be just as delicious. If purchasing
berries from the grocer, take care to make sure they are well ripened.*

INGREDIENTS | YIELD: 2 CUPS

1¼ pounds fresh blueberries, rinsed

¼ cup sugar

1½ teaspoons fresh lemon juice

1. Place all ingredients in a food processor and purée until smooth.

2. Refrigerate, covered, until needed, up to 3 days.

Blackberry Sauce

Seedless blackberries would be the best choice for this sauce, but large, juice-filled seeded berries are equally delicious. Just press the sauce through a strainer to remove the unwanted seeds.

INGREDIENTS | YIELD: 2 CUPS

1¼ pounds fresh blackberries, rinsed
½ cup sugar
2 teaspoons fresh lemon juice

1. Place all ingredients in a food processor and purée until smooth.

2. Press through a mesh strainer to remove seeds, if desired.

3. Refrigerate, covered, until needed, up to 3 days.

Raspberry Sauce

While fresh raspberries are preferable, frozen berries can be used successfully in this smooth and dreamy sauce.

INGREDIENTS | YIELD: 2 CUPS

1 quart fresh or frozen raspberries
5 tablespoons sugar
½ cup water
½ teaspoon fresh lemon juice

1. Place all ingredients in a food processor and purée until smooth.

2. Press through a mesh strainer to remove seeds, if desired.

3. Refrigerate, covered, until needed, up to 3 days.

Mixed Berry Sauce

The beauty of this sauce is that you can use any berry that is readily available. The recipe below combines berries that are typically the most readily available, but feel free to substitute with whatever bounty you happen to have.

INGREDIENTS | YIELD: 2 CUPS

½ pound fresh or frozen strawberries
1 cup fresh or frozen raspberries
1 cup fresh or frozen blackberries
¼ cup sugar
1 teaspoon fresh lemon juice

1. Place all ingredients in a food processor and purée until smooth.

2. Press through a mesh strainer to remove seeds, if desired.

3. Refrigerate, covered, until needed, up to 3 days.

Chunky Variation

You can easily opt to purée only half of the berries, and reserve the other half to stir into the prepared sauce.

Peach Compote

Vanilla brings out the flavor of ripened peaches in this sweet and gentle compote. It is superb served with Simple Vanilla Ice Cream (see Chapter 2), but it's a true delight with caramel-based ice creams or gelato.

INGREDIENTS | YIELD: 3 CUPS

1 pound peaches, peeled, pitted, and chopped
½ cup brown sugar
¼ cup water
1 teaspoon cinnamon
½ teaspoon nutmeg
¼ teaspoon ginger
1 teaspoon vanilla

1. Place all ingredients except the vanilla in a medium saucepan, and cook over medium-high heat. Allow to simmer for 13–15 minutes, until sauce is thickened.

2. Remove from heat and stir in vanilla. Let cool to room temperature.

3. Refrigerate, covered, until needed.

Lemon Curd

One should always have a jar of Lemon Curd on hand. A spoonful on cake, crackers, or especially on ice cream delivers a wonderful taste of freshness and decadence.

INGREDIENTS | YIELD: 2 CUPS

Zest and juice of 2 lemons

1 cup sugar

⅓ cup butter, softened

3 large eggs

Pinch salt

Storage

Kept refrigerated, Lemon Curd will keep for up to 2 weeks. If making large batches, cans of it can be processed for longer keeping.

1. Place lemon zest and sugar in a small bowl. Work the zest into the sugar with your fingers, until the sugar is yellow and aromatic.

2. Using a mixer, cream the butter in a separate medium bowl, then beat into the sugar mixture.

3. Add in eggs, one at a time, beating well after each addition. Add in lemon juice and salt, and mix until thoroughly combined.

4. Heat mixture over medium-low heat until thickened, about 10 minutes, or until it reaches 170°F.

5. Remove from heat and allow to cool. Refrigerate, covered, until needed.

Lime Curd

Lime makes for a delicious curd. Don't expect it to be green:
The yolks will inevitably turn your curd a luscious yellow.

INGREDIENTS | YIELD: 2 CUPS

Zest and juice of 3 limes
1 cup sugar
⅓ cup butter, softened
3 large eggs
Pinch salt

1. Place lime zest and sugar in a small bowl. Work the zest into the sugar with your fingers, until the sugar is yellow-green and aromatic.

2. Using a mixer, cream the butter in a separate medium bowl, then beat in the sugar mixture.

3. Add in eggs, one at a time, beating well after each addition. Add in lime juice and salt, and mix until thoroughly combined.

4. Heat mixture over medium-low heat until thickened, about 10 minutes, or until it reaches 170°F.

5. Remove from heat and allow to cool. Refrigerate, covered, until needed.

Cherry Compote

So, what is compote? Compote is a recipe consisting of fruit, whether fresh or dried, that is stewed in syrup and other complementary flavors.

INGREDIENTS | YIELD: 2 CUPS

4 cups sweet cherries, pitted and chopped

¼ cup sugar

2 tablespoons ice water

1 teaspoon orange juice

2 teaspoons cornstarch

½ teaspoon vanilla

1. Place all ingredients except vanilla in a medium saucepan, and cook over medium-high heat. Bring to a boil for 1 minute, stirring constantly.

2. Remove from heat and stir in the vanilla. Let cool to room temperature.

3. Refrigerate, covered, until needed.

Rhubarb Instead

The tartness of cherries is similar in nature to rhubarb, and equal parts rhubarb may be substituted into this recipe for the cherries. You could also use half cherries and half rhubarb for an intoxicating compote.

Spiced Apple Compote

This compote is as delicious as apple pie, and is as good with toast as it is on frozen desserts.

INGREDIENTS | YIELD: 2 CUPS

2 pounds tart apples, peeled, cored, and chopped

⅓ cup brown sugar

¼ cup water

2 teaspoons cinnamon

¼ teaspoon ginger

1 teaspoon vanilla

1. Place all ingredients except vanilla in a medium saucepan, and cook over medium heat. Allow to simmer for about 30 minutes, until apples are very tender and sauce is thickened.

2. Remove from heat and stir in the vanilla. Let cool to room temperature.

3. Refrigerate, covered, until needed.

Milk Chocolate Fudge Sauce

A little sweeter, this Milk Chocolate Fudge Sauce is a favorite for the kiddos, but grown-ups will enjoy it too. Poured over Peanut Butter Ice Cream (see Chapter 2) or bananas, you'll find it hard to resist!

INGREDIENTS | YIELD: 2 CUPS

¼ cup salted butter, cold
⅔ cup heavy cream
1½ tablespoons corn syrup
⅓ cup sugar
6 ounces milk chocolate chips
1 teaspoon vanilla extract

1. Cut the cold butter into pieces, then add to a saucepan with the cream, corn syrup, and sugar. Bring to a boil over medium heat. Allow to boil for 2–3 minutes, stirring occasionally.

2. Remove from heat and stir in the chocolate chips until smooth.

3. Once chocolate sauce is smooth, stir in vanilla extract.

Peanut Butter Topping

This is a delicious, peanut buttery treat to top your favorite scoop of homemade ice cream.

INGREDIENTS | YIELD: 2 CUPS

½ cup light brown sugar
½ cup granulated sugar
1 teaspoon sea salt
½ cup water
¾ cup peanut butter
1 teaspoon vanilla extract

1. Stir the sugars, salt, and water in a small saucepan over high heat. Boil for 2 minutes.

2. Remove from heat and stir in peanut butter and vanilla until the texture becomes silky. Allow to cool to room temperature. Store in refrigerator, covered, up to 2 weeks.

Try It in Milk

The next time you crave chocolate milk, try adding a few tablespoons of this Peanut Butter Topping to it. It's a great twist to the standard chocolate milk! Your kids will love it, too.

Dark Chocolate Fudge Sauce

*Deep, dark chocolate is a culinary delight. When paired with flavors
like raspberry, mint, or orange, the richness is unparalleled.*

INGREDIENTS | YIELD: 2 CUPS

¼ cup salted butter, cold
⅔ cup heavy cream
1⅔ tablespoons corn syrup
½ cup sugar
6 ounces dark chocolate, chopped
2 teaspoons vanilla extract

1. Cut the cold butter into pieces, then add to a saucepan with the cream, corn syrup, and sugar. Bring to a boil over medium heat. Allow to boil for 2–3 minutes, stirring occasionally.

2. Remove from heat and stir in the chocolate chips until smooth.

3. Once chocolate sauce is smooth, stir in vanilla extract.

Mixing It Up

This Dark Chocolate Fudge Sauce can be easily changed by adding ¼ teaspoon of additional extracts with the vanilla. Mint, orange, or raspberry are always favorites, but coconut or Irish crème would be delicious variations.

Marshmallow Topping

This fluffy confection is reminiscent of old-fashioned ice cream shops.

INGREDIENTS | YIELD: 4 CUPS

½ cup light cream
1½ cups granulated sugar
1 teaspoon sea salt
2 tablespoons light corn syrup
4 tablespoons unsalted butter
1 (16-ounce) package mini marshmallows
1 tablespoon vanilla extract

1. Combine cream, sugar, sea salt, corn syrup, and butter in a medium saucepan. Stir over medium-low heat until all the sugar is dissolved. Bring to a boil and continue the boil for 5 minutes.

2. Stir in marshmallows until smooth. Then add vanilla and stir until incorporated.

3. Allow to cool to room temperature. Store in refrigerator, covered, up to 2 weeks.

Milk Chocolate Ganache

*Milk Chocolate Ganache is a nice switch from deep dark chocolate ganache,
giving a lighter, more playful spin to the customarily fancy sweet.*

INGREDIENTS | YIELD: 2 CUPS

2 ounces finely chopped dark chocolate

8 ounces finely chopped milk chocolate

1 cup heavy cream

Pinch salt

2 teaspoons vanilla extract

Ganache

Ganache is an incredibly simple yet versatile dessert. Just by adjusting the ratio of cream to chocolate, you can make truffles, glazes, sauces, fillings, and frostings. This is a recipe that anyone can easily master.

1. Place dark chocolate and milk chocolate in a medium heat-proof bowl and set aside.

2. In a small saucepan, warm heavy cream and salt just until small bubbles begin to form in the cream, stirring constantly.

3. Immediately pour the cream over the chocolate, cover, and allow to stand for 2–5 minutes.

4. Stir the mixture until smooth and shiny.

5. Stir in the vanilla extract and allow to cool. Cover and refrigerate.

Toffee

Toffee is an amazing candy, great for toppings—but you may find you've eaten it all before you've had a chance to top your homemade ice cream!

INGREDIENTS | YIELD: ½ POUND

2 cups sugar

2 cups butter

1 teaspoon sea salt

1 teaspoon almond extract

1 tablespoon vanilla extract

¼ teaspoon baking soda

Make It Nutty

Feel free to add in your favorite toasted nut to make it even more flavorful. Almonds, pecans, and walnuts make wonderful additions, or try pistachios for a pop of color and an unexpected burst of flavor.

1. Cover a cookie sheet in aluminum foil and coat foil with a light layer of butter.

2. In a large, heavy-bottomed pot, melt the sugar, butter, and sea salt, stirring constantly just until it comes to a boil. Keep it at a boil while continuing to stir over medium heat, until the mixture turns a deep amber color and the temperature reaches 300°F.

3. Remove immediately from heat and add extracts. Be careful—the toffee will bubble and steam. Once it calms down, add the baking soda while stirring vigorously.

4. Pour immediately onto your prepared cookie sheet. Allow to cool and set for at least 2 hours, break into pieces, then store in an airtight container.

Marshmallow Meringue

Marshmallow Meringue is delicious, thick, silky, and oh-so delightfully sweet. Use this satisfying meringue to top ice cream pies, such as Lime Ice Cream Pie (see Chapter 13), or in your own baked pie recipes.

INGREDIENTS | YIELD: 4 CUPS

¾ cup sugar

1½ teaspoons light corn syrup

2 ounces water

6 egg whites

1. In a heavy-bottomed saucepan, stir sugar, corn syrup, and water to a boil. Bring temperature to 240°F (soft ball stage).

2. When sugar mixture reaches 220°F, begin to whip the egg whites on medium-high speed until soft peaks form. By the time you reach soft peaks, the sugar mixture should be at 240°F.

3. Turn the speed down to medium and pour the hot sugar in slowly and steadily, being careful to avoid the whisk if you can.

4. Once all the sugar mixture is incorporated, turn the speed back up to medium-high and beat for 15 minutes.

5. Cover and chill until ready to pipe.

APPENDIX A

Glossary

All-purpose flour

White flour that is a combination of soft and hard wheats, good for most types of baking. It is available in bleached and unbleached varieties.

Baking pan

Any flat, metal pan used for baking. Many baking pans have a lip around the edge.

Beat

The process of smoothing a mixture by rapidly whisking, stirring with a spoon, or using an electric mixer.

Blend

The act of gently combining ingredients until they are thoroughly mixed.

Boil

Bringing a liquid to a high enough temperature that it causes bubbles to rise to the surface and break.

Cream

A thick, high butter-fat dairy product. Heavy whipping cream is best for making ice creams and whipped toppings, as it has a higher butter-fat content.

Creaming

To beat or mix ingredients to a smooth, creamy consistency.

Drizzle

To quickly pour a liquid or glaze in a thin stream.

Dust

To lightly coat an item with a powdered substance, such as cocoa or sugar.

Fold

To carefully combine ingredients that are whipped or fragile. This is done by stirring from the bottom of the vessel with a large spoon or spatula, lifting the ingredients from the bottom, and "folding" them onto the top. This is done in many whipped desserts.

Food coloring

Food-safe dyes that are used to color edibles. Gel or paste colors are best, as they are highly concentrated and offer more intense colors.

Frozen yogurt

A creamy frozen dessert made from yogurt, though often containing additional cream.

Gelato

An Italian-born type of ice cream that incorporates less air than standard ice cream, resulting in a thicker, more intense flavor concentration.

Glaze

A thin frosting that is typically poured over a cake or confection.

Granita

Granitas are frozen juices, scraped into crystals.

Ice cream

A frozen dessert, typically containing cream. Two generic styles exist: French style, which is egg- or custard-based, and Philadelphia (or American) style. French style is often considered smoother, thanks to the yolks used to create the creamy custard base, though it is more complicated to make. Philadelphia style tends to be firmer in texture and lighter in taste, but is a lot easier and faster to produce.

Piping

The act of pressing icing or filling through a pastry bag to create designs or inject fillings.

Sherbet

A frozen dessert made primarily of fruit juice and sweetener, and also containing milk or cream, egg white, or gelatin.

Sift

To shake powdered sugar or flour through a sifter to remove any lumps.

Sorbet

A frozen dessert typically made of fruit, juices, and sweetener, without any dairy included. Often served between courses as a palate cleanser.

Whip

To vigorously beat a food or liquid, typically cream or egg whites, quickly enough to incorporate air, causing them to increase in volume.

Zest

The colored outer skin of a citrus fruit. It is flavorful and used in many recipes. Avoid the bitter white pith that rests just beneath it.

APPENDIX B

Resources

Amazon

A huge selection of ice cream machines can be found at discounted prices, from countertop to industrial models.
www.amazon.com

Beanilla

An online retailer specializing in high-quality vanilla beans and vanilla bean products from around the world. The prices are substantially less than can be found on supermarket shelves. Extracts, sugars, and other vanilla products abound here at very reasonable prices.
www.beanilla.com

Cuisinart

Large selection of ice cream makers, mixers, cookware, and other helpful tools.
www.cuisinart.com

KitchenAid

KitchenAid is well known for its high-quality stand mixers and attachments. Here you can purchase a variety of products, from the mixer to the ice cream bowl attachment, as well as a variety of other useful tools. Be sure to shop the weekly special and Outlet on the website for wonderful deals.
www.shopkitchenaid.com

Le Creuset

Excellent quality cookware treasured by chefs and home cooks alike. Known for heavy, enameled cast-iron cookware that is fantastic for making sauces, custards, and caramels.
http://cookware.lecreuset.com

Nudo

Nudo brand olive oils are top-quality imported oils. While they do carry standard olive oils, they also carry infused olive oils. Mandarin orange, lemon, thyme, and chili are just a few that make wonderful flavor profiles. *www.nudo-italia.com*

Peanut Butter & Co.

A variety of gourmet peanut butters, including white chocolate peanut butter. These flavored versions offer a way to easily change up your ice cream recipes. *www.ilovepeanutbutter.com*

SaltWorks

An online retailer specializing in a variety of sea salts and salt blends, many of which are excellent in ice cream, cookie, and cake recipes featured in this book. *www.saltworks.us*

Scharffen Berger

High-quality chocolates ranging from white to milk to the darkest varieties there are at very reasonable prices. *www.scharffenberger.com*

She's Becoming Doughmesstic

This is the author's website. Life, recipes, cooking solutions, and product reviews are shared. Giveaways are offered on a daily basis. *www.doughmesstic.com*

Tasty Kitchen

Created by Ree Drummond (a.k.a. The Pioneer Woman). Tasty Kitchen is an interactive database and recipe-sharing community that offers a wealth of information and entertainment.

www.tastykitchen.com

Wilton

Baking and cooking products of all types, including pans (even an ice cream sandwich pan), food colorings, pastry bags, piping tips, sprinkles, and more.

www.wilton.com

Standard U.S./Metric Measurement Conversions

VOLUME CONVERSIONS

U.S. Volume Measure	Metric Equivalent
⅛ teaspoon	0.5 milliliters
¼ teaspoon	1 milliliters
½ teaspoon	2 milliliters
1 teaspoon	5 milliliters
½ tablespoon	7 milliliters
1 tablespoon (3 teaspoons)	15 milliliters
2 tablespoons (1 fluid ounce)	30 milliliters
¼ cup (4 tablespoons)	60 milliliters
⅓ cup	90 milliliters
½ cup (4 fluid ounces)	125 milliliters
⅔ cup	160 milliliters
¾ cup (6 fluid ounces)	180 milliliters
1 cup (16 tablespoons)	250 milliliters
1 pint (2 cups)	500 milliliters
1 quart (4 cups)	1 liter (about)

WEIGHT CONVERSIONS

U.S. Weight Measure	Metric Equivalent
½ ounce	15 grams
1 ounce	30 grams
2 ounces	60 grams
3 ounces	85 grams
¼ pound (4 ounces)	115 grams
½ pound (8 ounces)	225 grams
¾ pound (12 ounces)	340 grams
1 pound (16 ounces)	454 grams

OVEN TEMPERATURE CONVERSIONS

Degrees Fahrenheit	Degrees Celsius
200 degrees F	95 degrees C
250 degrees F	120 degrees C
275 degrees F	135 degrees C
300 degrees F	150 degrees C
325 degrees F	160 degrees C
350 degrees F	180 degrees C
375 degrees F	190 degrees C
400 degrees F	205 degrees C
425 degrees F	220 degrees C
450 degrees F	230 degrees C

BAKING PAN SIZES

American	Metric
8 × 1½ inch round baking pan	20 × 4 cm cake tin
9 × 1½ inch round baking pan	23 × 3.5 cm cake tin
11 × 7 × 1½ inch baking pan	28 × 18 × 4 cm baking tin
13 × 9 × 2 inch baking pan	30 × 20 × 5 cm baking tin
2 quart rectangular baking dish	30 × 20 × 3 cm baking tin
15 × 10 × 2 inch baking pan	30 × 25 × 2 cm baking tin (Swiss roll tin)
9 inch pie plate	22 × 4 or 23 × 4 cm pie plate
7 or 8 inch springform pan	18 or 20 cm springform or loose bottom cake tin
9 × 5 × 3 inch loaf pan	23 × 13 × 7 cm or 2 lb narrow loaf or pate tin
1½ quart casserole	1.5 liter casserole
2 quart casserole	2 liter casserole

Index

Note: Page numbers in **bold** indicate recipe category lists.

Alcohol (liqueurs, etc.)
about: Chianti, 55; limoncello, 52
Caramelized Banana Rum Ice Cream, 86
Cherry Lime Smoothie, 254
Chianti Gelato (*Gelato di chianti*), 55
Chocolate Raspberry Ice Cream Cake, 201
Dark Chocolate Bourbon Gelato (*Gelato di cioccolato scuro borbone*), 58
Elvis Milkshake, 247
Limoncello Gelato (*Gelato di limoncello*), 52
Mudslide Ice Cream, 38
Orange Frozen Yogurt, 65
Rum Raisin Ice Cream, 40
Allergies, special diets and, 21
Apples
about: caramel, 42; Granny Smith, 133
Apple Pie Ice Cream, 80
Autumn Apple Ice Cream Cake, 198
Caramel Apple Gelato (*Gelato di caramello mela*), 42
Caramel Apple Smoothie, 254
Spiced Apple Compote, 278
Tart Apple Granita, 133
Tart Apple Sorbet, 110
Avocados, in Vegan Choco-Avocado Ice Cream, 157

Baked Alaska, Neapolitan, 236
Baking sheets, pans, muffin pans, 17
Bananas
about: caramelizing, 109
Banana Coffee Toffee Ice Cream Cake Roll, 197
Banana Frozen Yogurt, 70
Banana Pudding Ice Cream Pie, 216
Banana Sherbet, 122
Banana Split Trifle, 208
Banana Toffee Latté Smoothie, 257

Blue Banana Smoothie, 256
Caramelized Banana Rum Ice Cream, 86
Chocolate Covered Banana Cake, 200
Chocolate Covered Banana Ice Cream Pie, 222
Cocoa Banana Sherbet, 125
Frozen Bananas, 183
Good Morning Sunshine Smoothie, 262
Peanut Butter Banana Smoothie, 260
Purple Cow Milkshake, 244
Strawberry Banana Sherbet, 124
Strawberry Banana Sorbet, 109
Tropical Milkshake, 245
Basil
about: historical perspective, 45
Basil Gelato (*Gelato di basi*), 45
Cucumber Basil Granita, 129
Herbed Tomato Gelato (*Gelato di herbes e tomati*), 44
Berries. *See also* Blackberries; Blueberries; Cranberries; Raspberries; Strawberries
about: buying, 18
Fruity Whipped Cream, 267
Mixed Berry Sauce, 275
Mixed Berry Sherbet, 118
Blackberries
about: buying, 18
Blackberry Granita, 143
Blackberry Lemon Tea Sherbet, 120
Blackberry Lemon Tea Smoothie, 257
Blackberry Lime Frozen Yogurt, 64
Blackberry Lime Sorbet, 106
Blackberry Sauce, 274
Blackberry Sherbet, 114
Blackberry Sorbet, 106
Double Trouble Ice Cream Pops, 183
Fruity Whipped Cream, 267
Mixed Berry Sauce, 275
Mixed Berry Sherbet, 118
Sage Blackberry Swirl Gelato (*Gelato di leggenda e mora*), 54
Blenders, 16

Bloody Mary Smoothie, 255
Blueberries
about, 154; buying, 18
Blue Banana Smoothie, 256
Blueberry Frozen Yogurt, 63
Blueberry Granita, 141
Blueberry Muffin Ice Cream Pie, 223
Blueberry Peach Ice Cream Cake, 199
Blueberry Peach Sherbet, 119
Blueberry Sauce, 273
Blueberry Sherbet, 116
Double Trouble Ice Cream Pops, 183
Fruity Whipped Cream, 267
Mixed Berry Sherbet, 118
Vegan Blueberry Lavender Ice Cream, 154
Bombe, 238
Bowls, chocolate, 235
Brown butter, in Vanilla Brown Butter Ice Cream, 94
Bubble Gum Ice Cream, 81
Butterscotch Sauce, 271

Cake Batter Ice Cream, 82
Cakes, ice cream cakes, cupcakes, and trifles, **191**–209
about: mixing batters, 192
Autumn Apple Ice Cream Cake, 198
Banana Coffee Toffee Ice Cream Cake Roll, 197
Banana Split Trifle, 208
Blueberry Peach Ice Cream Cake, 199
Candy Ice Cream Cake, 200
Chocolate Cake, 196
Chocolate Caramel Ice Cream Cupcakes, 209
Chocolate Covered Banana Cake, 200
Chocolate Raspberry Ice Cream Cake, 201
Ice Cream Cupcakes, 180
Lemon Cake, 194
Lemon Cheesecake Ice Cream Cupcakes, 207
Red Velvet Cake, 193
Red Velvet Cake Ice Cream, 87

Red Velvet Lovers Ice Cream Cake, 202
Strawberry Cake, 195
Strawberry Cheesecake Ice Cream Cupcakes, 207
Strawberry Lemonade Frozen Trifle, 204
Strawberry Shortcake Ice Cream Cupcakes, 205
Tiramisu Ice Cream Cake Roll, 206
Triple Citrus Ice Cream Cake, 203
Turtle Ice Cream Cake, 202
Vanilla Bean Butter Cake, 192
White Chocolate Ganache, 199
Candy Ice Cream Cake, 200
Cantaloupe. *See* Melons
Caramel and toffee
    about: adding nuts to caramel, 268; caramelizing bananas, 109; turtles, 166
    Banana Coffee Toffee Ice Cream Cake Roll, 197
    Banana Toffee Latté Smoothie, 257
    Caramel Apple Gelato (*Gelato di caramello mela*), 42
    Caramel Apple Smoothie, 254
    Caramel Corn Milkshake, 248
    Caramel DeLite Milkshake, 247
    Caramelized Banana Rum Ice Cream, 86
    Caramel Pecan Ice Cream, 83
    Caramel Sauce, 272
    Chocolate Caramel Ice Cream Cupcakes, 209
    Coffee Caramel Milkshake, 250
    Crunchy Caramelized Nuts, 268
    Nutty Buddies, 178
    Sugar-Free Turtle Ice Cream, 166
    Sugar-Free Vanilla Caramel Swirl Ice Cream, 165
    Toffee, 282
    Turtle Ice Cream Cake, 202
Cereal, in Better Than Breakfast Cereal Ice Cream, 82
Cheese
    about: cheesecake history, 67, 218
    Cheesecake Milkshake, 248
    Cream Cheese Frozen Yogurt, 67
    Frozen Cheesecake Pops, 190
    Lemon Cheesecake Ice Cream Cupcakes, 207
    Pumpkin Cheesecake Ice Cream Pie, 227

Pumpkin Cream Cheese Ice Cream, 91
Strawberry Cheesecake Ice Cream Cupcakes, 207
Strawberry Cheesecake Ice Cream Pie, 218
Vegan Cinnamon Cheesecake Swirl Ice Cream, 156
Cherries
    about: cordials, 69; pitting, 35
    Bing Cherry Sorbet, 105
    Black Cherry Ice Cream, 35
    Black Forest Ice Cream Pie, 226
    Cherry Compote, 278
    Cherry Limeade Gelato (*Gelato di bere ciliegia e calce*), 57
    Cherry Lime Smoothie, 254
    Cherry Pie Milkshake, 250
    Chocolate Cherry Frozen Yogurt, 69
    Vegan Rhubarb Cherry Swirl Ice Cream, 155
Chipotle chiles, in Chocolate Chipotle Ice Cream, 74
Chocolate. *See also* White chocolate
    about, 18; Almond Joy bars, 151; Butterfinger bars, 96; chocolate chip cookies, 186; curls, 220; Dutch-processed cocoa, 18; malted milk powder and Ovaltine, 88; milk chocolate, 31; Nutella, 39, 47; s'mores, 79; sweetened cocoa powder, 26; Swiss, 93; turtles, 166
    Black Forest Ice Cream Pie, 226
    Brownies for Breakfast Ice Cream Sandwiches, 189
    Candy Ice Cream Cake, 200
    Chocolate Bowls, 235
    Chocolate Cake, 196
    Chocolate Caramel Ice Cream Cupcakes, 209
    Chocolate Cherry Frozen Yogurt, 69
    Chocolate Chipotle Ice Cream, 74
    Chocolate Chipwiches, 186
    Chocolate Covered Banana Cake, 200
    Chocolate Covered Banana Ice Cream Pie, 222
    Chocolate Crepes, 232
    Chocolate Espresso Sherbet, 122
    Chocolate Frozen Yogurt, 66
    Chocolate Ice Cream Sandwiches, 185
    Chocolate Malted Milkshake, 251
    Chocolate Mint Sherbet, 121

Chocolate Sherbet, 121
Chocolate Tart Crust, 213
Chocolate Whipped Cream, 267
Classic Chocolate Milkshake, 249
Cocoa Banana Sherbet, 125
Cookies and Cream Milkshake, 251
Dark Chocolate and Raspberry Ice Cream Pie, 222
Dark Chocolate Bourbon Gelato (*Gelato di cioccolato scuro borbone*), 58
Dark Chocolate Fudge Sauce, 280
Decadent Chocolate Ice Cream, 28
Deep Dark Chocolate Depths Milkshake, 249
Double Brownie Blast Ice Cream, 84
Double Trouble Ice Cream Pops, 183
French Twist, 237
Gianduja Gelato (*Gelato di gianduja*), 51
Gimme S'More Ice Cream, 79
Grasshopper Ice Cream Pie, 217
Hazelnut Nutella Swirl Gelato (*Gelato alla Nutella*), 47
Homemade Chocolate Magic Shell, 178
Hot Fudge Sauce, 272
Kit Kat Ice Cream, 88
Milk Chocolate Fudge Sauce, 279
Milk Chocolate Ganache, 281
Milk Chocolate Ice Cream, 31
Mint Chocolate Chip Ice Cream, 36
Mudslide Ice Cream, 38
Neapolitan Baked Alaska, 236
Nutella Ice Cream, 39
Peanut Butter Butterfinger Ice Cream, 96
Raspberry Dark Chocolate Swirl Ice Cream, 75
Rich Chocolate and Raspberry Frozen Yogurt, 66
Rocky Road Ice Cream, 39
Simple Chocolate Ice Cream, 26
Sugar-Free Chocolate Ice Cream, 171
Sugar-Free Coffee Chip Ice Cream, 169
Sugar-Free Dark Chocolate Orange Ice Cream, 168
Sugar-Free Decadent Dark Chocolate Raspberry Ice Cream, 173
Sugar-Free Mint Chip Ice Cream, 174
Sugar-Free Turtle Ice Cream, 166
Super Double Dark Chocolate Ice Cream, 93

Chocolate—*continued*
  3 Musketeers Candy Bar Ice Cream, 90
  Triple Chocolate Ice Cream Pie, 220
  Turtle Ice Cream Cake, 202
  Vegan Almond Joy Swirl Ice Cream, 151
  Vegan Choco-Avocado Ice Cream, 157
Cinnamon
  about, 156; Red Hots, 76
  Not-Too-Hot Red Hots Ice Cream, 76
  Vegan Cinnamon Cheesecake Swirl Ice Cream, 156
Citrus
  about, 18; clementines, 113; enhancing lemon flavor, 194; filling oranges, 237; lemonade stands, 101; lemon-lime soda trivia, 100; lemons, 112; limeade, 57; lime bowls, 106; limes, 78; limoncello, 52; Orange Julius drinks, 258; oranges, 168; pink lemonade, 221; zesting, 128
  Blackberry Lemon Tea Sherbet, 120
  Blackberry Lemon Tea Smoothie, 257
  Blackberry Lime Frozen Yogurt, 64
  Blackberry Lime Sorbet, 106
  Blood Orange Gelato (*Gelato di arancia rosso*), 59
  Candied Citrus Peels, 270
  Cherry Limeade Gelato (*Gelato di bere ciliegia e calce*), 57
  Cherry Lime Smoothie, 254
  Cranberry Orange Granita, 138
  Double Trouble Ice Cream Pops, 183
  Dreamsicle Heaven Ice Cream Pie, 219
  Dreamsicle Milkshake, 252
  Dreamy Orange Cream Ice Cream, 24
  Florida Ice Cream Pie, 224
  Frozen Strawberry Lemonade Ice Cream Pie, 221
  Lemonade Sorbet, 101
  Lemon Cake, 194
  Lemon Cheesecake Ice Cream Cupcakes, 207
  Lemon Cream Ice Cream, 97
  Lemon Curd, 276
  Lemon Granita, 128
  Lemon Ice Cream, 34
  Lemon Lime Soda Sorbet, 100
  Lemon Meringue Ice Cream Pie, 219
  Lemon Mint Granita, 146
  Lemon Sherbet, 112

Lemon Shortbread Ice Cream Sandwiches, 239
Lemon Simple Syrup, 203
Lime and Coconut Ice Cream, 78
Lime Curd, 277
Lime Frozen Yogurt, 65
Lime Granita, 132
Lime Ice Cream Pie, 215
Lime Sherbet, 112
Lime Sorbet, 100
Limoncello Gelato (*Gelato di limoncello*), 52
Mascarpone Ice Cream, 89
Orange Dream Smoothie, 258
Orange Frozen Yogurt, 65
Orange Granita, 130
Orange Infused Olive Oil Gelato (*Gelato di arancia olio d'oliva infuso*), 43
Pomegranate Orange Granita, 147
Popsicles, 178
Raspberry Lemonade Smoothie, 263
Sorbet-Filled Frozen Oranges, 237
Strawberry Lemonade Frozen Trifle, 204
Sugar-Free Dark Chocolate Orange Ice Cream, 168
Sugar-Free Dreamy Orange Cream Ice Cream, 170
Tangerine Sherbet, 113
Taste of the Tropics Ice Cream Pie, 225
Triple Citrus Ice Cream Cake, 203
Vegan Lemon-Infused Olive Oil Ice Cream, 161
Vegan Lemon Poppy Seed Ice Cream, 160
Zesty Lemon Frozen Yogurt, 64
Coconut
  about: name origin, 224; piña colada, 175; toasted, 95
  Caramel DeLite Milkshake, 247
  Double Trouble Ice Cream Pops, 183
  Florida Ice Cream Pie, 224
  Lime and Coconut Ice Cream, 78
  Piña Colada Ice Cream Pie, 226
  Pineapple Coconut Sorbet, 107
  Strawberry Coconut Smoothie, 262
  Sugar-Free Piña Colada Ice Cream, 175
  Toasted Coconut Gelato (*Gelato di noce di cocco tostata*), 56
  Toasted Coconut Ice Cream, 95
  Tropical Milkshake, 245

Coffee and espresso
  about: caffeine warning, 122; coffee, 158; flavored coffees, 32
  Banana Toffee Latté Smoothie, 257
  Chocolate Espresso Sherbet, 122
  Coffee Caramel Milkshake, 250
  Coffee Ice Cream, 32
  Double Trouble Ice Cream Pops, 183
  Espresso Frozen Yogurt, 70
  Espresso Gelato (*Gelato di espresso*), 53
  Sugar-Free Coffee Chip Ice Cream, 169
  Vegan Coffee Ice Cream, 158
Cones
  Waffle Cones, 181
Cookies and cookie dough
  about: cookie dough caution, 37; Girls Scout cookies, 247; shortbread history, 239
  Chocolate Chipwiches, 186
  Cookie Dough Ice Cream, 37
  Cookies and Cream Milkshake, 251
  Lemon Shortbread Ice Cream Sandwiches, 239
  Oatmeal Raisin Ice Cream Sandwiches, 188
  Sugar Cookie Cups, 184
Cranberries
  about: growing, 138
  Cranberry Orange Granita, 138
  Vegan Cranberry White Chocolate Chunk Ice Cream, 157
Cream
  about, 19
  whipped, recipes, 266–67
Cream cheese. *See* Cheese
Cream puffs, 230
Crepes, 231, 232
Crust. *See* Ice cream pies
Cucumbers
  about: coolness of, 260; nutritional value, 71
  Cucumber Basil Granita, 129
  Cucumber Mint Frozen Yogurt, 71
  Cucumber Mint Smoothie, 260
Cupcakes. *See* Cakes, ice cream cakes, cupcakes, and trifles

Decadent frozen confections, **229**–41
  Bombe, 238
  Chocolate Bowls, 235
  Chocolate Crepes, 232
  Crepes, 231

French Twist, 237
Fried Ice Cream, 234
Frozen Pumpkin Whoopie Pies, 241
Frozen Red Velvet Whoopie Pies, 240
Lemon Shortbread Ice Cream
  Sandwiches, 239
Neapolitan Baked Alaska, 236
Profiteroles, 230
Sorbet-Filled Frozen Oranges, 237
White Chocolate Mousse Cake, 233
Double Trouble Ice Cream Pops, 183
Dragonfruit Mint Ice Cream, 85
Dreamsicle Heaven Ice Cream Pie, 219
Dreamsicle Milkshake, 252
Dulce de Leche, 271
Dulce de Leche Ice Cream, 84

Eggs
  about: aging whites for meringue, 34;
    cookie dough caution, 37; types of,
    buying, 20
  Good Morning Sunshine Smoothie,
    262
Elvis Milkshake, 247
Equipment and supplies, 14–17
Espresso. *See* Coffee and espresso

Fanciful flavors, **73**–97
  Apple Pie Ice Cream, 80
  Better Than Breakfast Cereal Ice
    Cream, 82
  Bubble Gum Ice Cream, 81
  Cake Batter Ice Cream, 82
  Caramelized Banana Rum Ice Cream,
    86
  Caramel Pecan Ice Cream, 83
  Chocolate Chipotle Ice Cream, 74
  Concord Grape Ice Cream, 85
  Double Brownie Blast Ice Cream, 84
  Dragonfruit Mint Ice Cream, 85
  Dulce de Leche Ice Cream, 84
  Gimme S'More Ice Cream, 79
  Kit Kat Ice Cream, 88
  Lavender Honey Ice Cream, 77
  Lemon Cream Ice Cream, 97
  Lime and Coconut Ice Cream, 78
  Mascarpone Ice Cream, 89
  Not-Too-Hot Red Hots Ice Cream, 76
  Peanut Butter Butterfinger Ice Cream,
    96
  Pumpkin Cream Cheese Ice Cream,
    91

Raspberry Dark Chocolate Swirl Ice
  Cream, 75
Red Velvet Cake Ice Cream, 87
Super Double Dark Chocolate Ice
  Cream, 93
3 Musketeers Candy Bar Ice Cream,
  90
Toasted Coconut Ice Cream, 95
Vanilla Brown Butter Ice Cream, 94
White Chocolate Pretzel Ice Cream,
  92
Figs, in Fresh Fig Gelato (*Gelato di fichi*),
  44
Flour, 20
Food processors, 16
French Twist, 237
Fried Ice Cream, 234
Frozen yogurt, **61**–71
  about: definition of, 14; Greek yogurt,
    256; yogurt types, 20
  Banana Frozen Yogurt, 70
  Blackberry Lime Frozen Yogurt, 64
  Blueberry Frozen Yogurt, 63
  Cheesecake Milkshake, 248
  Chocolate Cherry Frozen Yogurt, 69
  Chocolate Frozen Yogurt, 66
  Cream Cheese Frozen Yogurt, 67
  Cucumber Mint Frozen Yogurt, 71
  Espresso Frozen Yogurt, 70
  French Twist, 237
  Lime Frozen Yogurt, 65
  Orange Frozen Yogurt, 65
  Peach Pie Frozen Yogurt, 68
  Peanut Butter Frozen Yogurt, 68
  Raspberry Frozen Yogurt, 63
  Rich Chocolate and Raspberry
    Frozen Yogurt, 66
  Strawberry Frozen Yogurt, 62
  Vanilla Frozen Yogurt, 62
  Yogurt Fruit Pops, 181
  Zesty Lemon Frozen Yogurt, 64
Fruit. *See also specific fruit*
  about: citrus, 18. *See also* Citrus; fresh
    vs. frozen or canned, 18
  Fruity Whipped Cream, 267
  Popsicles, 178
  Yogurt Fruit Pops, 181
Fudge sauces, 272, 279, 280

Ganache
  Milk Chocolate Ganache, 281
  White Chocolate Ganache, 199
Gelato, **41**–59

about: definition of, 13
  Basil Gelato (*Gelato di basi*), 45
  Blood Orange Gelato (*Gelato di
    arancia rosso*), 59
  Caramel Apple Gelato (*Gelato di
    caramello mela*), 42
  Cherry Limeade Gelato (*Gelato di
    bere ciliegia e calce*), 57'
  Chianti Gelato (*Gelato di chianti*), 55
  Dark Chocolate Bourbon Gelato
    (*Gelato di cioccolato scuro
    borbone*), 58
  Espresso Gelato (*Gelato di espresso*),
    53
  Fresh Fig Gelato (*Gelato di fichi*), 44
  Gianduja Gelato (*Gelato di gianduja*),
    51
  Hazelnut Nutella Swirl Gelato (*Gelato
    alla Nutella*), 47
  Herbed Tomato Gelato (*Gelato di
    herbes e tomati*), 44
  Honey Swirled Pear Gelato (*Gelato di
    miele roteato pera*), 50
  Limoncello Gelato (*Gelato di
    limoncello*), 52
  Orange Infused Olive Oil Gelato
    (*Gelato di arancia olio d'oliva
    infuso*), 43
  Pistachio Gelato (*Gelato di
    pistacchio*), 49
  Pumpkin Gelato (*Gelato di zucca*), 48
  Rice Gelato (*Gelato di riso*), 46
  Sage Blackberry Swirl Gelato (*Gelato
    di leggenda e mora*), 54
  Toasted Coconut Gelato (*Gelato di
    noce di cocco tostata*), 56
Ginger
  about: benefits of, 214
  Ginger Pear Sorbet, 102
  Gingersnap Tart Crust, 214
Glossary, 285–89
Graham Cracker Crust, 214
Granitas, **127**–48
  about: definition of, 14
  Blackberry Granita, 143
  Blueberry Granita, 141
  Cantaloupe Granita, 137
  Cranberry Orange Granita, 138
  Cucumber Basil Granita, 129
  Honeydew Melon Granita, 136
  Kiwi Granita, 148
  Lemon Granita, 128
  Lemon Mint Granita, 146

Granitas—*continued*
    Lime Granita, 132
    Orange Granita, 130
    Pear Granita, 145
    Pineapple Granita, 135
    Pomegranate Granita, 142
    Pomegranate Orange Granita, 147
    Raspberry Granita, 134
    Sparkling White Grape Granita, 144
    Strawberry Granita, 139
    Strawberry Kiwi Granita, 140
    Tart Apple Granita, 133
    Watermelon Granita, 131
Grapes
    about: Concord grapes, 85; sparkling
        juice, 102
    Concord Grape Ice Cream, 85
    Great Grapes Smoothie, 259
    Purple Cow Milkshake, 244
    Sparkling White Grape Granita, 144
    Sparkling White Grape Sorbet, 102
Grasshopper Ice Cream Pie, 217

Hand mixers, 16
Hazelnuts. *See* Nuts
Herbs, 20. *See also specific herbs*
Honeydew. *See* Melons
Honey Swirled Pear Gelato (*Gelato di
    miele roteato pera*)
    Honey, 50

Ice cream
    basics, 11–22
    definition and ingredients, 13
    history of, 12
    machines for making, 15–16
    tools and techniques, 14–17
    varieties/other frozen desserts, 12–13
Ice cream, essential recipes, **23**–40
    Black Cherry Ice Cream, 35
    Butter Pecan Ice Cream, 29
    Coffee Ice Cream, 32
    Cookie Dough Ice Cream, 37
    Decadent Chocolate Ice Cream, 28
    Dreamy Orange Cream Ice Cream, 24
    Fresh Peach Ice Cream, 33
    Lemon Ice Cream, 34
    Milk Chocolate Ice Cream, 31
    Mint Chocolate Chip Ice Cream, 36
    Mudslide Ice Cream, 38
    Nutella Ice Cream, 39
    Peaches and Cream Ice Cream, 30
    Peanut Butter Ice Cream, 32

Rich Vanilla Bean Ice Cream, 27
Rocky Road Ice Cream, 39
Rum Raisin Ice Cream, 40
Simple Chocolate Ice Cream, 26
Simple Strawberry Ice Cream, 25
Simple Vanilla Ice Cream, 24
White Chocolate Ice Cream, 40
Ice cream pies, **211**–27. *See also*
    Whoopie pies
    about: puffing crusts, 212
    Banana Pudding Ice Cream Pie, 216
    Black Forest Ice Cream Pie, 226
    Blueberry Muffin Ice Cream Pie, 223
    Chocolate Covered Banana Ice
        Cream Pie, 222
    Chocolate Tart Crust, 213
    Dark Chocolate and Raspberry Ice
        Cream Pie, 222
    Dreamsicle Heaven Ice Cream Pie,
        219
    Florida Ice Cream Pie, 224
    Frozen Strawberry Lemonade Ice
        Cream Pie, 221
    Gingersnap Tart Crust, 214
    Graham Cracker Crust, 214
    Grasshopper Ice Cream Pie, 217
    Lemon Meringue Ice Cream Pie, 219
    Lime Ice Cream Pie, 215
    Piña Colada Ice Cream Pie, 226
    Pumpkin Cheesecake Ice Cream Pie,
        227
    Strawberry Cheesecake Ice Cream
        Pie, 218
    Streusel Topping, 223
    Sweet Dough Tart Crust, 212
    Taste of the Tropics Ice Cream Pie, 225
    Triple Chocolate Ice Cream Pie, 220
    Vanilla Wafer Crust, 215
Ingredients, 18–21. *See also specific
    ingredients*

Jelly
    about: PB and J, 172
    Peanut Butter and Jelly Ice Cream
        Sandwiches, 187
    Sugar-Free Peanut Butter and Jelly Ice
        Cream, 172

Kids, ice cream for, **177**–90
    Brownies for Breakfast Ice Cream
        Sandwiches, 189
    Chocolate Chipwiches, 186

Chocolate Ice Cream Sandwiches,
    185
Double Trouble Ice Cream Pops, 183
Frozen Bananas, 183
Frozen Cheesecake Pops, 190
Homemade Chocolate Magic Shell,
    178
Ice Cream Cupcakes, 180
Nutty Buddies, 179
Oatmeal Raisin Ice Cream
    Sandwiches, 188
Peanut Butter and Jelly Ice Cream
    Sandwiches, 187
Popsicles, 178
Sugar Cookie Cups, 184
Waffle Cones, 181
Yogurt Fruit Pops, 181
Kit Kat Ice Cream, 88
Kiwi fruit
    about, 110; skin of, 140
    Kiwi Granita, 148
    Kiwi Sorbet, 110
    Strawberry Kiwi Granita, 140
    Strawberry Kiwi Smoothie, 261

Lavender
    about, 77
    Lavender Honey Ice Cream, 77
    Vegan Blueberry Lavender Ice Cream,
        154
Lemons and limes. *See* Citrus

Magic Shell, 178
Malted milk powder, 88
Mangoes
    Mango White Chocolate Smoothie,
        259
Mangos
    about: choosing, 176; tree as symbol,
        101
    Mango Sorbet, 101
    Sugar-Free Mango Ice Cream, 176
    Taste of the Tropics Ice Cream Pie, 225
    Tropical Milkshake, 245
Marshmallows
    about: s'mores, 79
    Elvis Milkshake, 247
    Florida Ice Cream Pie, 224
    Gimme S'More Ice Cream, 79
    Marshmallow Meringue, 283
    Marshmallow Topping, 280
    Piña Colada Ice Cream Pie, 226
    Rocky Road Ice Cream, 39

Taste of the Tropics Ice Cream Pie, 225
3 Musketeers Candy Bar Ice Cream, 90
Mascarpone Ice Cream, 89. *See also Tiramisu references*
Melons
about: cantaloupe, 137; choosing, 104; watermelons, 131
Cantaloupe Granita, 137
Cantaloupe Sorbet, 104
Honeydew Melon Granita, 136
Honeydew Sorbet, 104
Watermelon Granita, 131
Watermelon Smoothie, 261
Watermelon Sorbet, 103
Meringue, egg whites for, 34
Milk
about: fat content, 19
Dulce de Leche, 271
Milkshakes, **243**–52
about: malted milk powder, 88
Caramel Corn Milkshake, 248
Caramel DeLite Milkshake, 247
Cheesecake Milkshake, 248
Cherry Pie Milkshake, 250
Chocolate Malted Milkshake, 251
Classic Chocolate Milkshake, 249
Classic Strawberry Milkshake, 246
Classic Vanilla Milkshake, 245
Coffee Caramel Milkshake, 250
Cookies and Cream Milkshake, 251
Deep Dark Chocolate Depths Milkshake, 249
Dreamsicle Milkshake, 252
Elvis Milkshake, 247
Peachy Keen Milkshake, 244
Purple Cow Milkshake, 244
Tiramisu Milkshake, 246
Tropical Milkshake, 245
Mint
about: peppermint, 174; varieties of, 36
Chocolate Mint Sherbet, 121
Cucumber Mint Frozen Yogurt, 71
Cucumber Mint Smoothie, 260
Dragonfruit Mint Ice Cream, 85
Lemon Mint Granita, 146
Mint Chocolate Chip Ice Cream, 36
Sugar-Free Mint Chip Ice Cream, 174
Mixers, 16
Muffin pans, 17

Neapolitan Baked Alaska, 236

Nectarines, in Raspberry Nectarine Sorbet, 108
Nuts. *See also* Peanuts and peanut butter
about: adding to caramel, 268; allergies to, 21; Almond Joy bars, 151; cashews, 152; Nutella, 39, 47; omitting from recipes, 21; turtles, 166
Butter Pecan Ice Cream, 29
Candied Pecans, 269
Caramel Pecan Ice Cream, 83
Crunchy Caramelized Nuts, 268
Gianduja Gelato (*Gelato di gianduja*), 51
Hazelnut Nutella Swirl Gelato (*Gelato alla Nutella*), 47
Nutella Ice Cream, 39
Pistachio Gelato (*Gelato di pistacchio*), 49
Sugar-Free Turtle Ice Cream, 166
Turtle Ice Cream Cake, 202
Vegan Almond Joy Swirl Ice Cream, 151
Vegan Pineapple White Chocolate Macadamia Nut Ice Cream, 159
Vegan Raspberry Almond Ice Cream, 155
Vegan Vanilla Bean Ice Cream, 152
Walnuts in Syrup, 269

Oatmeal Raisin Ice Cream Sandwiches, 188
Olive oil
about, 43
Orange Infused Olive Oil Gelato (*Gelato di arancia olio d'oliva infuso*), 43
Vegan Lemon-Infused Olive Oil Ice Cream, 161
Onions, in Vegan Caramelized Onion Ice Cream, 150
Oranges. *See* Citrus

Pans, 17
Parchment paper, 17
Peaches
about: climates for growing, 117; yellow vs. white, 30
Blueberry Peach Ice Cream Cake, 199
Blueberry Peach Sherbet, 119
Fresh Peach Ice Cream, 33
Peach Compote, 275
Peaches and Cream Ice Cream, 30
Peach Pie Frozen Yogurt, 68

Peach Sherbet, 117
Peachy Keen Milkshake, 244
Raspberry Nectarine Sorbet, 108
Peanuts and peanut butter
about: Butterfinger bars, 96; natural vs. commercial butter, 32; PB and J, 172; protein content, 260; substituting for, 266
Elvis Milkshake, 247
Nutty Buddies, 179
Peanut Butter and Jelly Ice Cream Sandwiches, 187
Peanut Butter Banana Smoothie, 260
Peanut Butter Butterfinger Ice Cream, 96
Peanut Butter Frozen Yogurt, 68
Peanut Butter Ice Cream, 32
Peanut Butter Topping, 279
Peanut Butter Whipped Cream, 266
Sugar-Free Peanut Butter and Jelly Ice Cream, 172
Pears
about: nutritional value, 145
Ginger Pear Sorbet, 102
Honey Swirled Pear Gelato (*Gelato di miele roteato pera*), 50
Pear Granita, 145
Pies. *See* Ice cream pies; Whoopie pies
Pineapple
about: piña colada, 175; plantation history, 107; ripeness, 159; ripening quickly, 135
Double Trouble Ice Cream Pops, 183
Piña Colada Ice Cream Pie, 226
Pineapple Coconut Sorbet, 107
Pineapple Granita, 135
Sugar-Free Piña Colada Ice Cream, 175
Taste of the Tropics Ice Cream Pie, 225
Tropical Milkshake, 245
Vegan Pineapple White Chocolate Macadamia Nut Ice Cream, 159
Pizzelle makers, 17
Pomegranate
about: health benefits, 147; historical perspective, 142
Pomegranate Granita, 142
Pomegranate Orange Granita, 147
Poppy seeds, in Vegan Lemon Poppy Seed Ice Cream, 160
Popsicles. *See* Kids, ice cream for
Pretzels, in White Chocolate Pretzel Ice Cream, 92

Profiteroles, 230
Pumpkin
   about: purée, 91
   Frozen Pumpkin Whoopie Pies, 241
   Pumpkin Cheesecake Ice Cream Pie,
      227
   Pumpkin Cream Cheese Ice Cream,
      91
   Pumpkin Gelato (Gelato di zucca), 48
Purple Cow Milkshake, 244

Raisins, in Rum Raisin Ice Cream, 40
Raspberries
   about, 63, 75; buying, 18
   Chocolate Raspberry Ice Cream Cake,
      201
   Dark Chocolate and Raspberry Ice
      Cream Pie, 222
   Good Morning Sunshine Smoothie,
      262
   Mixed Berry Sauce, 275
   Mixed Berry Sherbet, 118
   Raspberry Dark Chocolate Swirl Ice
      Cream, 75
   Raspberry Frozen Yogurt, 63
   Raspberry Granita, 134
   Raspberry Lemonade Smoothie, 263
   Raspberry Nectarine Sorbet, 108
   Raspberry Sauce, 274
   Raspberry Sherbet, 115
   Rich Chocolate and Raspberry
      Frozen Yogurt, 66
   Sugar-Free Decadent Dark Chocolate
      Raspberry Ice Cream, 173
   Vegan Raspberry Almond Ice Cream,
      155
Red Hots, in Not-Too-Hot Red Hots Ice
   Cream, 76
Red Velvet
   Frozen Red Velvet Whoopie Pies, 240
   Red Velvet Cake, 193
   Red Velvet Cake Ice Cream, 87
   Red Velvet Lovers Ice Cream Cake,
      202
Rhubarb
   Rhubarb Sorbet, 105
   Vegan Rhubarb Cherry Swirl Ice
      Cream, 155
Rice Gelato (Gelato di riso), 46
Rum Raisin Ice Cream, 40

Sage Blackberry Swirl Gelato (Gelato di
   leggenda e mora), 54

Sandwiches
   about: extra touch for, 189
   Brownies for Breakfast Ice Cream
      Sandwiches, 189
   Chocolate Chipwiches, 186
   Chocolate Ice Cream Sandwiches,
      185
   Lemon Shortbread Ice Cream
      Sandwiches, 239
   Oatmeal Raisin Ice Cream
      Sandwiches, 188
   Peanut Butter and Jelly Ice Cream
      Sandwiches, 187
Saucepans, 17
Sauces. See Toppings and mix-ins
Sherbets, 111–25
   about: definition of, 14
   Banana Sherbet, 122
   Blackberry Lemon Tea Sherbet, 120
   Blackberry Sherbet, 114
   Blueberry Peach Sherbet, 119
   Blueberry Sherbet, 116
   Chocolate Espresso Sherbet, 122
   Chocolate Mint Sherbet, 121
   Chocolate Sherbet, 121
   Cocoa Banana Sherbet, 125
   Lemon Sherbet, 112
   Lime Sherbet, 112
   Mixed Berry Sherbet, 118
   Peach Sherbet, 117
   Raspberry Sherbet, 115
   Strawberry Banana Sherbet, 124
   Strawberry Sherbet, 123
   Tangerine Sherbet, 113
Silicone mats, 17
Smoothies, 253–63
   Banana Toffee Latté Smoothie, 257
   Blackberry Lemon Tea Smoothie, 257
   Bloody Mary Smoothie, 255
   Blue Banana Smoothie, 256
   Caramel Apple Smoothie, 254
   Cherry Lime Smoothie, 254
   Cucumber Mint Smoothie, 260
   Good Morning Sunshine Smoothie,
      262
   Great Grapes Smoothie, 259
   Mango White Chocolate Smoothie,
      259
   Orange Dream Smoothie, 258
   Peanut Butter Banana Smoothie, 260
   Raspberry Lemonade Smoothie, 263
   Strawberry Coconut Smoothie, 262
   Strawberry Kiwi Smoothie, 261

Watermelon Smoothie, 261
S'mores ice cream, 79
Sorbet, 99–110
   about: definition of, 13–14
   Bing Cherry Sorbet, 105
   Blackberry Lime Sorbet, 106
   Blackberry Sorbet, 106
   Bombe, 238
   Cantaloupe Sorbet, 104
   Ginger Pear Sorbet, 102
   Honeydew Sorbet, 104
   Kiwi Sorbet, 110
   Lemonade Sorbet, 101
   Lemon Lime Soda Sorbet, 100
   Lime Sorbet, 100
   Mango Sorbet, 101
   Pineapple Coconut Sorbet, 107
   Raspberry Nectarine Sorbet, 108
   Rhubarb Sorbet, 105
   Sorbet-Filled Frozen Oranges, 237
   Sparkling White Grape Sorbet, 102
   Strawberry Banana Sorbet, 109
   Strawberry Sorbet, 107
   Tart Apple Sorbet, 110
   Watermelon Sorbet, 103
Special diets, 21
Stand mixers, 16
Storing concoctions, 21–22, 178
Strawberries
   about: buying, 18; color of ice cream,
      25
   Classic Strawberry Milkshake, 246
   French Twist, 237
   Frozen Strawberry Lemonade Ice
      Cream Pie, 221
   Fruity Whipped Cream, 267
   Mixed Berry Sauce, 275
   Neapolitan Baked Alaska, 236
   Simple Strawberry Ice Cream, 25
   Strawberry Banana Sherbet, 124
   Strawberry Banana Sorbet, 109
   Strawberry Cake, 195
   Strawberry Cheesecake Ice Cream
      Cupcakes, 207
   Strawberry Cheesecake Ice Cream
      Pie, 218
   Strawberry Coconut Smoothie, 262
   Strawberry Frozen Yogurt, 62
   Strawberry Granita, 139
   Strawberry Kiwi Granita, 140
   Strawberry Kiwi Smoothie, 261
   Strawberry Lemonade Frozen Trifle,
      204

Strawberry Sauce, 273
Strawberry Sherbet, 123
Strawberry Shortcake Ice Cream
    Cupcakes, 205
Strawberry Sorbet, 107
Sugar-Free Strawberry Ice Cream, 167
Tropical Milkshake, 245
Vegan Strawberry Ice Cream, 150
Streusel Topping, 223
Sugar Cookie Cups, 184
Sugar-free ice cream, **163**–76
    about: recipes overview, 21, 164;
        Splenda, 167; sweeteners for, 164,
        167
    Chocolate Ice Cream, 171
    Coffee Chip Ice Cream, 169
    Dark Chocolate Orange Ice Cream,
        168
    Decadent Dark Chocolate Raspberry
        Ice Cream, 173
    Dreamy Orange Cream Ice Cream,
        170
    Mango Ice Cream, 176
    Mint Chip Ice Cream, 174
    Peanut Butter and Jelly Ice Cream,
        172
    Piña Colada Ice Cream, 175
    Strawberry Ice Cream, 167
    Turtle Ice Cream, 166
    Vanilla Bean Agave Ice Cream, 170
    Vanilla Caramel Swirl Ice Cream, 165
Sugars, 19
Sugar substitutes, 19–20
Supplies and equipment, 14–17

Tea
    Blackberry Lemon Tea Sherbet, 120
    Blackberry Lemon Tea Smoothie, 257
3 Musketeers Candy Bar Ice Cream, 90
Tiramisu Ice Cream Cake Roll, 206
Tiramisu Milkshake, 246
Toffee. See Caramel and toffee
Tofu
    about, 161
    Vegan Caramelized Onion Ice Cream,
        150
    Vegan Lemon-Infused Olive Oil Ice
        Cream, 161
Tomatoes, in Herbed Tomato Gelato
    (Gelato di herbes e tomati), 44
Toppings and mix-ins, **265**–83
    Blackberry Sauce, 274
    Blueberry Sauce, 273

Butterscotch Sauce, 271
Candied Citrus Peels, 270
Candied Pecans, 269
Caramel Sauce, 272
Cherry Compote, 278
Chocolate Whipped Cream, 267
Crunchy Caramelized Nuts, 268
Dark Chocolate Fudge Sauce, 280
Dulce de Leche, 271
Fruity Whipped Cream, 267
Homemade Chocolate Magic Shell,
    178
Hot Fudge Sauce, 272
Lemon Curd, 276
Lime Curd, 277
Marshmallow Meringue, 283
Marshmallow Topping, 280
Milk Chocolate Fudge Sauce, 279
Milk Chocolate Ganache, 281
Mixed Berry Sauce, 275
Peach Compote, 275
Peanut Butter Topping, 279
Peanut Butter Whipped Cream, 266
Raspberry Sauce, 274
Spiced Apple Compote, 278
Strawberry Sauce, 273
Sweetened Whipped Cream, 266
Toffee, 282
Walnuts in Syrup, 269

Vanilla
    about: beans, 20–21, 27, 62; extract, 20
    Classic Vanilla Milkshake, 245
    Double Trouble Ice Cream Pops, 183
    Neapolitan Baked Alaska, 236
    Rich Vanilla Bean Ice Cream, 27
    Simple Vanilla Ice Cream, 24
    Sugar-Free Vanilla Caramel Swirl Ice
        Cream, 165
    Vanilla Bean Agave Ice Cream, 170
    Vanilla Bean Butter Cake, 192
    Vanilla Brown Butter Ice Cream, 94
    Vanilla Frozen Yogurt, 62
    Vanilla Wafer Crust, 215
    Vegan Vanilla Bean Ice Cream, 152
Vegan ice cream, **149**–61
    about: overview of recipes, 21
    Almond Joy Swirl Ice Cream, 151
    Blueberry Lavender Ice Cream, 154
    Caramelized Onion Ice Cream, 150
    Choco-Avocado Ice Cream, 157
    Cinnamon Cheesecake Swirl Ice
        Cream, 156

Coffee Ice Cream, 158
Cranberry White Chocolate Chunk
    Ice Cream, 157
Lemon-Infused Olive Oil Ice Cream,
    161
Lemon Poppy Seed Ice Cream, 160
Pineapple White Chocolate
    Macadamia Nut Ice Cream, 159
Raspberry Almond Ice Cream, 155
Rhubarb Cherry Swirl Ice Cream, 155
Strawberry Ice Cream, 150
Vanilla Bean Ice Cream, 152
White Chocolate Ice Cream, 153

Waffle cone makers, 17
Waffle Cones, 181
Watermelon. See Melons
Whipped cream recipes, 266–67
White chocolate
    about, 40, 87, 153; garnishing with, 259
    Blueberry Peach Ice Cream Cake, 199
    Chocolate Bowls, 235
    Mango White Chocolate Smoothie,
        259
    Red Velvet Cake Ice Cream, 87
    Vegan Cranberry White Chocolate
        Chunk Ice Cream, 157
    Vegan Pineapple White Chocolate
        Macadamia Nut Ice Cream, 159
    Vegan White Chocolate Ice Cream,
        153
    White Chocolate Ganache, 199
    White Chocolate Ice Cream, 40
    White Chocolate Mousse Cake, 233
Whoopie pies, 240, 241

Yogurt. See also Frozen yogurt
    about: Greek, 256; types of, 20
    Banana Toffee Latté Smoothie, 257
    Cherry Lime Smoothie, 254
    Cucumber Mint Smoothie, 260
    Good Morning Sunshine Smoothie,
        262
    Peanut Butter Banana Smoothie, 260
    Watermelon Smoothie, 261

Zesters, 17
Zesting lemons, 128

We Have EVERYTHING® on Anything!

With more than 19 million copies sold, the Everything® series has become one of America's favorite resources for solving problems, learning new skills, and organizing lives. Our brand is not only recognizable—it's also welcomed.

The series is a hand-in-hand partner for people who are ready to tackle new subjects—like you!

For more information on the Everything® series, please visit *www.adamsmedia.com*

The Everything® list spans a wide range of subjects, with more than 500 titles covering 25 different categories:

Business	History	Reference
Careers	Home Improvement	Religion
Children's Storybooks	Everything Kids	Self-Help
Computers	Languages	Sports & Fitness
Cooking	Music	Travel
Crafts and Hobbies	New Age	Wedding
Education/Schools	Parenting	Writing
Games and Puzzles	Personal Finance	
Health	Pets	